When Reform Meets Reality

When Reform Meets Reality

The Power and Pitfalls of Instructional
Reform in School Districts

EDITED BY JONATHAN A. SUPOVITZ

HARVARD EDUCATION PRESS
CAMBRIDGE, MASSACHUSETTS

Copyright © 2025 by the President and Fellows of Harvard College

All rights reserved. No part of this publication may be reproduced or transmitted in any form or by any means, electronic or mechanical, including photocopy, recording, or any information storage and retrieval systems, without permission in writing from the publisher.

Paperback ISBN 9781682539347

Library of Congress Cataloging-in-Publication Data

Names: Supovitz, Jonathan A., editor.
Title: When reform meets reality : the power and pitfalls of instructional reform in school districts / [edited by] Jonathan A. Supovitz.
Description: Cambridge, Massachusetts : Harvard Education Press, [2024] | Includes bibliographical references and index.
Identifiers: LCCN 2024020016 | ISBN 9781682539347 (paperback)
Subjects: LCSH: Educational change—United States—Case studies. | Education, Urban—United States—Case studies. | Curriculum change—United States—Case studies. | Educational innovations—United States—Case studies. | Curriculum-based assessment—United States—Case studies. | Organizational learning—United States—Case studies.
Classification: LCC LB2806.23 .W54 2024 | DDC 370.973—dc23/eng/20240515
LC record available at https://lccn.loc.gov/2024020016

Published by Harvard Education Press,
an imprint of the Harvard Education Publishing Group

Harvard Education Press
8 Story Street
Cambridge, MA 02138

Cover design: Patrick Ciano
Cover image: Bridget Goldhahn

The typefaces in this book are Minion Pro and ITC Stone Sans.

Contents

1 Searching for Black Swans   1
   Jonathan A. Supovitz

2 The Ongoing Assessment Project (OGAP):
   A Mathematics Formative Assessment System   21
   Marjorie Petit, Elizabeth Hulbert, and Robert Laird

3 OGAP in Philadelphia: Adaptive Partnering
   in a Complex System   45
   Janine T. Remillard

4 How OGAP Made a Difference: Teacher and
   Student Impacts   73
   Jonathan A. Supovitz and Maurice Spillane

5 Not so Fast: Expectations for First-Year School
   Implementation   105
   *Adrianne Flack, Brittan Hallar, Brittany L. Hess,
   Katrina Morrison, Christian Kolouch, and Jordan D'Olier*

6 Teachers' Understanding of Learning Trajectory–
   Oriented Formative Assessment in Theory
   and Practice   129
   Caroline B. Ebby and Jordan D'Olier

7	The Logic of Benchmark Assessments *Jonathan A. Supovitz and Jordan D'Olier*	155
8	Leadership Moves: How Two School Leaders Organized the Schools for Deeper Implementation *Adrianne Flack and Brittany L. Hess*	181
9	Persisting with OGAP: Why Educators Valued the Reform, and How One School Organized for Persistence *Jill C. Pierce, Adrianne Flack, and Brittany L. Hess*	207
10	Supporting the Core *Jonathan A. Supovitz*	235

Notes	255
Acknowledgments	265
About the Editor and Contributors	267
Index	273

1

Searching for Black Swans

JONATHAN A. SUPOVITZ

The district leaders sat hunched around a conference table in the central office, poring over the latest state test results that encapsulated the performance of tens of thousands of students in hundreds of schools from different neighborhoods across the diverse city, looking for the "black swans" that indicated improvements in English language arts, mathematics, and/or science. The black swans were their name for that rare trend in improvements that seemed to show a connection between all the district's efforts up and down the system and steady increases in the performance of students.[1] They examined the data in all kinds of permutations—by grade level, subject area, and student subgroup—looking for indications that their strategies, resources, and supports for teachers and schools were paying off.

Meanwhile, in an elementary school about three miles north, a group of three fourth-grade teachers rearranged the undersized desks of a handful of students into a tight semicircle and pulled out packets of student solutions to a single open-ended mathematics problem they each had given to their class in the past couple of days. In their previous meeting they had carefully selected the math problem, which reflected where they were in the multiplication unit of the curriculum. The teachers weren't exactly in the same place in the four-week unit, so the problem reflected a somewhat different challenge for the students across the three classes. Nonetheless, it was a good indicator of the levels of student understanding at that juncture of their learning. As the teachers began to examine the student work, they began to notice the range of understanding that was reflected in the student responses, what misconceptions students shared, and which students seemed to have little idea about how to approach the problem. They also puzzled over a few of the student answers, which they passed around, trying to decipher what the student was thinking that produced the answer. Rather than sorting the student responses by whether they got the answer correct or not, the teachers grouped their piles to indicate students with different approaches to the problem, which reflected their stages of mathematics development. Based on their observations, the teachers shared ideas about how to instruct groups of students differently to deepen their understanding and move their learning forward. Meetings like this were a central approach of the Ongoing Assessment Project, or OGAP, which was the mathematics reform in which the school was participating, and which is the focus of this book.

Could these regular teacher meetings be connected to the state test results that the district leaders were examining? What exactly was the relationship, if any, between the array of experiences that these and other teachers across the city were providing for students and what was reflected on the state tests? In education, these are the proverbial million multibillion dollar questions. Indeed, states and districts around the nation spend billions of dollars each year trying to produce better student outcomes on state tests.

Like disentangling a ball of yarn after the cat has batted it around all day, tracing the trail from what teachers, schools, and districts do to what their efforts produce is incredibly difficult to follow. After decades of research studies and evaluations, the links connecting educational inputs and outputs are still hotly debated. In the early 1990s, investigations into the so-called education production function, which sought to link educational inputs to student outcomes, showed little systematic evidence of the connection between the educational expenditures and student outcomes.[2] In response, other researchers pointed out that of course resources mattered, but that it depended more on how and for what they were spent.[3] Since then, hundreds of studies have examined the impacts of programs, policies, resources, and supports, with mixed results. In many ways, we are still looking for the black swans.

It should not really be all that surprising that stable and systematic connections between students' schooling and education performance on standardized tests are inconsistent. The pathways that lead from what happens inside classrooms on a daily basis to the results on large-scale tests are long and winding and strewn with assumptions. Think of all the ingredients that we have deemed important enough to place along this pathway that reasonably might contribute to these connections—from curriculum and other materials to particular teaching practices to teacher professional development and support systems to computer programs to student socioemotional and behavioral support systems to parental and community engagement strategies to preparatory testing activities to leadership approaches and supports to breakfast and nutrition programs to afterschool programs—and even this is an incomplete list. Now add the developmental and psychological state of the students who are the focus (either directly or indirectly) of many of these activities, as well as what we know about the uneven progression of student learning, and you begin to get the idea of the complex chain of contributing factors that underlie educational support efforts in one site, not to mention across disparate geographic, socioeconomic, and demographic contexts.

Amid this profusion of factors, programs that show tangible and repeated effects on teachers and students should be celebrated. They represent an unfortunately all too rare circumstance in American education in which an instructional reform consistently produces positive impacts on teachers and students at scale relative to the status quo. Chapter 4 of this book is devoted to sharing the evidence of the persistent impacts of OGAP on teachers and students in the School District of Philadelphia (SDP). The story of OGAP in Philadelphia would be far less compelling if there was not substantial data that OGAP had significantly improved the instructional practice of almost one thousand teachers and the learning of their approximately twenty thousand students. This success also raises a host of questions, including:

- What is OGAP's instructional improvement strategy, and what are its particular qualities that contributed to the improvements in teaching and learning that might distinguish it from other efforts that have not shown improvements?
- How, if at all, did the reform adjust over time to better respond to the needs of teachers and schools?
- What challenges did the reformers face as they worked with teachers and school and district leaders?
- What factors within classrooms, schools, and the broader system elevated or hampered the instructional improvement efforts?

Answering these questions is the purpose of this book. It follows the arc of the ambitious mathematics instructional reform program, the Ongoing Assessment Project, as it was introduced and scaled up in the large urban school district of Philadelphia over the course of five years, from 2014 to 2019.

Philadelphia was a challenging environment to implement ambitious instructional reform. In 2015, the SDP was the eighth-largest school district in the United States. Philadelphia is also one of the most diverse and segregated cities in the United States, where two-thirds of the students are minority and virtually all students receive free or reduced-price lunch.[4] The district faced, and continues to grapple with, a number of intractable challenges, including budget and management. In 2015, for example, per-pupil funding in Philadelphia and Upper Darby was just over $14,000, barely half of what was spent in the nearby tony suburb of Lower Merion ($26,812) and a third less than its Pennsylvania urban sister city of Pittsburgh ($21,120).[5] Even with low per-pupil spending, the district has been chronically underfunded, running an $80 million deficit in 2015.[6] Due to low test performance and chronic financial problems, the SDP underwent state takeover from 2001 to 2017, moving from local control to oversight by a reform commission with three members appointed by the governor and two by the mayor. In addition to the political movement back to local control occurring in the midst of the project, the district was heavily focused on literacy, with much of the resources and attention focused on improving student reading capabilities by fourth grade.

Across the five years, the reform moved from an externally funded test of its efficacy to a program centrally supported by the district; innovated its training and support strategies to more effectively meet the needs of teachers, students, and school leaders; and expanded its focus from grades 3–5 to K–8 in the recognition that whole-school support was integral to both its continuation and school and district priorities. It is also the tale of a reform that, despite its documented success, failed to sustain the scope of its presence as times changed, priorities shifted, and central office champions moved on. The story also ends at a new beginning. At the time of this writing, in 2024, the reform continues in pockets within the district.

The broad brushstrokes of this story in the annals of education are all too familiar—the tale of reform promise, scale-up, and churn. Many authors have chronicled the rise and fall of educational reform approaches that seem to ebb and flow with the predictability of the tides.[7] But chalking this story up to well-known pitfalls misses several crucially important lessons that provide insights into the challenges that reformers will continue to face as they seek to recraft education for the postpandemic world. Indeed, the failure to acknowledge these lessons reveals several of the reasons why this story is so familiar, and until we acknowledge and make headway on them, we are all too likely to repeat the past. For within this story course the undercurrents of several fundamental dynamics that flow within the education system that will continue to play out as educators seek to increase the ambition of teaching to prepare students for the rapidly changing and increasingly interconnected world.

Across the chapters of this book, we examine three larger themes about instructional reform, its implementation, and the surrounding context that either ease or hinder efforts to introduce meaningful pedagogical change into school systems.

The first theme is what we think makes OGAP impactful. We argue that the construction of OGAP combines two essential ideas: first, specific research-informed knowledge about the developmental progressions along which students typically evolve to gain a deeper conceptual understanding of mathematics content areas and, second, iterative formative assessment techniques; together, these provide teachers with crucial insights into student thinking that gives them perspective on what to do next to develop student understanding. Collectively, we view this approach, which we call *learning trajectory–oriented formative assessment*, to be a powerful instructional reform design.[8] OGAP embodies a powerful instructional design because it helps teachers to improve upon many of the traditional ways that teaching has come to be delivered in this country. Traditional approaches to teaching generally involve a teacher-centered environment in which information is delivered based on a predetermined curriculum and/or scope and sequence. Teaching, in this sense, is a planned exchange between teacher and student, where the role of the student is to adapt to the teacher's plan. Formative assessment practices provide the opportunity to invert this relationship. Through the analysis of student understanding represented in their work, teachers can responsively adapt their approaches more tightly to the needs of their students. The potential for this shift in the instructional dynamic opens up the opportunity for different teaching and learning experiences but also challenges a host of other implicit dynamics that are embedded in education today, including the habits and beliefs of teachers and the ways in which the system surrounding classrooms is organized.

The second theme of the book is the ways that the major actors in support of the reform collaborated to engage in ongoing learning and deeper implementation of the program at different levels of the system over time. We call this multilevel learning. Success rarely comes right out of the gate but requires ongoing adjustments to refine a reform in a particular context. Five groups of actors had major roles in the implementation of the instructional reform: the OGAP providers themselves, committed teachers, school leaders, district leaders, and our organization, the Consortium for Policy Research in Education (CPRE), as the research and support partner. Just like the axiom that it takes a village to raise a child, it takes a community of learners at different levels and in different positions of the education ecosystem to make ambitious reform successful (which is itself part of the ambition of the reform). As we will see in the coming chapters, the different actors all needed to make adjustments as they learned about the reform's progress over time. When we looked back at the times and places in which the reform had the most momentum, we saw learning and change happening at multiple levels of the system.

The third theme that we examine in this volume is the identification and implications of what happens when ambitious instructional reforms seek to take root in education systems that are fundamentally shaped by learning conceptions of the past. Instructional reforms that are based on contemporary ideas about how both children and adults learn and change often face obstacles that are deeply ingrained within the structures and dynamics of the ways that schooling is structured and supported. If you look closely enough, you can see these frictions at different levels of the education system—including classroom dynamics, the ways that schools are organized, and the district systems that are designed to support teaching.

Let's examine these themes in a bit more depth and introduce where they are discussed in chapters in this book.

THEME 1: THE POTENTIAL OF AMBITIOUS INSTRUCTIONAL REFORM

To begin, we must define what we mean by an "ambitious instructional reform." An ambitious instructional reform is one that develops teacher knowledge and skill to diagnose and respond to student learning needs in ways that target instruction at the developmental levels of individual students at that particular time, rather than generically delivering a sequence of content. This is easier said than done and has a host of implications for teachers, schools, and systems. The ambitious instructional reform that is the centerpiece of this book is called the Ongoing Assessment Project, or OGAP. In chapter 2, Marge Petit, Bob Laird, and Beth Hulbert, members of the original Vermont-based OGAP development team, provide a primer on the basic tenets of the mathematics formative assessment system they have developed and refined over the past twenty years. The reform combines two key ingredients: longstanding evidence of the efficacy of formative assessment combined with a more recent research-based understanding of how students develop understanding in mathematics, which together we call *learning trajectory-oriented formative assessment*.

OGAP's ambition is rooted in its powerful underlying learning theory, which asks teachers not just to teach students differently, but to shift their understanding of *how* students learn, which is a precursor to their instructional approach. Formative assessment is based on the theory of how instructors gain access to the current state of learners' understanding and move them toward a goal. According to Sadler, "Formative assessment is concerned with how judgments about the quality of student responses (performances, pieces, or works) can be used to shape and improve the student's competence."[9] The essential activity of formative assessment is the use of some assessment mechanism to identify and reduce the gap between a learner's current knowledge and a desired goal.[10] That is, the assessment becomes "formative" when its information is activated as feedback to the learner, either directly or through a teacher, and in doing so shortens the gap between their present state of understanding and the goal. As Ramaprasad stated, "Feedback is information about the gap between the actual level and the reference level of a system parameter which is used to alter the gap in some way."[11] The formative assessment process involves one or more of three different types of feedback, as shown in figure 1.1.

The first type of feedback is feedback from the assessment directly to the learner, as in the case of self-assessment. The second type of feedback is from the assessment to the teacher. The third type of feedback is the feedback provided by the teacher to the learner. These three types of feedback are distinct from each other, to some extent dependent on the form of the assessment (i.e., the instrument used to collect data from the learner), and require a different skill set on the part of the teacher. The process of assessing the gap between the learner's current state of knowledge and the goal—via an assessment of some form—is done repeatedly, either as the gap shrinks or as the learner progresses to newer or deeper content.

The seminal summary of the literature on the efficacy of formative assessment was conducted in 1998 by Black and Wiliam, who examined a wide range of studies about the effects of formative assessment.[12] The

Figure 1.1 A framework for learning trajectory–oriented formative assessment

```
                    Feedback (1)
         ┌─────────────────────────────────┐
         ↓                                 ↓
   Learner's         ASSESSMENT
   Current       ─ ─ ─ ─ ─ ─ ─ ─ ─ ─ →   Learning
   State         LEARNING TRAJECTORY        Goal
         ↖                             ↙
            Feedback (3)      Feedback (2)
                     ↘      ↙
                     Teacher
```

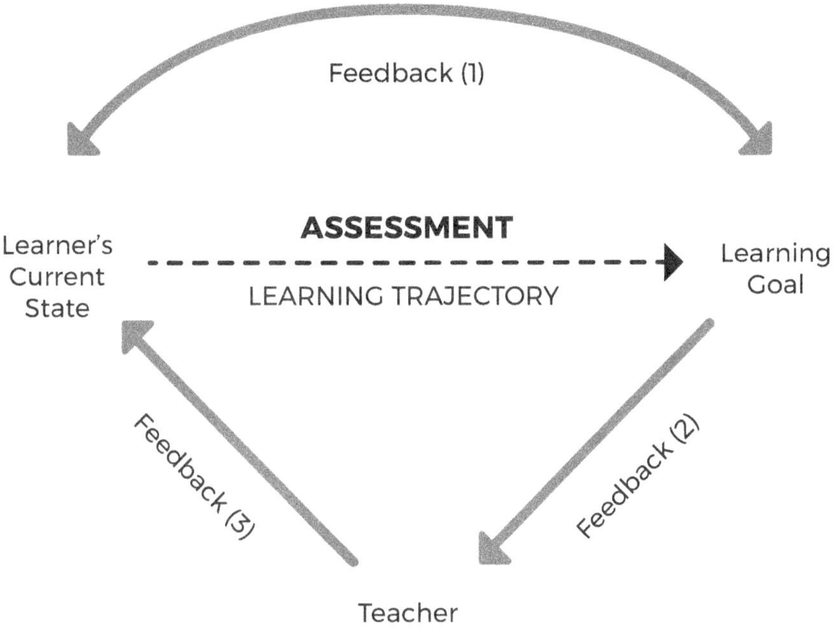

Source: This figure and the associated explanation are drawn from Jonathan A. Supovitz, Caroline B. Ebby, and Philip Sirinides, *TASK Teacher Analysis of Student Knowledge: A Measure of Learning Trajectory-Oriented Formative Assessment* (Philadelphia: Consortium for Policy Research in Education, 2013).

efficacy of feedback from teachers to learners is well documented, with a number of meta-analyses on the topic. In the largest research review to date, Kluger and DeNisi identified 131 studies of "feedback interventions," which they defined as "actions taken by (an) external agent(s) to provide information regarding some aspect(s) of one's task performance."[13] The studies contained over six hundred effect sizes, and Kluger and DeNisi reported average effect sizes of a robust 0.40, but more than one-third of the feedback interventions actually decreased performance. They concluded that feedback interventions that focused on the learner and away from the task had reduced effectiveness. In another large meta-analysis, the authors reviewed forty reports and fifty-eight effect sizes and found a statistically significant 0.26 effect of feedback on student achievement.[14]

They also found that eighteen of the fifty-eight effects were *negative*, with four being significantly so, indicating that not all types of feedback were conducive to learning.

A weak point in the theory of formative assessment is the guidance to teachers about what they should focus their feedback on that will help learners move toward the goal or standard. While the formative assessment process provides information about where students are relative to the goal, there is little suggestion about what to do next. This is where research-informed learning trajectories provide a valuable complement. Learning trajectories, represented by the dashed line in figure 1.1, are "descriptions of the successively more sophisticated ways of thinking about a topic that can follow one another as children learn about and investigate a topic over a broad span of time."[15] Research on the development of students' understanding of math content areas indicates that students move from basic strategies to more sophisticated approaches as their mental structures evolve.[16] The sophistication of students' strategies develops over time as they interact with different problem structures and develop stronger multiplicative reasoning.[17] However, this is not strictly a linear process, as they may oscillate between more and less sophisticated approaches as they encounter different problem structures and complex numbers.[18]

Multiple studies have found that knowledge of and use of learning trajectories positively impacts teachers' knowledge and instructional practices.[19] Yet few studies focus on the impact on student learning and achievement. One notable exception is the work by Clements and Sarama on the longitudinal effects of an early childhood curriculum developed around learning trajectories on children's learning.[20] Thus, the combination of formative assessment and learning trajectories is the central component of OGAP.

Rather than a curriculum, OGAP is a curricular complement designed to provide teachers with actionable feedback on student thinking in mathematics to inform subsequent instructional responses. But what does this approach look like in practice? This is the main focus of two chapters in the volume. In chapter 5, Adrianne Flack and colleagues look at OGAP implementation in grades 3–5 in twelve schools and give us a picture of what first-year implementation looked like across a range of schools. They found that after one year, teachers were beginning to use central components of the program, including the item banks and learning progressions, but that schools had more difficulty implementing OGAP professional learning communities, and that the focus on grades 3–5 made it difficult for principals and math leads to support a model that was only in a subset of the school's grades. They discuss factors that impeded implementation and call into question a support model that assumes a one-year implementation window.

In chapter 6, Caroline Ebby and Jordan D'Olier investigate how teachers understood OGAP's underlying theory of learning trajectory–oriented formative assessment and how they enacted it in practice. By interviewing a sample of thirty-two teachers and asking them to both explain OGAP's approach and show how they sorted and analyzed their students' work, they exposed (in)consistencies between espoused views and applications in practice. In doing so, they reveal both the challenges of changing prior teacher beliefs and the different stages that teachers might go through as they seek to incorporate the ambitious instructional reform into their everyday teaching practices.

THEME 2: THE IMPORTANCE OF MULTILEVEL LEARNING

The second theme of the book is the importance of what we call multilevel learning. This refers to the ongoing refinement of both an instructional reform and its support by relevant actors at different levels of the education system. These changes are sometimes motivated by the reformers and, at other times, by system actors' recognition of the best way to support reform implementation in their particular context.[21] Implementation improvements can also be influenced by others beyond the program's provider. To make instructional reforms work at any scale also requires crucial adjustments at the school and district levels. School and district leaders also played an important part in the story of OGAP. Their adjustments to OGAP, including changes to its professional development and ongoing support model, shifts in the way the district supported implementation, and the ways in which many schools adapted their supports, are described in chapter 3, where Janine Remillard lays out the journey of OGAP in Philadelphia.

Remillard chronicles the multiple changes to OGAP and the system surrounding it that both eased and impeded implementation and describes the journey as a process of design-based implementation research.[22] She describes the ways in which OGAP started as an external district reform focused on conducting a rigorous test of its efficacy and morphed into a partnership among the program, district, and research team called the Philadelphia Mathematics Leadership Collaborative (PMLC), in which the program was integrated into many of the district's offerings and support systems.

Her story features the many adjustments that occurred across the years. At the programmatic level, there were several important refinements that became central to OGAP's continued success. Foremost was OGAP's decision after its first year in Philadelphia to move ongoing professional development down to the school level and to customize it to the needs of the school rather than keep it centralized. The summer professional development continued to be conducted at a centrally located district site, but thereafter, OGAP trainers visited schools at least three times a year and provided additional training and ongoing support to schools' math coaches. These visits were highly customized to teacher needs: the OGAP trainers might facilitate an OGAP professional learning community meeting to demonstrate OGAP's routine of teachers bringing and sorting completed student work on a chosen math item, discussing what this says about student understanding, and using this knowledge to plan the next day's lesson; teach a class based on analyzed student work; they might lead a conversation about how to choose assessment items that target specific curricular areas or student skills; and/or they might rotate and work individually with small groups of teachers.

Another example of the refinement of programmatic supports was the decision to build a connection between the district-predominant math curriculum, enVision, and the OGAP process, beginning in 2016. During site training, teachers described the challenge they felt connecting OGAP to the curricular units in their textbooks. Each unit in the textbook began with a preassessment, or an item that assessed student prior knowledge entering the unit. However, the text's guidance to teachers for scoring the item and the provided examples of student work focused on whether students answered the item correctly or incorrectly. To align the item with OGAP, the CPRE research team collected student workbooks from teachers from the previous year and built an interactive website that provided information about the preassessment from multiple units at each grade level that showed student solutions to the preassessment item at different levels of understanding that were aligned with the OGAP frameworks, sortable interactive web-based practice activities for teachers to place the student solutions at different levels on the OGAP progressions, explanations of where and why experienced OGAP users would place the students on the progressions based on evidence from the student work, as well as a suggested set of items in the OGAP item bank that would provide further practice for students at different developmental levels. On follow-up survey measures, teachers reported that the connection between the curriculum and OGAP's approach was highly helpful in their efforts to adopt OGAP practices.

Sometimes the programmatic refinements removed things that were intended to facilitate implementation but did not pan out as hoped. A prime example of this was a web-based e-tool for OGAP that we designed for teachers to collect and store their student data so they could identify trends in student solution approaches over time. The OGAP e-tool was a major element of our grant from the National Science Foundation in 2013, and we spent two years designing and developing it. As part of the grant, CPRE bought over two hundred iPad minis and used them as inducements for teachers to enroll in the initial study as part of our recruitment process. We intended that teachers would use the mobile tool to help them assess students and track their work on the fly. But it turned out that teacher experiences in the first year were disappointing. Teachers and trainers reported that the procedures of using the e-tool were getting in the way of easy implementation, and the e-tool was not increasing implementation as we hoped. After much debate, we decided to encourage teachers to use the e-tool as an electronic item database, but not to push teachers to use the tool in recording and tracking student work. Sometimes, addition comes from subtraction.

The district also made several changes to support the reform, which reflected learning on the part of the district leaders. In 2015, for example, the district recognized the promise of OGAP. This was in part due to their internal analyses of improvements in benchmark test scores in OGAP schools relative to other district schools. Based on these promising results, and positive reports from teachers and school leaders, the district decided to fund OGAP summer professional development as part of the district's mathematics support initiative. In the summers of 2016 and 2017, the district offered OGAP to grades 3–5 teachers in their summer professional development and paid for ongoing support across the school year. In 2018, the district expanded OGAP professional development to grades K–8.

Two additional chapters look at the effects of the changes sought by PMLC, whose findings also were infused back into redesign efforts. In chapter 8, Adrianne Flack and Brittany Hess closely follow the leadership efforts of the principals in two schools that were among the first cohort of K–8 schools to adopt OGAP schoolwide in 2018 to understand the principal's role in supporting implementation. This was also the second year that PMLC provided ongoing support for principals, so the authors were able to see how the supports for leadership were translated in schools. In their chapter, they discuss how principals protected opportunities for teacher collaboration, a key aspect of OGAP's theory of change, and how they used internal school capacity to support implementation. Through their investigation, they identify many of the key strategies that principals can use to foster and support deeper engagement with ambitious instructional reforms like OGAP that were shared with other principals in leader meetings.

Finally, in chapter 9, Jill Pierce, Adrianne Flack, and Brittany Hess examine why teachers and schools chose to persist with OGAP after their year of initial training and support. At that point, teachers and schools had flexibility to decide whether to continue their implementation of OGAP and to receive ongoing support from PMLC. Given this choice, some schools and pockets of teachers within schools chose to persist. In this chapter, the authors examine how a sample of these teachers and schools organized for persistence. Their investigation leads them to important elements of persistence, including ongoing professional learning and continuous new training to account for teacher turnover, the protection of time and space for ongoing engagement with the reform ideas, efforts to align the new teaching ideas with teachers' existing practices to avoid overload and the typical churn of reforms, and the importance of principal engagement and distributed leadership for broader buy-in and coherence.

THEME 3: ELEMENTS OF THE EDUCATION SYSTEM THAT IMPEDE INSTRUCTIONAL IMPROVEMENT EFFORTS

The third theme of this book is the identification and examination of elements of the larger education system that are inconsistent with ambitious instructional reform. Over the past fifty years, learning theories have evolved substantially. The field has increasingly come to understand how the didactic delivery of knowledge (behaviorism) and the construction of meaning through problem-solving (constructivism) and interacting with others (socioculturalism) are all appropriate learning experiences in different subject areas, at different times, and for different-minded individuals.[23] More recently, cultural and socioemotional factors have become increasingly prominent instructional elements.[24] Yet in many ways, the surrounding education system is still designed to support outdated notions of teaching and learning as a strictly linear transmission of knowledge. This creates tensions for teachers and school leaders who must grapple with the implications of misalignments with system support efforts as they seek to adopt new ways of teaching.

The implementation of OGAP brought many of these tensions to the fore. The fundamental premise of OGAP is to iteratively develop students' conceptual understanding through multiple experiences with repeated exposure and practice with problems of different degrees of complexity and from different contexts. This multiexperienced approach is designed to build a deeper understanding and fluency in students, which creates an essential foundation for engaging with more advanced concepts as they matriculate through school. This theory of learning eschews the linear notion of teaching and learning which has been, and continues to be, the dominant mode of instruction in American schools.[25] When you look for them, the tensions between the timeworn structures of the education system and more contemporary instructional approaches quickly become apparent.

There are several ways in which these tensions play out in educational organizations. First is the way that district guidance systems like curriculum pacing guides reify linear conceptions of learning that emphasize instruction as the straightforward transmission of knowledge from teacher to learner. Pacing guides, which are mapped to standards and end-of-year state tests, provide teachers with expectations of what to cover and how briskly to work their way through the curriculum. The challenge for teachers is to meet both coverage expectations and the depth of understanding that is advocated by ambitious instructional approaches to give students strong subject-based foundations. This problem is often exacerbated as students advance through the grades and teachers find they have to backfill areas of weak understanding in students. This puts teachers in a squeeze between spending more time to provide students with the experiences to deepen their understanding that will be necessary for success when they engage in more advanced topics, and the demands to "keep up" with the pacing guidelines. This problem is further exacerbated by current student capabilities, which are often behind the starting point assumed by both the curriculum and the pacing guidelines, particularly in poor communities with perennially underfunded systems.

A second way that district systems are misaligned with current learning theories is the way that teacher professional development is often structured using the model of one year of training for teachers to absorb new approaches, despite the field's acknowledgement of the importance of ongoing and sustained support.[26] Adult learning and change, similar to that of students, requires repeated opportunities to grapple with concepts and develop understanding over time, yet teacher professional development too often cycles across content areas and is focused on curriculum implementation. For cash-strapped districts, this is exacerbated by the dilemma of how to reach all teachers equitably while providing something robust enough to influence practice.

As a third example, district benchmark/interim assessment systems, which are intended to provide formative feedback to teachers, inadvertently reify behaviorist notions of teaching in their structure, the form of data they provide, and the ways their uses are advocated. These systems, which typically provide numerical representations of student responses to items representing content coverage, are presented as formative for teachers even though some of the topics they cover are old (since they are only administered three to four times a year) and lack feedback on *how* students understand the content that makes their data formative for teachers to use to guide instructional next steps. Due to the relative lack of insight they provide for teachers, their advocated uses are grouping students into subsets of those that answered problems incorrectly (regardless of the multitude of reasons that could underlie student misunderstanding) and reteaching the content. Absent more refined guidance about the underlying reasons why students are not answering correctly, the reteaching that occurs tends to repeat the initial instruction, reinforcing behaviorist notions.

Considering these examples together, I encapsulate the misalignment between support systems and learning expectations as a fundamental confusion between learning processes and performance outcomes. Learning occurs in the ongoing interactions among teachers, students, and materials, and classroom-based formative assessment practices by teachers are an especially powerful way to enhance learning. Performance, by contrast, is a measure of the outcome of learning. Performance metrics like benchmark assessments and end-of-year state tests are limited tools to inform learning. While they can give teachers and administrators some sense of what areas might need more attention and support, they cannot provide enough actionable information for teachers to use in anything but the broadest sense. The confusion between performance and learning also exacerbates inequalities, since it is the schools and students who are the lowest performing who are the targets of accountability and feel the most pressure to gravitate toward performance.

The ways that district systems support performance rather than learning come out in several chapters. In Flack and coauthors' chapter 5, we see the limitations of progress that teachers and schools make in implementing OGAP in their first year, yet their professional development and support are limited to one year. In Ebby and D'Olier's chapter 6, we see how teachers continue to hold a performance orientation despite their introduction to OGAP's developmental approach, which leads us to ask what kinds of sustained supports and consistent messages teachers need to durably shift their practice.

In chapter 7, Jonathan Supovitz and Jordan D'Olier examine SDP's benchmark system and how district leaders, principals, and teachers viewed the purpose and utility of the benchmarks. Tellingly, district leaders tended to view the benchmarks as formative for teachers, while teachers viewed the benchmark system as largely an accountability system to check on their work. Principals had mixed views, and many sought to protect teachers from the scrutiny of their performance based on the benchmark data. As the authors show in their chapter, most (OGAP-trained) teachers recognized the design flaws in the benchmarks that crimp their utility as formative feedback for instructional improvement.

Introducing and sustaining reforms that change the core instructional practices of hosts of teachers has a long and uneven history in the annals of education reform. We should learn from those that succeed. To illuminate the successes and challenges of enacting instructional change in a large urban school system, this chronicle weaves together the stories of the implementation journey and substantial impacts of an ambitious mathematics instructional reform from the vantage points of different stakeholders, including the program developers, teachers, school and district leaders, and the researcher team.

From these experiences across five years, we have distilled three central themes that we will explore across the chapters of this book. First, we describe the essential elements of the mathematics reform itself, which has distinctive qualities that make it both ambitious and pragmatically useful for teachers. Its ambition comes from the ways in which it changes traditional instructional dynamics by providing training, tools, and resources to help teachers to continually diagnose their students' current learning needs and target individualized instructional responses. Teachers readily recognized the utility of OGAP's formative assessment system, yet employing it with skill takes ongoing work.

Second, we depict the ongoing adjustments that the project team made to continually situate the instructional reform in ways that fit best within the particular school and district contexts. From these experiences, there are important lessons about the need for ongoing adjustments and refinements. And third, but not least, we identify entrenched practices within the education system itself that are inconsistent with the contemporary learning ideas embedded within the instructional reform and that we have come to see as predictable impediments to the introduction of different ways of teaching. After describing the journey of OGAP across the chapters, we will return to these three topics in the concluding chapter and ask what it will take to support the instructional core to fulfill the mission of education organizations to improve the teaching and learning experiences of all students.

Collectively, these themes encapsulate the central power and pitfalls of introducing ambitious instructional reforms into today's school systems, and through the lessons conveyed in the following chapters, we contribute to the growing understanding of the many factors that facilitate and impede enduring change. Through these insights, we seek to help school and system leaders increase their sightings of black swans in the results of their efforts.

2

The Ongoing Assessment Project (OGAP)

A Mathematics Formative Assessment System

MARJORIE PETIT, ELIZABETH HULBERT,
AND ROBERT LAIRD

Sometimes timing is everything. That was the case with the development of the Ongoing Assessment Project (OGAP) in 2003. No Child Left Behind became law in 2002, and teachers and district leaders were feeling the pressure from large-scale assessment and accountability systems. Findings from a meta-study by Black et al. about the potential impact of formative assessment on student learning was just beginning to make its way into practitioners' hands but not their classrooms.[1] The National Research Council had recently published several summative reports with recommendations focused on assessment and student learning. In the recently updated *Principles and Standards for School Mathematics*, the National Council of Teachers of Mathematics was calling for "a carefully organized system of assessment of student learning."[2] The stage was set for a project to bring this growing research on formative assessment and mathematics teaching to practitioners and classroom instruction.

THE INCEPTION OF OGAP: RESPONDING TO NEEDS IN THE FIELD

In the fall of 2003, a Vermont statewide committee (hereafter referred to as the Committee) consisting of mathematics coaches, mathematics classroom teachers, and a mathematician was convened by the Vermont Mathematics Partnership (VMP) to respond to two needs:[3]

- improving mathematics learning for all students as it related to state standards and grade-level expectations
- providing teachers with quality information on student understanding to make on-time interventions for a class as a whole and for individual students

This marked the beginning of what would later become the Ongoing Assessment Project (OGAP), a mathematics formative assessment system based on the mathematics education research related to how students develop understanding and fluency of specific concepts, common errors that students make, and preconceptions or misconceptions that can interfere with learning new concepts or solving related problems. OGAP is supported by tools and routines designed for teachers to elicit and act on evidence of student learning.

The early work of the Vermont Mathematics Partnership was informed by recommendations from the National Research Council reports on student learning and assessment, as well as findings from interviews with educators and observations in classrooms.[4] Based on these data, the Committee identified the following challenges:

- Teachers often misused results of both external and classroom-based summative assessments for instructional decisions.

- Mathematics education research was either inaccessible to classroom teachers or teachers did not realize the importance of the research.
- Some teachers used questioning to probe for understanding but often used the strategy haphazardly. Questions were often used for students to convey "correct answers" and were rarely strategically placed to collect information about students' developing conceptual understanding.
- Teachers' content knowledge gaps, particularly at the elementary level, impacted the effectiveness of the questions they asked.
- Teachers celebrated the range of strategies students used to solve problems but often did not realize the potential of using the progression of strategies to inform instructional decisions.
- Teachers were often aware of the final mathematical goal related to a concept but struggled with how to provide timely and informed instruction that deliberately supports all student's reaching the goal, particularly when students falter.

The Committee created an overarching conceptual framework comprising four guiding principles (figure 2.1) that still anchors the foundation of OGAP.

Central to this conceptual framework is the understanding that students come to a new topic or concept with preexisting knowledge. For students to effectively learn a new topic or concept, instruction should build upon that preexisting knowledge; otherwise, the instruction might not result in the intended learning. In addition to the importance of prior knowledge, learning and assessing for understanding are essential for student learning. The framework also recognizes that only through ongoing formative assessment can teachers be clear about the nature of a student's preexisting and developing understandings. Finally, assessments should build upon mathematics education research on the topic or concept and be designed to probe for student understanding on an ongoing basis.

The Committee agreed that the "ideal" model would be one in which teachers were trained to use formative assessment techniques, including effective questioning, for formative and instructional purposes. Based on

Figure 2.1 OGAP guiding principles

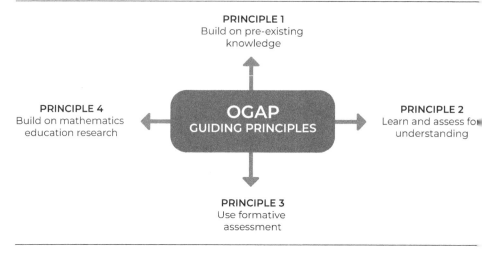

existing research and standards, the decision was made to focus on core mathematical ideas at the different grade spans: additive reasoning in the primary grades, multiplicative reasoning and fractions in the intermediate grades, and proportionality for middle school grades.[5] Since reports and interviews indicated that students consistently struggled with fractions, the work began there, later expanding to multiplicative reasoning and proportionality and, finally, to additive reasoning.

Informed by these guiding principles and needs, the Committee distilled hundreds of mathematics education research articles, wrote hundreds of formative assessment items sensitive to research, and developed tools for collecting and analyzing evidence in student work. Initially, the project focused on using mathematics education research to develop formative assessment questions and professional development that was focused on helping teachers understand how to use the items and sort student solutions. However, early users of OGAP asked for deeper understanding of the research. As teachers became aware of the mathematics education research, they wanted to know more.

During the first phase of development, the research for each mathematics topic was organized into frameworks for each content area: (1) the trajectories of strategies students use to solve problems and (2) problem contexts and structures. Over time, the frameworks were refined and made more user-friendly with examples of student work exemplifying strategies along the progression. Notably, at the time this shift was made, the Committee was not aware of the evolving research on mathematics learning trajectories.

For many teachers, the early OGAP progressions helped to explain evidence of student thinking they observed but did not understand. These observations led the Committee to develop professional development activities, essays, and case studies to illuminate the mathematics education research and potential evidence-based instructional responses to evidence in student work. These materials ultimately resulted in a series of books written for practitioners:

- *A Focus on Addition and Subtraction: Bringing Mathematics Education Research to the Classroom*[6]
- *A Focus on Multiplication and Division: Bringing Research to the Classroom*[7]
- *A Focus on Fractions: Bringing Research to the Classroom*[8]
- *A Focus on Ratios and Proportions: Bringing Mathematics Education Research to the Classroom*[9]

OGAP'S CONTINUOUS IMPROVEMENT MODEL

Mirroring the continuous learning model of formative assessment, OGAP has sought to use research to continuously improve the program. Based on emerging understandings about effective professional development in the field, and participant feedback over time, OGAP's professional development expanded to include specific sessions addressing mathematics content knowledge, knowledge of the related content-specific mathematics education research, and the tools and strategies to gather, interpret, and act on evidence of student learning as shown in figure 2.2. OGAP professional development currently involves four days of direct professional development and ongoing implementation support. The ultimate goal of OGAP

Figure 2.2 Informed instructional decision-making

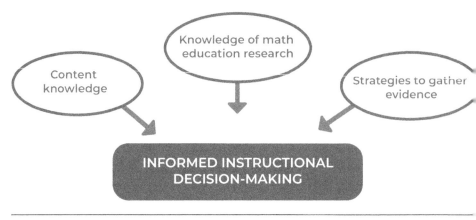

Source: From *A Focus on Fractions: Bringing Mathematics Education Research to the Classroom*, 3rd Edition, by Marjorie Petit, Robert Laird, Caroline Ebby, and Edwin Marsden, Copyright 2022 by Routledge. Reproduced by permission of Taylor & Francis Group.

professional development is to provide teachers with the information they need to make informed instructional decisions.

THE EVOLUTION OF OGAP

Since 2003, OGAP has been developed and refined. The initial development period, which occurred roughly between 2003 and 2008, focused on the design of the OGAP frameworks in fractions and multiplicative reasoning for grades 3–5 and proportional reasoning for grades 6–8. Research in both Vermont and Alabama on both the frameworks and associated professional development included cognitive labs, the collection of student work samples associated with OGAP items, the development of pre- and postassessments, small-scale studies of classroom teachers, and action research projects.

The second phase of OGAP development ran roughly from 2008 to 2014. During this phase OGAP developed a partnership with the Consortium for Policy Research in Education (CPRE) at both Teachers College–Columbia University and the University of Pennsylvania. This partnership allowed OGAP to collect and analyze artifacts to build an e-tool and refine the tools, resources, and professional development of the project. The e-tool included an electronic version of the item bank and an electronic system to sort through the item bank and to record the evidence in student work.

From 2014 to 2016, in partnership with CPRE at the University of Pennsylvania, OGAP was funded to deliver and support OGAP implementation in thirty-one schools in the School District of Philadelphia and a neighboring district. This project was part of a National Science Foundation funded study of the impacts of OGAP on teacher and student learning. The promising results of this work led to a partnership with the School District of Philadelphia and CPRE from 2016 to 2019. The Philadelphia Mathematics Learning Collaborative provided different supports to OGAP teachers and school leaders in Philadelphia area schools and studied approaches to systemic instructional reform.

Simultaneously, from 2016 to 2018, OGAP and CPRE received another grant from the National Science Foundation to develop an additive reasoning framework and item bank to provide support for grades K–2.

Over the past two decades, OGAP has worked with thousands of teachers in schools and districts in Alabama, Delaware, Kentucky, Maryland, Michigan, Minnesota, Nebraska, New Hampshire, Vermont, New York, Pennsylvania, and South Carolina and internationally. OGAP oversees a team of thirty National Facilitators and over a hundred site-based facilitators, providing training in districts across the country.

In the next section we provide an overview of the key elements of OGAP's formative assessment system and approach to helping teachers use formative assessments and learning progressions to inform improvements in teaching and learning.

INTEGRATING FORMATIVE ASSESSMENT AND LEARNING TRAJECTORIES TO INFORM INSTRUCTION AND STUDENT LEARNING

OGAP is an intentional and systematic approach to formative assessment based on mathematics education research. The key concepts addressed in the OGAP system include (1) how students develop understanding and fluency of specific mathematics concepts, (2) common errors that students make, (3) preconceptions or misconceptions that may interfere with students learning new concepts or solving related problems, (4) how teachers can make instructional decisions based on evidence of student understanding, and (5) how teachers can vary structures of math problems. OGAP is supported by tools and routines designed for teachers to elicit and act on evidence of student learning, including item banks, learning trajectories at a granular size usable at the classroom level for both teachers and students, a series of books for practitioners, extensive professional development, and ongoing support.

The OGAP formative assessment process is cyclical. It involves eliciting and acting on evidence of student thinking and strategies using short, focused assessment items based on mathematics education research and designed to elicit developing student understandings, common errors, preconceptions, and misconceptions. The items are strategically used as an entrance card, during the lesson, or as an exit card at the end of a lesson. As teachers internalize the OGAP progressions and the interaction of the progression of strategies with problem structures, they begin to collect and act on evidence in real time as students are learning.

In OGAP professional development, teachers are introduced to the OGAP cycle through an iterative sequence of assessing, analyzing, and responding, as shown in figure 2.3. Teachers select items from the OGAP item bank, or another carefully chosen item, administer the item to students (assess), sort the student results based upon the OGAP framework, and develop an informed response based on the evidence of student thinking represented by their work (analyze). Based on their analysis and guided by the OGAP framework and other instructional resources, teachers enact an informed instructional response to evidence of student thinking.

OGAP frameworks, for each content strand, communicate the relationships among the progression, problem contexts, and problem structures. The progressions offer a visual representation of a learning trajectory of student strategies for solving problems in a specific area. The OGAP

Figure 2.3 The OGAP cycle

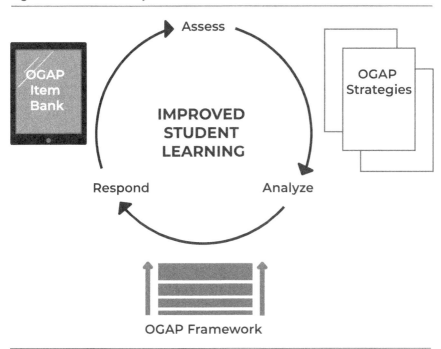

progressions and problem structures and contexts work in concert with each other, as we will illustrate shortly.

It is worth noting that the terms *learning trajectory* and *learning progression* are often used interchangeably even though each has its unique origin. Unfortunately, researchers do not clearly agree on the differences between learning trajectories and learning progressions. A learning trajectory was originally defined to include "the learning goal, the learning activities, and the thinking and learning in which students might engage."[10] One definition of a learning progression describes it as a succession of increasingly more complex ways of reasoning about a related set of ideas.[11] In this way of thinking, a learning progression proposes a learning pathway students can follow as they develop deeper understanding and increased facility within a particular domain.[12] To make the distinctions between a learning trajectory and a learning progression more uncertain, Lobato and Waters introduced the term *learning trajectory/progression* (LT/P) to acknowledge the difficulties in differentiating between the two terms.[13] In materials and training, OGAP uses the term *learning progression*.

Consider the OGAP Ratio and Proportion Progression shown in figure 2.4. The OGAP progressions have several distinct features:

- The different levels on the progression reflect movement from less sophisticated to more sophisticated and more efficient strategies. Each level is briefly described in the callouts on the right side of figure 2.4.
- The two-way arrow on the left side of the progression is an important reminder that learning progressions are not linear. Rather, as students learn new concepts and/or interact with problem structures, their solution strategies may move back and forth across the progression.
- The arrow on the right provides some potential instructional strategies to address students' understanding (e.g., instructional focus on visual models, multiplicative relationships, equivalence, unit rate, contexts, and the coordinate plane). There is not one right path to help move students toward more efficient and sophisticated strategies; rather, the path is dependent on a student's strengths and weaknesses in understanding, and in this way the progressions provide equity access and multiple entry points for all students.
- At the bottom of the progression is a list of underlying issues and errors that teachers may find in student work.

UNDERSTANDING THE INTERACTION OF PROBLEM STRUCTURES AND CONTEXTS

This section focuses on the impact that problem contexts, topics, and structures have on problem difficulty, using ratio and proportion problems as an example. Problem structures refer to how problems are built—that is, "how the features of the problems are organized and interact with each other."[14] Problem context and topics refer to the range of situations in which proportionality is evidenced (e.g., constant speed, scale, slope, similarity).

Figure 2.5 shows the problem context and problem structures of the OGAP Ratio and Proportion Framework. Notice the range of problem contexts that involve understanding and fluency of ratios and proportions. The contexts span algebra, geometry, statistics, probability, percents, measurement, and consumerism and are not just part of a unit of instruction called ratios and proportions. Rather, they are an integral part of mathematics at the middle school level. Notice the different problem structures (e.g., problem types, types of numbers, language).

Researchers have found that depending on the strength of proportional reasoning and the problem structure and context, student solutions may vary between proportional, transitional, and nonproportional strategies.[15] Ultimately, a strong proportional reasoner should not be influenced by context or problem structures.[16]

To better understand how problem structures and contexts interact with each other, consider the three problems in figure 2.6. How are the problems alike? How are they different? Which problems may be easier for students? What structures do you think influence the difficulty?

Even though all three problems involve the same context, constant speed, each represents a different problem type with different mathematical demands. Figure 2.7 explains how these problems differ.

These problems involve the same context, but each of these problem types (missing value, unit rate, rate comparisons) can be situated in different contexts such as density, buying and consuming, and so forth. Besides varying the context and problem type, other features can be engineered to impact the difficulty of ratio and proportion problems (e.g., number type).

A Focus on Ratios and Proportions: Bringing Mathematics Education Research to the Classroom dedicates four chapters to helping teachers understand the mathematics education research related to these ideas.[17]

Teachers use their understanding of the problem contexts and problem structures to select OGAP formative assessment items from the OGAP item bank, from their mathematics instructional materials, or from problems they strategically developed.

Figure 2.4 OGAP Ratio and Proportion Progression

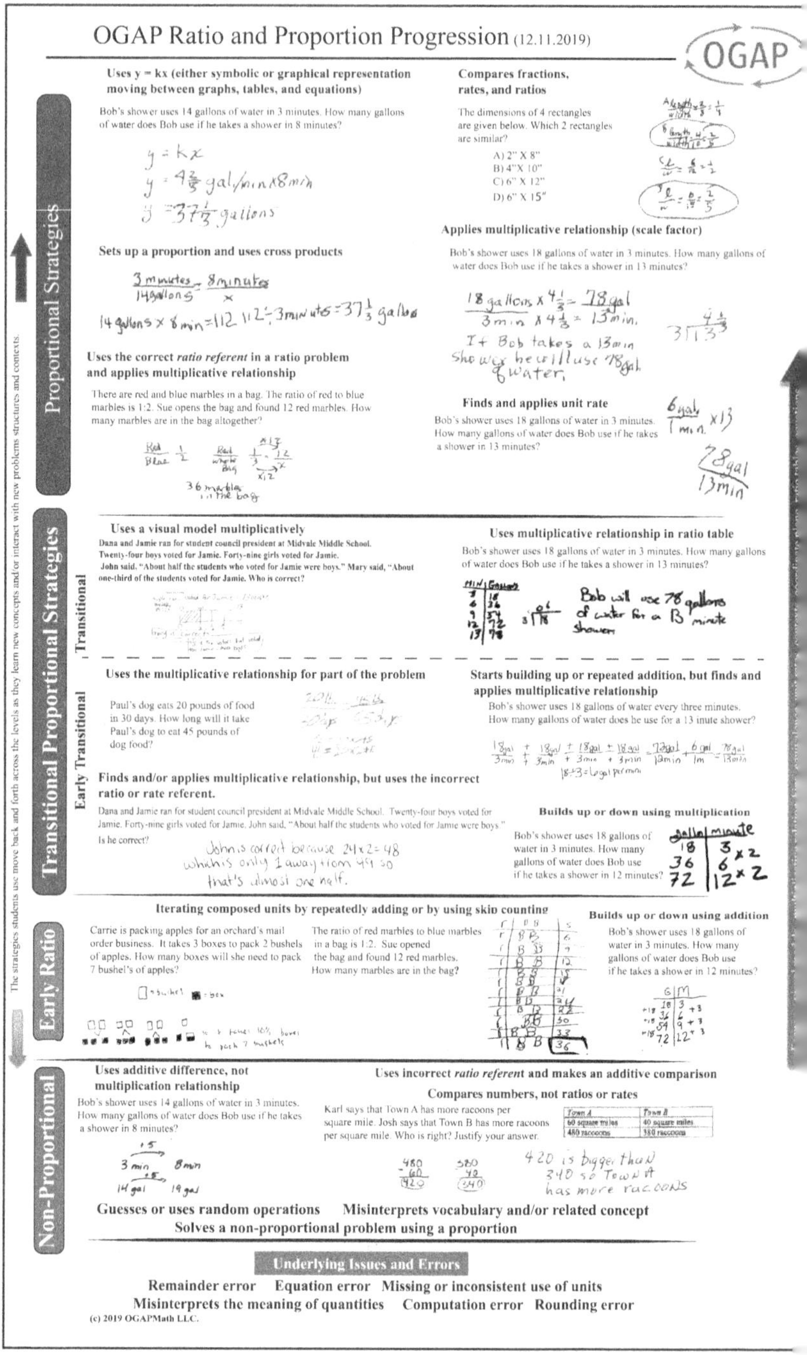

Proportional Strategies are efficient and generalizable

Finding and applying:

- ✓ scale factors
- ✓ unit rates
- ✓ multiplicative relationships and compaing ratios or rates, and using the cross-products procedure

Transitional Strategies show evidence of using the multiplicative relationships between quantities, but the strategy many not be efficient.

Early Transitional Strategies show evidence of using the multiplicative relationship for part, but not the entire problem.

Early Ratio Strategies show evidence of iterating composed unit and/or using an additive rather than multiplicative strategy.

Nonproportional Strategies show evidence of using the additive differences between quantities, comparing numbers not quantities in ratio, guessing or uses random operation.

g Issues or Errors uses repeated addition, remainder error, equation error, inconsistent use of units, misinterprets the quantities in the problem, ion error, rounding error, others.

Figure 2.5 OGAP Ratio and Proportion task considerations and progression

Task Considerations

Problem Context

*Ratios
*Density
*Constant speed
*Buy/consume
*Concentrations
*Measurement conversions
*Similarity
*Scale
*Probability
*Percents
*Slope
*Sampling

Problem Structures

*Problem types
*Internal structure
*Multiplicative relationships
*Types of number
*Ratio referent
*Language
*Ratio relationships
*Representations

Figure 2.6 Problem contexts and problem types

Problem 1:
Sally walks 2 miles every day. It takes her 30 minutes. Ashley walks 5 miles every day, and it take her 2 hours. Who walks faster?

Problem 2:
Donna runs at an average rate of 6 miles per hour. At this rate, how many miles can she run in 2 hours?

Problem 3:
Tanya walks 3 miles in 30 minutes. If Tanya maintains this rate, how many miles can she walk in 60 minutes?

Source: Marjorie Petit et al., *A Focus on Ratios and Proportions: Bringing Mathematics Education Research to the Classroom* (New York: Routledge, 2020), 131.

Figure 2.7   Three problem types and the features that distinguish them from each other

Problem 1 is a *rate comparison problem*. In this example, the distance and time are given for both walkers. To solve this problem one must compare each ratio and choose the one that indicates a faster speed.

Problem 2 is a *unit rate problem*. That is, the unit rate of 6 miles per hour is one of the quantities given. To solve this problem, one has to use the unit rate as well as the amount of time stated in the problem to determine how far one might run in a different amount of time.

Problem 3 is a *missing value problem*. That is, three quantities are given (in this case two amounts of times and one distance) and the student is asked to find the missing quantity (distance for walking 60 minutes).

Source: Marjorie Petit et al., *A Focus on Ratios and Proportions: Bringing Mathematics Education Research to the Classroom* (New York: Routledge, 2020), 132.

USING THE OGAP PROGRESSION TO GATHER EVIDENCE OF STUDENT THINKING

An important principle of OGAP is that a focus only on the correctness of a student's answer may provide the teacher with limited evidence on which to base future instruction. For example, examine the problem and a sixth-grade student solution in figure 2.8.

> Max and Thomas each delivered vegetables to a store. Max delivered 8 bags of vegetables with 40 pounds in each bag. Thomas delivered 9 bags of vegetables with 35 pounds in each bag. How many pounds of vegetables were delivered by Max and Thomas altogether?

Notice that the solution is correct. If the focus was just on the correctness of the answer, a teacher might overlook the evidence that the student

36 WHEN REFORM MEETS REALITY

Figure 2.8   Repeated addition to solve a multiplication problem

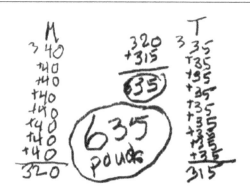

used addition rather than multiplication to solve the problem. Research shows that if repeated addition is a student's default strategy when solving multiplication problems, it is likely that the student will be at a significant disadvantage when working with ratios and proportions, as they move to more advanced mathematics topics.

Focusing on student work from a perspective of a learning progression keeps the initial analysis on the sophistication of the strategy. A technique to help teachers first focus on the learning progressions rather than the correctness of student responses is the OGAP Sort. In the OGAP Sort, the first level of analysis of student work is organizing the responses into groups representing the different levels on the progression as shown in figure 2.9.

The next level of analysis is on the specific strategy that students used, followed by identifying any underlying issues or concerns. Finally, correct and incorrect solutions are identified. Figure 2.10 shows the result of an OGAP Sort summarized in an OGAP evidence collection sheet. Notice that the students' strategies, issues or concerns, and correctness are recorded. Incorrect answers are circled.

OGAP, like all formative assessments, is only formative if action is taken based on the evidence that results in modifying instruction and/or student

Figure 2.9 Sorting student work into piles representing the different levels on the Ratio and Proportion Progression.

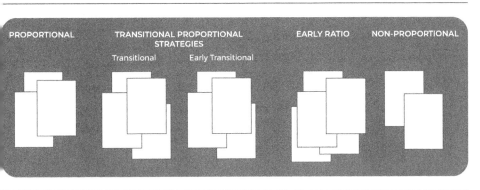

Figure 2.10 OGAP completed evidence collection sheet

ITEM #	PROBLEM STRUCTURES	PROPORTIONAL	TRANSITIONAL PROPORTIONAL		EARLY RATIO	NON-PROPORTIONAL
			Transitional	Early Transitional		
1	Raccoons Density	Harper, Amelia, Mason } unit rate Michael, Amy } Mult Relation ship	William, Mia } Visual Model James, Elijah, Evelyn } ratio table	Ava, Charlotte, Oliver } Builds Multipl. Sophia, Isabelle, Lucas } used result for part of the problem	Noah, Olivia } Iterates a composed unit	Liam, Ben, Emma } Added factors
	Uses additive strategy to find multiplicative relationship:		Remainder Error: Sophia Isabelle Lucas Ava	Error in equation:	Computational error: Mia Evelyn Ava	
	Misinterprets the meaning of quantities: Noah Olivia Liam Ben		Missing or inconsistent use of units: Harper James Mason William Amelia Elijah	Rounding error:	Other:	

learning.[18] To help teachers begin to think about next instructional steps after the evidence is recorded, the analysis then focuses on looking across the evidence for the whole class. The following three questions are posed after a student work sort to help teachers use the evidence they have collected to make informed instructional decisions:

- What are the developing understandings that can be built upon?
- What issues or concerns are evidenced in student work?
- What are potential next instructional steps for the whole class, for small groups, and/or for individuals?

Addressing these questions helps teachers focus on the instructional next steps.

TAKING ACTION: USING FORMATIVE ASSESSMENT AND LEARNING PROGRESSIONS TO INFORM INSTRUCTION

In OGAP professional development, teachers practice sorting, analyzing, and developing instructional responses for sets of student work that have been carefully constructed from authentic student solutions that represent the range of student strategies and errors likely to be elicited in any classroom. To help teachers think about different ways to engage students individually, in small groups, or as a whole class in the context of classroom instruction, they also engage in exploring case studies.

The case studies have the following general format:

- A teacher's lesson goal is presented with a general description of the lesson planned.
- An exit or entrance question that will be a part of the lesson or at the end of the lesson is presented.
- Participants solve the entrance or exit question and then provide an explanation as to why the teacher may have chosen this question, what evidence it might provide, and any errors that students might make.

- Participants then analyze and record a sample set of student work using the OGAP Sort and record the evidence as described on the evidence collection sheet.
- Participants then engage in planning, practicing, or learning about one of the following instructional activities: (1) facilitating a discussion strategically using some of the solutions from the set they analyzed, (2) facilitating a mini-lesson on a concept or strategy, 3) modifying the structures of a problem in order to collect additional evidence, and (4) helping students make sense of word problems.

THE IMPORTANCE OF ONGOING SUPPORT: PROFESSIONAL LEARNING COMMUNITIES (PLCS)

Realizing that professional development alone would not necessarily get the intended result of teachers intentionally and systematically implementing the OGAP formative assessment system, OGAP facilitators provided ongoing support as teachers implemented OGAP in their classrooms. OGAP facilitators also worked with school leadership to plan for thoughtful ongoing support designed to meet the needs of the staff and the unique needs of the school.

Connecting the work done during the initial training to ongoing support is a key element of OGAP. Throughout OGAP training, teachers learn to analyze and respond to evidence in student work using the OGAP progressions. The student work sets used in OGAP training are designed to provide teachers with an opportunity to examine an authentic set of work that represents the range of student responses found to be typical in most classrooms. During the initial training it is made clear to teachers that the process used to analyze students' work and make instructional decision mirrors that which happens in a school-level PLC. Providing support within a school/district allows teachers to replicate this process *using their own student work and planning for their own classrooms* in PLCs.

In many cases OGAP has capitalized on the existing grade-level PLCs in many schools and districts. With assistance from school leaders,

OGAP works with teachers in PLCs to support their implementation of different aspects of the OGAP process such as analyzing student work and making instructional decisions, intentionally selecting items from the item bank for formative assessment purposes, or examining instructional materials.

The opportunity to meet with colleagues in a PLC facilitated by an OGAP trainer helps support teachers at intervals throughout the year. Ideally, between meetings with an OGAP facilitator, teachers regularly monitor their students' understanding, meet in PLCs to analyze and plan for instruction with their colleagues, and then return to their classrooms to implement their instructional response to the evidence. In districts with instructional coaches, OGAP facilitators often train coaches on how to facilitate PLCs and meet with them throughout the school year to troubleshoot issues and help them improve their ability to effectively facilitate OGAP PLCs. Districts without formal instructional coaches often identify a small group of teacher leaders, who with the support of OGAP staff, become PLC facilitators. These OGAP facilitators can support district instructional coaches by providing additional training on how to facilitate PLCs and support teachers in successfully using formative assessment practices in math classrooms. In this way, implementation of OGAP is continually supported throughout the school year. Of course, this happens best in schools with strong support from school leaders.

Occasionally districts do not have a PLC process in place, and OGAP works with the district/school leadership to build a PLC structure that is responsive to the needs of the district and helps supports the implementation of OGAP.

In addition to a focus on PLCs, ongoing support can take several other forms:

- after-school workshops
- meetings with grade-level teams during PLC time
- all-day or half-day topic-specific workshops
- school visits
- modeled instruction in classrooms

- help for coaches to integrate OGAP concepts into upcoming math trainings
- virtual meetings with teachers or coaches
- help for districts to integrate OGAP into their existing mathematics instructional materials
- meetings with administrators
- for administrators, observable evidence of implementation of OGAP, such as:
  - teachers regularly using OGAP progressions
  - students being familiar with the progressions
  - teachers regularly administering and analyzing formative assessment questions and acting on the evidence
  - teachers using formative assessment questions from the OGAP item bank
  - teachers using some of the instructional strategies modeled in PLCs or the professional development, such as selecting and sequencing student work and using think-pair strategies
  - teachers and students using the language of OGAP progressions

Regardless of the format of the follow-up support, the goal is always to support implementation of OGAP and formative assessment strategies.

SCALING UP OGAP FOR A LARGE URBAN DISTRICT

OGAP has worked in several large urban districts, including Philadelphia, Minneapolis, and Charleston, South Carolina. Not surprisingly, each district comes with its own challenges and opportunities that must be considered when thinking about how to implement OGAP effectively. Scaling up in a large district can be daunting. While general follow-up goals are the same for all districts, the opportunities are different. OGAP's preference is to meet with every teacher a number of times throughout a school year to help them implement OGAP routines in their classrooms. While this is doable in smaller schools and districts, large districts likely require a different approach. In larger districts OGAP facilitators may need to support school math leads, grade-level leads, or district coaches to support the teachers while occasionally meeting directly with the classroom teachers.

Together, OGAP staff and district personnel adjust for district needs in terms of both initial training and follow-up. This can take many forms but will involve these aspects as well as others:

- timing of training: summer or school year
- configuration of training: days concurrent or divided into different configurations such as two-two or two-one-one
- number of follow-up days: has ranged from two to three days of follow-up to thirty in one district (The number of follow-up days is often reliant on the kind of support districts want during follow-up.)
- focus and goals of follow-up: direct support for teachers, administration, and/or math coaches, implementation of PLCS or workshops extending and deepening content from the initial training

It is often necessary to look for creative ways to build ongoing support. Examples of strategies that districts have used include after-school workshops, meeting with grade levels during planning time, all-day or half-day workshops that are topic-specific to content teachers have identified as needing more support, school visits, planning with coaches for upcoming math training they are responsible for to help keep focus on OGAP, and meeting virtually with teachers or coaches. No matter the format of the follow-up, the goal is always to support implementation of OGAP and formative assessment strategies.

As an example, in one urban district teachers meet regularly with their instructional coaches to sort, analyze, and respond to the evidence in their student work. The coaches receive regular training from OGAP facilitators to support their work with teachers. Additionally, teachers have a number of options throughout the school year to attend OGAP workshops facilitated by OGAP trainers that have been designed to respond to the unique structure of the district. They may go to a session titled OGAP Boost, which reviews some content or practice introduced in initial training that would benefit from a deeper understanding, or teachers may choose to go to a workshop designed to help them embed formative assessment tasks into their math program materials.

Another important aspect of OGAP support is a focus on observable implementation to help administrators develop a sense of what OGAP is and what it will look like in a classroom. Classrooms that are implementing OGAP practices should be using the OGAP learning progressions to analyze evidence of student thinking and to make instructional decisions based on that evidence. Administrators might recognize some of the tasks as being from the OGAP item bank, should see teachers using strategies such as select and sequence or warm-ups in response to their students' thinking and may hear the language of the OGAP learning progressions used by teachers and students.

Ultimately, OGAP is focused on helping districts help teachers to become more effective instructors of K–8 mathematics. To this end, OGAP encourages districts to make a long-term plan to maintain the progress made with initial OGAP training by training some coaches or teachers to be OGAP trainers in-district, thereby sustaining the work for many years to come. In this way, as new teachers enter the district, receiving OGAP training can be one aspect of their orientation. Districts often take a multifaceted approach to accomplishing the goal of sustainability of OGAP. Whatever pathway a district chooses, OGAP works with them to accomplish independence and success with long-term sustainability.

FINAL THOUGHTS

This chapter provided an overview of the development and structure of OGAP's content-based formative assessment system and implementation strategies. The OGAP knowledge base, tools, and routines were built on the emerging research about the effectiveness of formative assessment and the mathematics education research on how students learn specific mathematics concepts. OGAP focuses its work on additive reasoning, multiplicative reasoning, fractions, and proportionality. Initial development was supported by the Vermont Mathematics Partnership National Science Foundation (NSF) grant spanning the years 2003–2008.

Partnerships with CPRE at Teachers College at the University of Pennsylvania supported the additional analysis of artifacts collected during two Vermont-based studies to build an e-tool and refine the tools, resources, and professional development of the project. In 2014 CPRE at the University of Pennsylvania was awarded an NSF grant to conduct a large-scale study of the effectiveness of OGAP on teacher and student learning. Other chapters in this book provide in-depth discussion of the results of this study and other substudies conducted during the life of the grant.

Since 2005 OGAP has provided professional development to schools and districts across the country. One important piece of learning from this work is that ambitious instructional reform, such OGAP implementation in a school or district, requires intensive professional development, effective tools, systems and routines, and ongoing support. Interestingly, OGAP facilitators continue to find that the mathematics education research and the intentional and systematic approach to content-based formative assessment upon which OGAP was founded is new to most teachers that we work with today. Yet teachers continue to be eager and excited to learn this research, to develop deeper understanding of mathematics content, and to embrace the opportunities to use OGAP tools and routines to help all students learn important mathematics.

3

OGAP in Philadelphia

Adaptive Partnering in a Complex System

JANINE T. REMILLARD

INTRODUCTION

Researchers and commentators offer many explanations for why reforms are or are not taken up. Another approach is to ask *how* reforms are taken up. In their analysis of the history of reforms in US schools, Tyack and Cuban assert, "It is the rare reform that performs and persists precisely according to plan. Even long-lasting reforms are not static but evolve in ways often not foreseen by its proponents."[1] Some may view such revision as failure. Tyack and Cuban see it as *tinkering*—a natural and inevitable process of adapting reforms to fit schools, when making schools fit reforms is out of reach.

This chapter describes a five-year project aimed at introducing the Ongoing Assessment Project (OGAP) to teachers in the School District of Philadelphia (SDP). In collaboration with OGAP developers, a team of researchers and educators from the Consortium for Policy Research in

Education (CPRE) brought OGAP to SDP, first through a two-year experimental study and then through a collaborative partnership with district leaders to support the use of formative assessment in elementary school mathematics. An overarching theme in our work was change. In response to challenges and new learning, we adapted our approach—to how we supported teachers, connected with schools, and partnered with district leaders—to remain true to our aims. In Tyack and Cuban's words, we tinkered. Tinkering, however, can be interpreted as haphazard; yet we see this adaptive work as strategic and responsive. This chapter tells the story of this process and asks, What can we learn from how we adapted the reform design? This retrospective analysis makes evident the intricate and multilayered nature of working toward instructional improvement within a large school district.

PERSPECTIVES

The introduction of OGAP to SDP was initiated by a team of CPRE researchers. Members of this team had worked with the developers of OGAP for over five years and, seeing its potential, wanted to see it implemented in a district like SDP. This team secured funding from the National Science Foundation (NSF) to support the research and development activities and made overtures to district leaders to enlist their participation and engagement. Throughout the five-year period, members of this team, in collaboration with OGAP developers, worked on multiple fronts to keep the OGAP work moving forward and secure its place in the district. The story of the partnership activities in this chapter reflects the perspective of the CPRE and OGAP teams, which I refer to as "we." I use "I" when presenting my perspective or analytical decisions.

I begin by outlining the framing lenses guiding my analysis. I then provide a brief overview of the activities spanning the five-year project, before detailing the major adaptations that took place. I then examine these adaptations thematically, considering their implications for our evolving partnership with the district and nurturing instructional reform more generally.

FRAMING LENSES

The analysis in this chapter is guided by lenses drawn from design-based implementation research (DBIR) and research on instructional improvement within school systems.[2] The term *design-based implementation research*, coined by Penuel et al., refers to a strategy increasingly taken up by researchers in partnership with practitioners to support sustained, system-level change in educational practices.[3] DBIR builds on design research in classrooms, which involves short cycles of instructional design activities followed by revision, applying this approach to work within larger systems. While there is not a single approach to DBIR, most efforts involve a "model of collaborative, iterative, and systematic research and development."[4] In contrast to research that seeks to test an approach to implementing new ideas in a system, DBIR focuses on addressing "persistent problems of practice from multiple stakeholders' perspectives" and embraces a commitment to iterative cycles of design, learning, and revision as more is learned about the problem and the system.[5]

We did not begin the project with a DBIR lens. But, early on, we found ourselves using a number of DBIR principles and strategies and eventually began to understand our work from this vantage point. In particular, the focus on developing a capacity for sustaining change within the system and the concern for developing and testing theory related to classroom-level and system-level learning aligned with our growing understanding of our work. At many junctures along the way, our partnership with the district felt precarious and required ongoing design to navigate it. The DBIR lens was also helpful in understanding these challenges.

The DBIR lens is complemented by research on instructional improvement within school systems, which offers insight into the complexity of school districts and their impact on classroom practices or efforts to influence them. Researchers in the MIST project, a multiyear instructional improvement partnership with four school districts, argue that most instructional improvement efforts do not take into account the importance of the system in which teaching happens—teachers are organized within schools, which are nested within districts.[6] Instructional improvement efforts are profoundly impacted by school and district policies and leadership practices.[7] In other words, efforts to support significant instructional change must be informed by both research on teaching and learning and research on instructional improvement systems.

Researchers who study instructional change within complex school systems have offered several insights that are brought into sharp relief when examining our work with the district over time. First, there is considerable agreement that school districts are typically not structured to support instructional improvement. They tend to be organized in bureaucratic ways that distance management from the on-the-ground practice of teaching and learning, and thus efforts to improve it, whereas meaningful instructional improvement must be supported by a coherent system at all levels.[8] Cobb and colleagues further argue that support for instructional improvement is most effective when these efforts focus on schools and classrooms, where instruction takes place.[9] At the same time, accomplishing instructional change requires the support of leadership systems and organizational structures outside of schools.[10] In short, staying focused on the classroom but remaining cognizant of the ways classroom practices are supported or constrained by different levels of the system is critical.

It is also critical to acknowledge that *people* occupy the different levels of any school system, and it is their perspectives, decisions, actions, and interactions that propel the system forward. While the role of people is obvious, the way they interact within a system has been highlighted by analytical lenses that look past formal organizational structures and positions. Some people are skilled in traveling across communities (boundary crossers or brokers) and can facilitate communication and engagement across often stratified systems. Stein and Coburn theorize that the presence of brokers and boundary objects (tools and resources that have meaning within different communities of practice) can foster greater alignment across a system.[11]

Finally, instructional reforms call on teachers to work in new ways, which generally require new learning.[12] Teachers must learn new routines and strategies, and in the case of OGAP, they need opportunities to learn about how children's mathematical understandings develop and how to interpret students' work within this framework. Most likely, they also need support to deepen their mathematics knowledge. As Stein and Coburn explain, most reform efforts "fail to account for the role that teachers' learning plays in the implementation of new programs and practices."[13] Extrapolating out, a system not set up to enable learning is unlikely to support instructional reform. This approach to instructional reform dovetails with theories underlying OGAP.

The description and analysis that follow incorporate these lenses. I examine the iterative process of design, learning, and revision of our approach to support the use of OGAP in SDP schools, and in this process, I bring attention to how our work was influenced by our developing awareness of the system, the people, and the opportunities for learning.

OVERVIEW OF THE FIVE-YEAR PARTNERSHIP

CPRE's relationship with SDP around the use of OGAP began in 2014. This relationship, however, was preceded by a long-standing history of collaborative activities. SDP has often served as a site for research and professional development initiated by CPRE or others in the University of Pennsylvania's Graduate School of Education (GSE), and many teachers, principals, and central office leaders in the district have had relationships with GSE programs and projects. In fact, two key players in the OGAP partnership, the chief academic officer and newly hired director of mathematics, were doctoral students in GSE programs at the time. Moreover, work at CPRE that is focused on deepening and extending the use of OGAP in district schools has continued in various forms since the five-year partnership covered in this volume officially concluded.

The five-year OGAP project can be divided into two parts, each having its own purpose and underlying theory of action. The first two years (2014–2016) were designed as an external study, testing the impacts of the

OGAP approach on students' mathematics outcomes in both SDP and an adjacent smaller district, using a randomized controlled trial (RCT) design. RCTs are considered the gold standard of educational research because the design allows researchers to make causal claims about the effect of an intervention. While RCTs are highly desirable in the research and policy worlds, they are challenging to implement in the hustle and bustle of the real world of schools. Prior to this time, OGAP developers and collaborators had undertaken descriptive research of its tools and instruments, but the approach had not been rigorously studied, especially as an intervention that could systematically improve teaching or student learning. In order to advocate for efforts to implement the program in school systems under extreme pressure to improve student test scores, we understood that evidence of impact would be pivotal to gain traction. SDP more than fit the bill of a struggling urban district. Plagued with low test scores, the district operated under the weight of accountability measures in place since the No Child Left Behind (NCLB) period, which included tight regulation of teaching and favored rote instruction of isolated skills.

The last three years of the project (2016–2019) reflected a major transition in the relationship and focus of the partnership. Funded by a new NSF grant, our work focused on building capacity within the school system, in order to support the use of OGAP in deeper and coherent ways. Our initial approach during this period was largely informed by challenges we confronted during the RCT, which included our developing understanding of the need for systemwide coherence and vision around the learning principles underlying OGAP and the instructional approach it promoted. We saw principal and district leader engagement as pivotal to the take-up of OGAP. To this end, we sought to forge a deeper partnership with district and school leaders aimed at developing what we referred to as a "formative assessment mindset" toward learning across the system, rather than simply inserting this lens into teachers' instructional routines.

This second phase of the project co-occurred with a new period in the district's investment in mathematics teaching and curriculum. Mathematics, which had long played second fiddle to literacy and reading, received renewed attention and funding in 2016. The district hired a director of mathematics (DoM), a position that had been vacant for many years, and added two additional math specialists to the curriculum office within the first year. Through the relationships we had built with district leaders and supported by the NSF grant, the CPRE/OGAP team had a seat at the table for some of the plans that followed.

In 2016, the district launched a new initiative, entitled MathCounts. A major pillar of MathCounts was the Summer Math Institute (SMI), an intensive week of professional development for K–12 teachers and leaders, accompanied by school-based coaching during the school year. About one-quarter of the district's 160 plus schools were accepted to participate in the first year, with the expectation that the remaining schools would participate in the following two years. Acceptance was contingent on full principal participation in the summer institute and attendance of at least 65 percent of the teachers. The district contracted with Carnegie Learning to provide professional development and follow-up coaching for SMI participants but also contracted with OGAP to provide the professional development for all grades 3–5 teachers. The SMI also included sessions for principals and time for school teams to meet, reflect on their learning, and set goals for the coming year.

Additionally, each school in the district was required to identify a *math teacher leader*, who would have some responsibilities for supporting the math instruction among their colleagues, although criteria for selection and the extent of their responsibilities were underspecified. In the same year, leveraging funds from a city-wide cigarette tax before they expired, the curriculum office purchased and rolled out new reading and mathematics textbook series throughout the district, which further increased the focus on mathematics (and pressures faced by teachers).

MAJOR ADAPTATIONS

Throughout these two stages in Philadelphia, our commitment to the use of learning trajectory–oriented formative assessment to improve elementary mathematics teaching remained constant. We viewed OGAP resources and processes as a vehicle to support teachers' learning about and use of both specific learning progressions and formative assessment. Over the five years, and particularly in the last three, our approach evolved in both responsive and intentional ways. These evolutions were guided by a persistent problem of practice: fostering an approach to formative assessment in elementary mathematics instruction that centered teacher practice and decision-making. This approach to instructional improvement differed from the district's standard, top-down approach. Addressing this problem of practice involved making incremental changes and then gathering formal and informal evidence to inform the next iteration. Because we were working in and alongside, a large, struggling school district, much of our learning shed light on the uncertain work of supporting instructional improvement in a large school system.

In this section, I highlight the major structural adaptations that we made in the design of our work. Later, I discuss what these adaptations capture about our supporting instructional reform in a large, complicated, school district. Table 3.1 summarizes the five years of the project with respect to several key structural characteristics: focal grade levels, number of schools involved, the summer institute offering, the site-based support provided to each school, how principals and teacher leaders were involved, and our relationship to the systems for mathematics instruction in the district. The arrows indicate the notable adaptations in these characteristics from one year to the next.

As shown in table 3.1, many characteristics of the project remained the same during the RCT, years 1 and 2. We worked with thirty treatment schools in the two districts, all of which agreed to support grades 3–5 teachers to use OGAP resources regularly in their mathematics teaching. Teachers were introduced to OGAP through a three-day summer institute, taught by OGAP trainers, held at the district central office. Two half-day additional training sessions took place during the school year at times designated by the district for professional development. Principals were introduced to the philosophy and approach of OGAP through a ninety-minute meeting prior to each school year. Each principal agreed to identify a teacher leader who would serve as the point person and agreed to facilitate OGAP professional learning communities (PLCs), which is where teachers discuss what they are learning from student work on

Table 3.1 Key characteristics of CPRE-SDP partnership and major structural adaptations over time

	RCT Study of Impact of OGAP		Philadelphia Math Leadership Collaborative		
Year	2014–2015	2015–2016	2016–2017	2017–2018	2018–2019
Funding source	National Science Foundation		National Science Foundation		
Grade levels	3–5 only	3–5 only	3–5 only ➡	All grades—K–8	
Number of schools	31 treatment schools[a] ➡		16 school teams	15 new schools; 12 returning	9 new schools; 20 returning
Summer Institute	3 full-day teacher PD sessions, held at district central office; 1 full-day for teacher leaders ➡		5 full-day teacher PD sessions offered as part of Summer Math Institute, held at district school Leaders attended some sessions and had other district PD as well		
School-year PD	2 half-day sessions for teachers ➡ 3 full-day sessions for teacher leaders		2 after-school PD sessions; 2 school team ➡ meetings		
Site-based support	None ➡	OGAP coaches ➡ assigned to visit schools	2 half-day school visits ➡ by OGAP trainers	5 half-day school visits by OGAP trainers	5 half-day school visits by OGAP trainers
Principal involvement	Minimal ➡		Principal seen as leader of OGAP work in schools Required to attend Summer Math Institute 2–4 professional development sessions for school leader each year		
Teacher leader/math liaison role	Appointed by principal Asked to lead PLCs ➡		Teacher leaders seen as key guide for using OGAP in each school, often through PLCs Teacher leaders invited to attend school leader PDs		
Project relationship with district	Outside provider ➡		Partner in district's new MathCounts initiative Provided OGAP PD at Summer Math Institute and ongoing support for schools		

[a] Twenty-six of the thirty-one treatment schools were from SDP public and charter schools. The other five were from Upper Darby, an adjacent district.

OGAP tasks. These teacher leaders received a targeted day of professional development (PD) at the end of the summer institute. We learned through school visits during year 1 that these PLCs were infrequent occurrences in many schools. As a result, we added three full days of PD for teacher leaders during the year. In the 2015–2016 school year hired three OGAP coaches who were tasked with visiting schools, making contact with teacher leaders, and encouraging the use of OGAP, particularly through PLCs where teachers could analyze student work together.

The project evolved considerably in years 3–5. With support of the second NSF grant, we pursued a collaborative partnership with district leaders, which we called Philadelphia Mathematics Leadership Collaborative (PMLC). Under the PMLC umbrella, the CPRE-OGAP-SDP relationship transitioned from an external research and reform effort to a partnership in which efforts to improve math teaching were integrated into many district's offerings and support systems. We supported district leaders in the launch of the MathCounts initiative while negotiating a place for OGAP in these activities.

Key characteristics of the partnership also underwent several substantial changes, shown by the arrows in table 3.1, many of which involved nurturing a school team, including principals and teacher leaders, around the use of OGAP. In year 3 we worked with sixteen schools, continuing our focus on the use of OGAP resources in grades 3–5. These schools were among the forty K–8 schools that attended the Summer Math Institute, where all grades 3–5 teachers received OGAP professional development. All schools from the SMI were invited to participate in "ongoing support opportunities." The sixteen school teams that opted in agreed to host two half-day school visits by OGAP trainers to work with their staff, in December and February, and send teachers to two additional OGAP workshops, held at a local school, in January and March. Principals and math leads also agreed to participate in two leadership meetings, framed as helping them "explore ways to foster a school environment that is supportive to OGAP and the continuous learning mindset." School teams were also asked to attend a workshop cohosted by the district and OGAP trainers, aimed at connecting district and OGAP resources, and a final session, in May, aimed at celebrating their successes and discussing plans for the following year.

In year 4, we continued our approach of working with school teams, but we were able to expand this work in a critically important way—encompassing all grade levels, from kindergarten to eighth grade. This adaptation became possible when a CPRE/OGAP team of developers completed a suite of OGAP resources for grades K–2, focused on additive reasoning.[14] Thus, beginning in 2017, the OGAP suite of resources included frameworks and item banks for the following domains and grades: additive reasoning (K–2), multiplicative reasoning (3–5), fractional reasoning (3–5), and ratios and proportions (6–8). From this point forward, our efforts focused on extending the use of OGAP across the entire K–8 range, allowing whole elementary schools to adopt OGAP, regardless of their grade configuration.

Unlike the previous year, we contacted schools planning to attend the 2017 SMI in advance and invited them to participate in OGAP's summer professional development and year-long follow-up support. Fifteen schools chose to participate for the first time in 2017–2018 and agreed to send teachers from all grades to the OGAP sections of the SMI. Twelve schools from the previous year also continued their involvement, and we were able to open some institute spots to K–2 and 6–8 teachers from this cohort, since these teachers had not yet been introduced to OGAP.

The follow-up support activities were similar to the previous year but more intensive. New schools received five half-day visits by an OGAP trainer during the year; returning schools received two visits. We also held four professional development sessions for principals and math leads, aimed primarily at helping them support the formative assessment work being undertaken by teachers in their schools. In response to concerns raised by teachers the previous year, we threaded explicit connections between OGAP and the approaches of the newly adopted textbooks into the professional development for teachers and leaders across the year and introduced a new platform to support teachers in making these connections.

In year 5, we continued our approach of supporting the use of OGAP within K–8 schools, using a similar approach as the previous year. Our sights were set on building capacity and sustainability within schools, knowing that our funding was coming to an end. (We also worked toward maintaining a commitment to OGAP by the district, which I discuss later.) Nine new schools opted to join in the partnership, beginning with sending teachers and principals to OGAP professional development during the 2018 Summer Math Institute. Twenty schools continued from the previous year. As shown in table 3.1, much of the site-based support was similar to the previous year, primarily comprising school trainer visits and sessions for leaders.

As already noted, Carnegie Learning was contracted to lead the bulk of the professional development during the Summer Math Institutes. They also provided coaches to visit schools during the year following their participation in the SMI. Beginning in 2017, OGAP was funded through a subcontract with Carnegie Learning, which included support for Carnegie coaches on using OGAP tools, allowing them to align their support for teachers using OGAP. In this way, our partnership with the district allowed us to subtly extend the reach of OGAP into schools we were not directly supporting.

ANALYSIS OF MAJOR ADAPTATIONS

The changes in structural features of the partnership, summarized in table 3.1 and described in the previous section, were often responsive in nature, reflecting learning and challenges from the previous year. Some were born out of an effort to address immediate problems or gain traction among many competing demands; others were influenced by changing initiatives in the district. Looking across these adaptations, I identified four interrelated trends in how we worked with the district. First, over the five years, we located more of our work in schools and *with* schools. Second, through the development of new OGAP tools and frameworks, we were able to focus our capacity-building work on the entire school. A third evolution was in the innovations and tools we developed to support the use of formative assessment in classrooms. Finally, these shifts necessarily had implications for our ongoing relationship with the district, which underwent changes for other reasons, as well. Ultimately, we found that maintaining a flexible and adaptive approach to our relationship with the district was critical, given the churn and competing demands common to large, underresourced districts. In the sections that follow, I elaborate on each of these trends, providing more details about the story of OGAP in Philadelphia and the major evolutions of our work.

Anchoring the Work of Instructional Improvement in Schools

From the very beginning, OGAP professional development and resources focused directly on teachers and teaching. Over the five years of the project, the focus of our partnership evolved in two ways that had the impact of solidly anchoring our work in partner schools and leveraging their ecology to support instructional improvement. The first change involved locating more support and professional development at the school, as opposed to at a central location; the second change involved increasing the participation of school leaders from each school.

Locating Efforts in Schools Initially, the RCT (project years 1 and 2) supported teachers from a central location. Teachers attended OGAP professional development at the school district central office, and additional or make-up sessions were available at central locations during the year. We did not plan any site-based support, although, following the design of OGAP, we expected that PLCs, led by teacher leaders, would provide ongoing opportunities for teachers to learn to use OGAP tools.

Through a set of school visits in December of 2014, we found that the use of OGAP resources was modest at best. Typical teacher turnover and grade-level changes meant many teachers and even teacher leaders who had received training were no longer teaching grades 3–5. Many were distracted by other demands and were challenged to see the relevance of the OGAP resources for their math teaching. Some teacher leaders reported limited success in coordinating schedules so that they could hold regular PLCs, and for many principals, supporting the use of OGAP lacked urgency when weighed against the long list of procedures and programs required by the district, which favored literacy. While the district supported the study, teachers and school leaders did not receive any consistent messaging from the district about OGAP. All communication came from CPRE, reflecting our role as outside providers.

Our efforts were also affected by other tensions in the district. A longstanding contract dispute resulted in the district canceling the teachers' contract in mid-fall, the night before a teacher in-service day during which we were scheduled to offer additional professional development. Many teachers called out in protest. In some ways, our relationship with district curriculum leaders positioned us on the wrong side of this dispute. We also learned that many teachers whose understanding of OGAP was limited, interpreted "formative assessment" as another accountability measure being imposed on them and their students by district administrators.

Recognizing these challenges, we began to work more directly with schools, beginning in the spring of 2015, by providing support for teacher leaders as requested. We added the school-based OGAP coaches in the fall of 2015, whose role was to connect with principals and teacher leaders, visit each school site every few weeks, and provide encouragement, support, and general nudging. Through the coaches, we were able to establish more supportive relationships with some teachers and school leaders and provide targeted support. We also gained insight into the real struggles and barriers teachers faced as they tried to use OGAP resources. Learning to use OGAP alongside their textbook and while meeting other district-imposed requirements was challenging, and we found that principals and teacher leaders were not prepared to provide the support that was needed. Additionally, their understanding of what the program required was shaped by beliefs about math learning that conflicted with OGAP. While OGAP conceptualizes learning as developing over time, deepening along a progression, approaches commonly embraced in the school district focused on mastery of discrete skills that are either right or wrong.

The design of PMLC, covering years 3–5 of the project, was informed by evidence that the procedural views of learning held by teachers, principals, and district leaders stymied teachers' use of OGAP. The PMLC partnership was intertwined with the launch of the district's MathCounts initiative in the summer of 2016. Recognizing the importance of schoolwide commitment to instructional change, district leaders required all schools wishing to participate in the SMI to commit to full participation by the principal and 60% of the teaching staff. This arrangement laid the groundwork for our work with school teams. After the SMI, we invited school teams to opt into ongoing OGAP professional development during the 2016–2017 school year. Sixteen schools agreed to participate. OGAP trainers visited each school during two half-days during the year. In subsequent years, we added new schools—fifteen in 2017 and nine in 2018—and increased the number of coaching visits to five half-days for each new school.[15]

Attending to the Role of School Leaders   The school visits by OGAP coaches were critical to anchoring the professional development work within project schools. Of equal importance was the role that principals played in this process. In a letter to principals considering joining the project in year 3, we wrote, "Leader support for OGAP is *essential* for the solid implementation needed to improve student achievement." Through the leadership strand of PMLC, we intentionally and explicitly positioned principals as leaders of the OGAP work at their schools.

We nurtured principal engagement in two related ways. First, we created a community of principals and their school-based math leads and provided professional development around the work of supporting OGAP. These sessions took the form of two-hour, after-school sessions held at one of the school sites between two and four times each year. We also held introductory sessions for new principals at each summer institute. Our aim was to engage principals substantively in OGAP and to extend the formative mindset philosophy to their work with teachers. Following this aim, we designed the leadership professional development sessions to mirror and reinforce the formative assessment cycle at the heart of OGAP. Just as teachers were learning to recursively gather evidence of their students' understanding, analyze the evidence, and decide how to respond to further their learning along a progression, we wanted principals to consider a comparable approach to supporting their teachers. We designed the sessions to introduce leaders to the components of OGAP and engage them in assessing and supporting teacher development from a similar perspective. We were explicit about our intention of promoting a "formative leadership mindset," and we introduced tools and strategies that they could use to gather evidence on the use of OGAP in their schools and support further development.

Second, we also nurtured principals' engagement by looking to them, often in collaboration with the math lead, to structure the school coaching visits. With support of a CPRE coordinator, the visiting OGAP trainers, principal, and often the math teacher leader collaboratively designed the visit to meet the specific needs of the school's teachers in their work with OGAP. The visits might include the OGAP trainer leading a PLC, teaching a lesson, or spending part of the time working with teachers who had missed the summer institute or needed additional support. This approach was both pragmatic and strategic. Naturally, the principal had the authority and knowledge of the context necessary to make these visits work, which often included rearranging schedules, freeing up specific teachers, and designating necessary space. More importantly, however, we believed that the principal's on-the-ground participation signaled commitment to using OGAP. Further, we found that taking part in OGAP-related professional development alongside teachers deepened their learning about the program and its underlying philosophy. When possible, we provided opportunities for principals to share insights from school visits during the principal sessions.

Taken together, the moves to locate more of the professional development in participating schools and to integrate principals more fully into the OGAP work at each school across the five years of the project had the effect of anchoring the work of capacity-building around the use of OGAP in the schools. In so doing, we were able to use the ecosystem of the school in these efforts, including the leadership of the principal and math leads and professional relationships among the school staff. This approach was not without challenges, and the results varied. Principals are typically pulled in multiple directions. Keeping OGAP on the list of priorities required support and persistence.

This shift toward anchoring the professional development work in schools had the effect of rebalancing our partnership with the district. Working in schools and working directly with school leaders became the focus of our practical efforts. Still, positioning our team to do this work required ongoing communication and negotiation with district leaders, particularly those in the curriculum office who oversaw mathematics and the MathCounts initiative. It was due to the trust established with these leaders (and our persistence) that OGAP PD was incorporated into the SMIs, and we were able to contact participating schools in advance of the 2017 and 2018 SMIs to invite them to join the OGAP cohort. As described in a later section, we were able to maintain a level of trust, even as both the chief academic officer and director of mathematics departed.

Building Capacity: Taking a Full-School Approach

Working with schools directly increased interest and engagement among grades 3–5 teachers at each site. At the same time, OGAP PD was initially limited to upper elementary-grade teachers, leaving out a substantial portion of the teachers in K–8 schools. Professional development during the SMI and throughout the year separated grades 3–5 teachers and all others at the school. As a result, the progress we made in year 3 was uneven. Principals felt this disjuncture most potently, and many, recognizing progress with the use of OGAP, pressed for the opportunity to engage more of their faculty.

The project undertook two related shifts in year 4 that extended our work in each partner school to the full grade range. The first shift was made possible by ongoing work by a team of CPRE/OGAP developers who completed work on a suite of OGAP tools for grades K–2 (additive reasoning). As described in chapter 2, OGAP had resources for grades 3–5 (multiplicative reasoning, fractions) and grades 6–8 (ratio and proportions). The availability of grades K–2 resources, we believed, would create an opportunity to support the use of formative assessment across entire K–8 schools.

The second shift was made possible by the first. Once we had the tools and resources in place for grades K–8, we negotiated with the district to create a cohort of partner schools who would be fully engaged in OGAP PD during the SMI. We recruited schools in advance that agreed to send teachers of all grade levels to the institute and participate fully during the school year. We also convinced district leaders to allow for K–2 and 6–8 teachers from year 3 schools to attend the institute, giving them access to OGAP PD and resources. Ensuring that each school's math lead, some of whom were also grade-level teachers, while others were fully released, could participate fully in OGAP PD was critically important to the full-school strategy. We also encouraged principals to attend portions of the institute sessions with their teachers. Each afternoon of the institute, following the morning of OGAP training, teachers and the principal met together to discuss the implications of what they were learning and to plan for the coming school year.

These two shifts—the completion of OGAP materials for grades K–2 and expanding to grades 6–8, thereby making the OGAP reform fully available to grades K–8—cemented the transition from working with individual teachers to partnering with entire schools and supporting them over several years. Retrospectively, it is apparent that providing a resource that could be introduced to the entire school was critical to building a coherent system at the local level.[16] These resources could be viewed as boundary objects that fostered collective work among teachers and leaders at a single school.[17]

Introducing New Tools: Finding Traction

Formative assessment tools, including curated assessment items, learning progressions, and procedures for examining student work, are at the heart of OGAP. As Cobb and colleagues point out, "Instructional improvement efforts almost invariably involve the introduction of a range of new tools."[18] While new tools do not cause teachers to embrace new teaching practices, they can support teachers' engagement with new teaching ideas and scaffold their learning. They can also serve as boundary objects, engaging members of different communities of practice in common work.[19] As described in chapter 2, the primary OGAP tools are both vehicles for undertaking cycles of formative assessment and potential pathways for teachers to develop new lenses on student learning. For this reason, the core task of introducing OGAP into a school or district involves supporting teachers' developing use of these tools in their mathematics teaching.

Despite their potential, we know that introducing new tools into a system is fraught with challenges. When introduced to an already complex and resource-saturated system, new tools are often not taken up at all or their use is not sustained long enough to make a difference. Over the five years of the project, the CPRE team developed two additional tools (digital platforms) aimed at facilitating the use of OGAP tools. These two platforms were introduced at different points in the partnership and were designed to solve different problems, and they were taken up differently by teachers.

We initially developed the e-tool for OGAP use in other settings, but it was featured prominently in the original RCT proposal to NSF. The e-tool had a tablet-based interface that integrated the core OGAP resources and offered several additional features to scaffold teachers through formative assessment cycles (see figure 3.1). It contained the OGAP item bank in searchable form, which allowed teachers to create and print assessment items and tasks to give to students. It also allowed teachers to record results of these assessments and supported the analytical process, mapping student results to key features of the OGAP frameworks. The e-tool also included features that guided teachers to make responsive instructional decisions, before selecting new formative assessment items, to begin the next cycle. Prior to launching the RCT in 2014, the e-tool was preloaded onto iPads, and we presented them to teachers at the rollout of the project, seeing the e-tool as a way to generate initial interest in the project. We also hoped to use back-end data on search results, assessments created, and other uses of the tool to track and understand how teachers were using OGAP.

Take-up of the e-tool did not go as planned. Within the first six months of year 1, we observed minimal use of the e-tool across teachers in the thirty treatment schools. This small number of regular users were typically teacher leaders, who used the tool to select and download assessment items for other teachers in the school. The e-tool was not used for the remaining phases of the formative assessment cycle. We ultimately realized that it was a solution to a problem teachers did not yet have and decided to de-emphasize its use. Many teacher leaders continued to use it, but only for its bank of items. Eventually, we created a website that served as a hub for schools using OGAP and where teachers could access the item bank, the OGAP frameworks, and other OGAP resources. The e-tool was no longer needed.

The second platform we developed, the OGAP Curriculum Connection, came as a direct response to concerns many teachers and teacher leaders

Figure 3.1 Screenshot of the e-tool landing screen

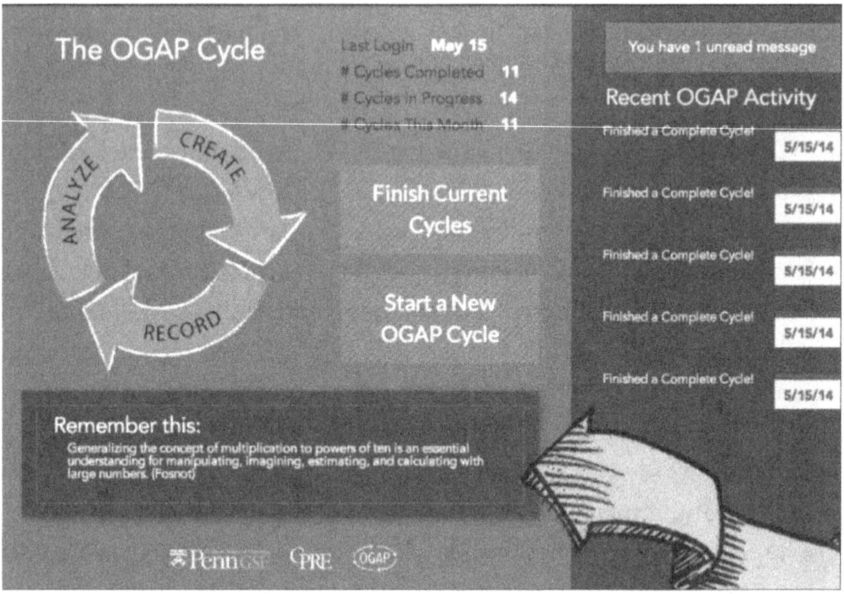

shared during year 3 of the project. At that point, teachers were struggling to learn to use a new mathematics curriculum while also learning to use OGAP. The district had purchased two new elementary curriculum programs, enVision and Expressions, and was rolling them out in the fall of 2016. We made every effort to communicate with teachers and school leaders that OGAP was *not* a curriculum and that it could be used alongside their primary curriculum program. Still, learning both systems simultaneously was overwhelming for many teachers. They felt pulled between two centers of gravity: adhering to the pacing of daily lessons and activities prescribed by their new textbook and using OGAP items to assess student understanding and make instructional decisions accordingly. While we understood this tension, our analyses of the approaches of both textbook series suggested that there was potentially more overlap with the OGAP frameworks than many initially saw, and we believed we could leverage these connections to enhance teachers' use of both.

Figure 3.2   Solve & Share

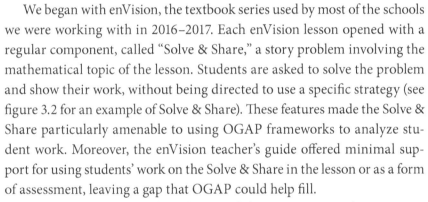

Li made 12 tacos. He wants to give some of his friends 2 tacos each. If Li does not get any of the tacos, how many of his friends will get tacos?

Solve this problem any way you choose.

We began with enVision, the textbook series used by most of the schools we were working with in 2016–2017. Each enVision lesson opened with a regular component, called "Solve & Share," a story problem involving the mathematical topic of the lesson. Students are asked to solve the problem and show their work, without being directed to use a specific strategy (see figure 3.2 for an example of Solve & Share). These features made the Solve & Share particularly amenable to using OGAP frameworks to analyze student work. Moreover, the enVision teacher's guide offered minimal support for using students' work on the Solve & Share in the lesson or as a form of assessment, leaving a gap that OGAP could help fill.

A team of CPRE researchers developed the OGAP Curriculum Connection platform using sample student work collected from partner schools on selected Solve & Share problems in grades 3–5. The platform guides teachers through the process of using the OGAP assessment cycle with many Solve & Share problems in their textbook. After selecting an enVision lesson from a dashboard for their grade, they are shown five varied (and likely) examples of student work for the Solve & Share problem that begins the lesson. They practice sorting the work, using an OGAP framework, and receive feedback on their decisions. They are also offered support for identifying trends in the student work and provided with several potential instructional responses they could try, depending on the trends in their own students' work on the problem. Finally, they are shown a menu of OGAP items they might give subsequently, based on a range of criteria.

The OGAP Curriculum Connection platform was received with enthusiasm by many teachers in the project when we introduced it during the SMI that began year 4 of the project. By allowing teachers to analyze student work from the textbook using an OGAP framework, the OGAP Curriculum Connection addressed a true problem of practice—learning to use and integrate two new resources. While the e-tool was designed to support teachers to use OGAP tools more efficiently and with greater ease, the connections platform helped teachers see the applicability of OGAP tools to problems in the new curriculum. The differences in the relevance of these two tools for teachers also highlights important learning in our work as partners. Over time, we learned to listen to teachers and understand the specific challenges they were facing. The Curriculum Connection platform reflected a response to *their* challenges. The e-tool, on the other hand, was designed in response to what the CPRE team perceived would be useful.

A Changing Relationship with the District: Brokering Through Precarity

The final evolution of the project occurred in our relationship with school district leaders. Across the five years, as our work with teachers became more focused on whole schools and school leaders, the nature of our partnership with district leadership shifted. In table 3.1, we characterize our relationship during the first two years as one of "outside provider." When we began the OGAP study, the program was new to the district leaders we interacted with, who cautiously agreed to the trial. By the end of the year 2, a number of synergies occurred that led to a deeper partnership. First, the OGAP RCT was beginning to show positive impacts on student learning, lending credibility to the resources. Second, regular interactions with instructional leaders in the district resulted in deeper levels of trust. Third, the district was ready to turn its attention to math, and we were there at the right time to support the effort. Thus, in the following three year of the project, the CPRE/OGAP team took on a role as partner in the new MathCounts initiative. In addition to providing OGAP training during the

Summer Math Institute and ongoing support during the academic year, our team was able to play a consultative role with district leaders. Importantly, this deepening relationship with district leaders was the result of extensive and ongoing effort from our team. Still, constantly shifting dynamics within the district meant this relationship always held a sense of precarity.

Two themes stand out in how we navigated our shifting relationship with district leaders: an ongoing need to be both responsive and opportunistic and the role that champions played in this evolving partnership. Through this work we gained insight into the complexity of the system, which seemed to work against coherence.[20] We also learned to work with and as boundary brokers in order to address shared challenges.[21]

Brokering Toward Common Ground Like all other evolutions described in this chapter, the shifts in our relationship with district leaders were infrequently by design. More often, they were in response to new opportunities or challenges as they emerged. Our aim in these interactions was to support the district's mathematics initiative and advocate for the role of OGAP in this initiative. Looking through a communities of practice lens, our work could be described as brokering—operating across multiple communities of practice to share resources and solve shared problems.[22]

By 2016, we found that the trust we had established after the two-year RCT had earned us a seat at the figurative table during discussions about mathematics instruction and PD, but that seat did not come with any special authority or privileges. We still needed to understand district leaders' intentions and decisions and negotiate a place for OGAP within or alongside these plans. In some cases, we did this through formal processes; for instance, OGAP made a bid to provide PD in the first SMI. In most cases, however, we did this work through less formal means, by participating *with* district leaders to identify and address shared goals. For instance, working as brokers across communities, we arranged for OGAP trainers to provide PD for Carnegie coaches who would be providing support to OGAP schools after the 2017 SMI. Engaging district leaders in this way would not have happened if we did not have a place at the table or were not willing to come to the table to listen, work to find common ground, and respond.

The Role of Champions   Our seat at the table with the math curriculum team was cemented by relationships with two leaders within the district who championed the OGAP cause. They were both students in different doctoral programs within the Graduate School of Education, and as such, held membership with us in an academic community of practice. One was the district chief academic officer (CAO), who oversaw the curriculum office during the RCT (years 1–2) and the beginning of PMLC (years 3–5) while pursuing a doctorate in educational leadership. Even though she did not have a mathematics background, she led the charge to elevate mathematics in the district. It was under her leadership that MathCounts was launched and the director of mathematics (DoM) position was filled after standing vacant for years. In late spring of 2016, The CAO hired a former high school math teacher and a doctoral student in a different Penn-GSE program. He was known to district curriculum leaders because he had voluntarily supported the district's efforts to direct attention toward mathematics for several years. He was familiar with OGAP because he served as an OGAP coach during year 2 of the project, having had a brief position in the CPRE/OGAP community of practice.

The DoM was a particularly strong advocate of OGAP; the instructional approach was aligned with his philosophy, and it is likely that his relationships with the CPRE team further encouraged his support. Early in his time in the district, he brought together a cadre of partners to share his vision for math instruction and to solicit support for moving district practices forward. Leaders from Carnegie Learning, CPRE, and OGAP were among the group. It looked and felt like math instruction in the district was about to change, and the CPRE team was available to support his efforts and advocate for our work. He endorsed our transition to working with full schools, which began with the SMI in 2017, and we worked with him and his team to structure the SMI to accommodate the growing OGAP cohort.

The DoM quickly discovered that his location in the district's organizational chart did not position him well to usher in a new vision. His curricular autonomy was constrained by his superiors in the curriculum office, particularly after his strongest advocate, the CAO, accepted a superintendency in another city and was replaced by a less-than-enthusiastic acting director. He also learned that district leaders who had the most direct influence on instructional practices in schools were the fifteen or so assistant superintendents, each of whom oversaw a network of schools. Assistant superintendents were empowered to require that schools under their jurisdiction use specific instructional routines, and many of them prioritized various testing protocols used in the district, which were managed by the assessment office. For just under two years, the DoM worked within the curriculum office and across other lines of district management to advance the new vision, which included OGAP. But progress was gradual and not without considerable effort. It was tensions within the curriculum office, however, that led to his departure in April of 2018.

Unsurprisingly, the loss of both of our original champions made our partnership work with district leaders more precarious. We worked to maintain ongoing communication with the acting director of the curriculum office and a remaining member of the mathematics team, and these interactions were always cordial and generally productive; at the same time, it was clear to us that a shared commitment to OGAP or appreciation of its contribution to elementary mathematics instruction had been lost. As we moved into year 5 of the project, our work directly with school teams was in full swing, and in June of 2018, we were working with nine new schools and twenty that were returning. Our interactions with district leaders focused primarily on advocating for this work and its continuation beyond the five-year project.

In 2018, the SDP reviewed the impacts of Carnegie's work and found little evidence of widescale improvements in math outcomes, concluding that Carnegie's professional development was not effective. As a subcontractor to Carnegie, OGAP was painted with the same brush. Knowing that support from NSF was ending, we marshalled a campaign to raise awareness of the effectiveness of OGAP on teachers, teaching, and learning, and on schools in the district. We created a short report of the number of teachers and students served by OGAP between 2014 and 2018 and the resources we had developed to support teachers and schools, and summarized the findings of the impact of OGAP on state test results (see chapter 4) in a short, nontechnical brief that also included testimonials from teachers and principals in the district. We created a mailing list of district leaders (superintendent, chief academic officer, deputy chief of teaching and learning), school board members, members of the curriculum office and office of research and evaluation, and regional superintendents and sent electronic and hard copies to each. We enlisted supportive teachers and principals to advocate for OGAP to their regional assistant superintendents and other district leaders. These efforts we not enough, and the district decided to work with teachers to create their own new math framework and curriculum.

In the summer of 2019, the district held a final, pared-down MathCounts Institute. Because they were no longer working with Carnegie Learning, sessions were run by district curriculum officials and teachers. OGAP led sessions on additive reasoning for K–2 teachers from schools they were already working with who had not had an opportunity to come to training yet.

As schools recovered from the COVID-19 pandemic in 2021, OGAP continued to have support in pockets of the district. Teachers were still using what they had learned and sought additional training and support. A few schools used their own funding to pay for OGAP training. A math lead from a school that adopted OGAP was promoted to a district math curriculum specialist position, enabling her to advocate for OGAP in the district. A partnership between this curriculum specialist and an assistant superintendent led to a new opportunity for schools in one network to receive OGAP training beginning in 2020. In unpredictable ways, the experience of OGAP in Philly traveled to other districts. As several former district leaders moved to other districts and states, including Nebraska and Maryland, they contracted with OGAP to provide support to their schools.

CONCLUDING REFLECTIONS

This exploration of how we adapted the OGAP-CPRE-SDP partnership over five years yields valuable insights into facilitating instructional improvement within a large, intricate school district. Drawing from Penuel and colleagues' conceptualization of design-based implementation research

(DBIR), we embrace a mindset that normalizes change within school-research collaborations.[23] This perspective invites a flexible approach to work within schools and school systems. We found that our inclination to take stock, learn, and make modification to improve the work was pivotal to fostering productive relationships with schools and district leaders. Successful efforts to support instructional reform must anticipate and plan for such evolutions as new and deeper understandings emerge.

Scholars have also argued for the importance of locating the work of improvement in schools where teaching and learning take place.[24] This insight rang true in our work. We also found that nurturing new instructional ideas in schools can be enhanced when, to the extent possible, the entire school community is engaged and moving toward a common aim. Further, positioning principals and teacher leaders as partners and guides in this endeavor can deepen school-wide engagement and sustainability. These two factors—whole-school participation and the centrality of leaders—can create opportunities for collaboration and learning across multiple communities of practice.[25] Understanding the critical role of teacher leaders in this work informed the design of a related project, the Responsive Math Teaching Project.[26]

Introducing new tools can scaffold new learning, particularly when they serve as boundary objects, supporting work across communities of practice toward shared aims.[27] At the same time, new tools are more likely to gain traction if they address problems that teachers and leaders are experiencing.[28] Designing relevant tools, we found, begins with listening to and accommodating the real concerns of teachers and leaders in schools and then tailoring supports to address them.

Finally, the complexity and precarity of partnering with a large, complex school district cannot be overstated. Looking under the hood of any such partnership, as I have done in this chapter, exposes a messy, multi-layered, and dynamic web of relationships—with individual schools and leaders, as well as with various district leaders—which are distinct yet interdependent. In essence, there is never a single partnership at play. Partnering with schools and leveraging their ecology is critical, as is simultaneously maintaining relationships with the district.[29] Above all, while these relationships exist across institutional structures, they are also with people. Many contend that teaching is fundamentally about building relationships with learners. Similarly, fostering instructional reform in school districts hinges on cultivating meaningful relationships with all stakeholders.

4

How OGAP Made a Difference

Teacher and Student Impacts

JONATHAN A. SUPOVITZ AND MAURICE SPILLANE

The story of the Ongoing Assessment Project (OGAP) in Philadelphia would be far less compelling if there were not substantial evidence that OGAP had significantly improved the instructional practice of teachers and the learning of their students. In this chapter we describe the impacts of the different permutations of OGAP on teachers and students. These results set the stage for subsequent chapters examining implementation efforts and challenges, the experiences of teachers and school leaders, and influences of the surrounding system.

To examine the impacts of OGAP, we organize this chapter into three sections. First, we report the impacts of OGAP on teachers using an authentic assessment of teachers' learning trajectory–oriented formative assessment practices. Second, we assess the impacts of OGAP on students using an OGAP-aligned assessment that was specifically developed for this project to examine student performance on two dimensions: correctness (accuracy) and solution sophistication (efficiency). The distinction between a student answering a mathematics problem correctly and the sophistication by which a student approaches solving the problem grows directly out of OGAP's theory that students develop understanding by going through a developmental progression that roughly aligns with increasing sophistication. Third, we examine OGAP's impacts on student performance on the Pennsylvania state test, the state's accountability metric.

The data we use for this chapter come largely from three sources. First, each year from 2014 to 2019 we conducted a survey of both teachers in schools participating in OGAP and a comparison set of teachers in a parallel set of schools. The survey featured an assessment of teacher knowledge of formative assessment practices called the Teacher Assessment of Student Knowledge (TASK), as well as demographic and opinion questions. The second data source was a student assessment called the Learning Trajectory Assessment (LTA), which was developed specifically by the research team to assess student problem-solving on item accuracy (correctness) and solution sophistication. This proximal assessment was designed to closely align with OGAP's instructional approach. The third data source was the Pennsylvania System of School Assessment (PSSA), the state's high-stakes assessment that is of most interest to policymakers and the public.

The analyses presented in this chapter are largely the results of statistical evaluations of the impacts of OGAP on teachers and students. Despite this, our goal is to present the evidence of OGAPs impacts in an accessible and nontechnical way. Therefore, we present the findings graphically and have put the underlying statistical models into appendices for those who want to get into the weeds.

Over the course of the five years of the program that are chronicled in this book, the schools and grade levels that OGAP worked with changed. This led to different samples of participating schools, teachers, and students, as well as different research designs. As shown in table 4.1, In years 1 and 2 (studies 1-4, years 2014-2016), the research was designed as an experimental study to test the efficacy of OGAP on teachers and students in grades 3-5 in the same sample of schools in Philadelphia and the neighboring district of Upper Darby. In those years we conducted separate impact studies in 2014-2015 and 2015-2016, as well as a study of the "stable"

Table 4.1 Studies of OGAP and samples, 2014–2019

Study	School year	Grades	Focus of analysis within mathematics	Research study design	Measures	OGAP sample (schools, teachers, students)	Comparison sample (schools, teachers, students)
1	2014–2015	3–5	Multiplication	Experiment	TASK, LTA, PSSA	Schools: 30 Teachers: 228 Students: 5,700	Schools: 31 Teachers: 207 Students: 5,175
2	2015–2016	3–5	Multiplication	Experiment	TASK, LTA, PSSA	Schools: 28 Teachers: 92 Students: 2,300	Schools: 23 Teachers: 55 Students: 1,375
3	2015–2016	3–5	Fractions	Experiment	TASK, LTA, PSSA	Schools: 25 Teachers: 83 Students: 2,075	Schools: 30 Teachers: 74 Students: 1,850
4	2014–2016	3–5	Multiplication	Experiment	TASK, LTA, PSSA	Schools: 27 Teachers: 84 Students: 2,100	Schools: 23 Teachers: 45 Students: 1,125
5	2016–2017	3–5	Multiplication	Quasi-experiment	TASK	Teachers: 106	Teachers: 148
6	2017–2018	K-2	Addition	Quasi-experiment	TASK	Schools: 20 Teachers: 90 Students: 2,250	Schools: 15 Teachers: 47 Students: 1,175
7	2017–2018	3–5	Multiplication	Quasi-experiment	TASK, PSSA	Schools: 20 Teachers: 60 Students: 1,500	Schools: 13 Teachers: 34 Students: 850
8	2017–2018	6–8	Proportions	Quasi-experiment	TASK, PSSA	Schools: 14 Teachers: 32 Students: 800	Schools: 11 Teachers: 17 Students: 425
9	Baseline–2019	3–5	Multiplication	Quasi-experiment	TASK	Schools: 36 Teachers: 89	Schools: 20 Teachers: 45

Note: The numbers in this table depict the samples of teachers and approximate numbers of students included in analyses. They may differ from those cited in other chapters.

subsample of students who were in the participating grades and schools in both years.

In the three school years from 2016–2017 to 2018–2019, OGAP was incorporated into the School District of Philadelphia's (SDP's) mathematics professional development offerings. In each of these three years (studies 5–9) we conducted a series of quasi-experiments that compared teachers in schools who chose to participate in OGAP with a comparison group comprising teachers in schools that attended the summer professional development in literacy and volunteered to complete the survey in exchange for a $25 Amazon gift card. In these quasi-experiments we used statistical adjustments to make the comparisons as fair as possible.

In 2016–2017 (study 5) we only conducted teacher impact analyses but did not investigate student impacts because we wanted to allow OGAP a year to adjust their offerings to new circumstances as the reform design shifted and it moved from an external program to a district offering. In the 2016–2017 analyses, due to the design of the SDP summer training, we did not have data on the schools of the comparison teachers. That year, due to the evolving supports developed by Philadelphia Mathematics Leadership Collaborative (PMLC; see chapter 3), we broke the teacher analysis into a comparison between three groups: (1) teachers who participated in the summer professional development and continued to receive ongoing OGAP support; (2) teachers who participated in summer professional development but received minimal support over the school year; (3) teachers in the comparison group.

In 2017–2018, OGAP expanded its training and support from grades 3–5 to grades K–8, and we likewise expanded our analyses to include both teachers and students in the broader set of participating grades (table 4.1, studies 6–8). The student data for these analyses were provided by the SDP at the individual student level.

Finally, in 2018–2019, the final year of our research, we shifted our analysis from one-year impacts to investigate the sustained impacts of OGAP by surveying teachers who had participated in prior years to look for persistent effects (table 4.1, study 9). To do so, we collected updated rosters from all the OGAP and comparison schools that had previously participated in a prior wave of the teacher assessment and reached out to those teachers still in their school via email. Using the Amazon gift card incentive, we again asked teachers to complete the survey.

In the description of the results that follow, we first describe the assessment that was developed or used to assess impacts on teachers and students and then depict the results in easily digestible graphs. We provide the multilevel regression results in the chapter appendixes for those who want more details.

IMPACTS OF OGAP ON TEACHERS

Each year from 2014 to 2019 teachers participating in OGAP and teachers in a comparison group were given an online survey that included a performance assessment called the Teacher Assessment of Student Knowledge, or TASK.[1] The TASK was administered to both groups of teachers in the summer (i.e., before OGAP training for the OGAP teachers) and in the following spring at the end of the school year. This research design allowed for a pre-post assessment for both OGAP teachers and comparison group teachers.

Overview of the Teacher Assessment of Student Knowledge (TASK)

TASKs are grade-specific, open-ended assessments for teachers of mathematics that measure teachers' knowledge of learning trajectory–oriented formative assessment (LTOFA). A TASK presents teachers with six different student solutions to a grade-appropriate mathematics problem and asks them to describe the different students' understanding based upon the evidence presented in the student solution, to rank the student solutions based upon their mathematical sophistication, and then to suggest appropriate instructional responses. By giving teachers authentic representations of student work and asking for open-ended explanations, the TASK is a more authentic assessment than multiple-choice renditions of teacher formative assessment knowledge.

An example of a grades 3–5 multiplication TASK is shown in figure 4.1. The item provides teachers with six student responses to an open-ended

Figure 4.1 Example TASK

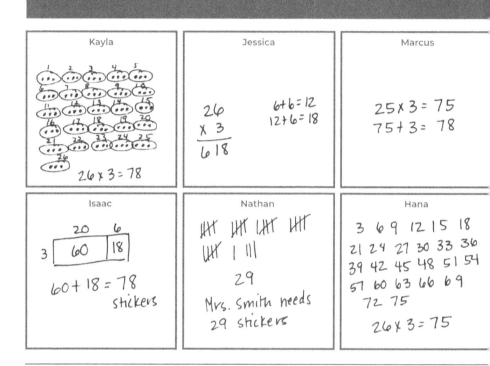

mathematics problem. The student responses are carefully crafted to provide different types of strategies that represent different levels of student solution sophistication. In the example, Nathan uses a nonmultiplicative strategy, adding the numbers in the problem instead of understanding the multiplicative relationship in the situation. Kayla uses a model to employ an additive strategy of subitizing in small groups. Hana and Isaac demonstrate transitional approaches between addition and multiplication. Hana uses an early transitional strategy of skip counting, while Isaac uses an area model to decompose 26 into 20 and 6. Marcus is utilizing a multiplicative strategy, relying on a known fact, 25 × 3, and using his understanding of multiplication to derive the answer to 26 × 3 from that. Jessica appears to be trying to use the traditional multiplication algorithm, which is a multiplicative strategy, but without an understanding of the procedure she is using, she makes a serious place value error.

Table 4.2 shows the prompts that teachers are asked to respond to for the TASK item, the domains that the item represents, the way it is scored, and the scale the scores were assessed upon. The domain "analyzing student thinking" includes three open-ended questions that ask teachers to explain what the work of the student suggests about their understanding of numbers and operations. The domain "learning trajectory orientation" asks teachers to rank the sophistication of students' solution responses and explain their rankings (note, the explanations are based on the rankings that teachers give). The third domain, entitled "instructional decision-making" asks teachers to provide an informed instructional

Table 4.2 TASK prompts, domains, and scoring

Item no.	Domain	Prompt	Scoring	Scale
1–3	Analyzing student thinking	1–3. Please comment on each student's solution process in terms of what the work suggests about the student's understanding of numbers and operations. *Please be as specific and detailed as you can.* (For 3 of the students)	Scored by rater	Rubric score (1–4)
4–7	Learning trajectory orientation	4. Please order each student's solution process below according to the **sophistication of mathematical thinking** involved. 5. Please explain why you ordered ___ as more sophisticated than ___. 6. Please explain why you ordered ___ as more sophisticated than ___. 7. Please explain why you ordered ___ as more sophisticated than ___.	Automated	Rubric score (1–4)
8–9	Instructional decision-making	8–9. As their teacher, what would you do next with the two students below? Please explain your rationale for the steps you suggest. *Please be as specific and detailed as you can.* (For 2 of the students)	Scored by rater	Rubric score (1–4)

Table 4.3 TASK scoring scale

Score	Rating	Description
1	General	Teacher response is general or superficially related to student work in terms of the mathematics content.
2	Procedural	Teacher response focuses on a particular strategy or procedure without reference to student conceptual understanding.
3	Conceptual	Teacher response focuses on underlying concepts, strategy development, or construction of mathematical meaning.
4	Learning trajectory	Teacher response draws on developmental learning trajectory to explain student understanding or develop an instructional response.

response based on their assessment of student understanding provided in the students' response.

TASK Scoring

TASKS were scored by trained raters who were experienced teachers of mathematics. In preparation, raters complete a four-hour training session and achieved greater than 80% agreement with an expert rater. The items from each of the three domains were scored on a four-point rubric, as shown in table 4.3. A teacher's overall score was their average of the three domains.

Impacts of OGAP on Teacher TASK Performance

Each year from 2014 to 2019, we administered the appropriate grade-level TASK to teachers in a pre-post format, with the premeasure of the TASK serving as a baseline of teacher knowledge before participation in OGAP and the postmeasure of the TASK serving as the teacher knowledge assessment at the end of the school year.[2] For each of these years, teachers in the comparison group also completed the beginning and end-of-year TASK assessments. With the gift card incentives, the response rates were between 75 and 90 percent across the years. This approach produced a series of one-year impacts of OGAP on different samples of teachers under different implementation conditions in different grades and different subjects.

To estimate TASK impacts for each year, we specified a multilevel model that nested teachers within schools. The outcome in each model was end-of-school-year TASK performance. At the teacher level, we included variables for OGAP teacher (or comparison school teacher), English language learner (ELL) teacher (or not), special education teacher (or not), female teacher (or male), as well as baseline TASK performance and years of teaching experience. At the school level, we included variables for school size (number of students enrolled), percentage of students on free or reduced lunch, and percentage of students of different ethnicities. The teacher-level variables and TASK performance were derived from the survey administered to teachers. The school-level variables came from publicly available data from the National Center for Education Statistics. The purpose of including these teacher- and school-level variables was to adjust for any differences between the individual and school characteristics in the OGAP and comparison schools, particularly in the quasi-experimental study years.

Figure 4.2 depicts the differences in TASK performance between OGAP and comparison school teachers across the different permutations of OGAP from 2014–2015 to 2018–2019. Below the year, we show what subject the TASK performance focused on. We have chosen to represent these TASK scores as the performance of a "typical" or average OGAP and comparison school teacher. These graphs therefore show the predicted performance of a female regular education teacher (as opposed to a special education or ELL teacher) of average experience with average prior TASK performance from a school with average school size, an average free/reduced lunch percentage, and average student ethnic composition. The models that produced these graphs are presented in greater detail in Appendix A.

The results show that in all years and across all the different permutations of OGAP, the TASK performance of OGAP teachers was statistically significantly greater than that of comparison school teachers, indicating that OGAP teachers performed significantly higher on the TASK than comparison teachers, after controlling for prior TASK performance and differences in individual and school characteristics.

Over the two years from 2014 to 2016, OGAP was funded externally and delivered in both the School District of Philadelphia and the adjacent small district of Upper Darby. The results of TASK comparisons in the first four sets of bars in figure 4.2 show OGAP TASK impacts based on the randomized experiment of OGAP. During this phase of OGAP, the first year of OGAP professional development and support focused on multiplicative reasoning, and the second year focused on fractional reasoning, both in grades 3–5. In the first year (2014–2015), all teachers took the TASK in multiplication. In the second year, teachers in the OGAP cohort were randomly assigned to take the TASK in multiplication (using a different form of the TASK assessment) or in fractions. Comparison school teachers were similarly randomly assigned to one of the two math areas.

In 2014–2015, the typical OGAP teacher scored 2.60 on the four-point TASK assessment (i.e., averaging between a procedural score of 2 and a conceptual score of 3), compared to the typical comparison group teacher's score of 2.27 (closer to a procedural score of 2). In 2015–2016, the OGAP teachers were a combination of the same teachers and teachers who were new to grades 3–5. In that year, fractions were introduced as the summer professional development, and on the end-of-year assessment we randomly assigned teachers to take either the multiplication or fractions TASK. Those who took the multiplication TASK scored slightly lower (2.48) than the previous year, but still significantly higher than the comparison group (who again averaged 2.27). On the fraction reasoning (FR) TASK, the OGAP teachers scored 2.25, which was significantly higher than the comparison group of teachers, who scored an average of 2.08. Finally, the results for 2014–2016 show the impacts for students who had teachers who participated in OGAP in both years.

In 2016, with the experimental study completed, OGAP was sponsored by the SDP as part of their math offerings in summer institutes over the next three years. In 2016–2017 OGAP focused again on teachers in grades 3–5 in multiplicative reasoning. In that year, teacher experiences could be organized into three groups. The first group were teachers who participated in OGAP in the summer institute and whose schools opted to continue OGAP support over the school year. A second group of schools participated in the summer professional development but received moderate support over the school year through Carnegie Learning. These are noted as

Figure 4.2 OGAP impacts on teacher TASK performance

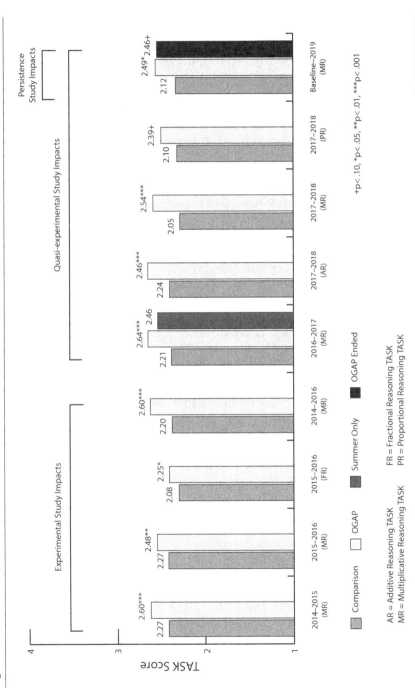

Note: TASK scores depict the average predicted performance of a female regular education teacher with average experience and average prior TASK performance from a school with an average school size, an average free/reduced lunch percentage, and average student ethnic composition.

"summer only" in figure 4.2.[3] A third group of teachers served as a comparison to the other two groups. These were teachers who attended the summer institute in literacy and whom we incentivized to complete the TASK survey.

As can be seen in figure 4.2, those who participated in OGAP in 2016–2017 with ongoing support scored an average of 2.64 on the multiplicative reasoning TASK, which was consistent with the previous cohorts. This was statistically significantly higher than both the comparison group (2.21) and the group that participated in the summer institute with minimal ongoing support (2.46). Additional analysis (not shown) indicated that the summer-only group scored significantly higher on the TASK than the comparison group (and significantly lower than the full treatment group), suggesting that teachers who were introduced to OGAP and received moderate ongoing support, retained their understanding of the Learning Trajectory–Oriented Formative Assessment (LTOFA) concepts at the end of the school year, but not to the degree of those with stronger ongoing support.

In 2017–2018 OGAP expanded to support math teacher development in grades K–8, providing training and support to teachers in grades K–2 in additive reasoning, grades 3–5 in multiplicative reasoning, and grades 6–8 in proportional reasoning. The results for that year showed that at all three grade levels, teachers in the OGAP schools had statistically significantly higher TASK scores than comparison school teachers. Again, grades 3–5 OGAP teachers' multiplicative reasoning scores (2.54) were on par with previous cohorts of grades 3–5 teachers. Since this was the only year we administered the TASKs in the other grades, we are unable to draw comparisons either over time or across mathematics content areas.

The final set of bars in figure 4.2 reflects a different research design than in previous years. Rather than conducting another one-year comparison, we investigated the persistent effects of OGAP on teachers' LTOFA knowledge. We wanted to see if the influence of OGAP on teachers' knowledge of formative assessment and learning trajectories persisted over time. To accomplish this, we first requested roster data from the SDP on the 2019 teachers in all of the treatment and comparison schools. We compared these rosters to the data from the original experiment (2014 and 2015 teachers) and identified the teachers who were part of the first two years of the study (both treatment and comparison) and were still teaching in the same school. We then emailed them and asked that they complete the TASK in the spring of 2019. We ended up with 45 comparison group teachers, 42 teachers who reported that they continued to use OGAP, and 47 teachers who said they no longer used OGAP.[4] We analyzed these data in the same modelling approach described previously, controlling for teacher and school background characteristics and nesting teachers within schools. The results show that both those who continued to use OGAP (who averaged a 2.49 on the four-point TASK scale) and those who reported they no longer used OGAP (2.46) performed significantly better on the TASK than teachers who had never participated in OGAP (2.12). It is also important to note that there was not much difference in the performance of teachers who reported that they continued to use OGAP and those who did not. This suggests that, whether or not teachers continued to use the OGAP items and learning progressions, their knowledge of the concepts of learning trajectory–oriented formative assessment persisted.

Overall, the results from 2014 to 2019 indicate the impacts of OGAP on teachers LTOFA knowledge regardless of their administration conditions, locus of support (internal or external), math content area, grade level, or research design (experimental or quasi-experimental).

IMPACTS OF OGAP ON STUDENTS

We assessed the impacts of OGAP on students in two different ways. The first assessment, called the Learning Trajectory Assessment (LTA) was specifically designed for the study to align with the OGAP theory that students' correctness in solving problems was distinct from their sophistication in solving problems. That is, students could get the same answer (either correct or incorrect) using a range of different strategies. The second assessment was the Pennsylvania State System of Assessment (PSSA) in mathematics. In the following sections we describe each assessment and its scoring and then present the results of the impacts of OGAP on students for each assessment approach.

Overview of the Learning Trajectory Assessment

To assess the intervention's impact on both students' problem-solving accuracy and their strategy sophistication, the project team developed the Learning Trajectory Assessment (LTA) for multiplication and division, a measure with three vertically equated grade-specific forms composed of open-ended multiplication and division items for grades 3,4, and 5. The assessment items consisted of a set of word problems that could be solved with multiplication or division. Students were asked to show their work to allow for analysis of both correctness and sophistication of solution strategies. The items were constructed around a range of problem structures and complexity in alignment with existing research on problem difficulty and the grade-level expectations of the Common Core State Standards for Mathematics.

The twelve items used in the final version of the LTA were selected from an extensive pilot test conducted the year before the study. The pilot test was administered in predetermined permutations of items to a sample of 1,400 students from two states outside of Pennsylvania. For these analyses, problem-solving accuracy was scored on a 0–1 scale of 0 = incorrect answer and 1 = correct answer. Solution strategy was scored on a 0–5 scale of 0 = inappropriate or nondiscernable strategy, 1 = early additive strategy, 2 = additive strategy, 3 = early transitional strategy, 4 = transitional strategy, and 5 = multiplicative strategy.

We used item response theory (IRT) modeling to analyze the full pilot sample and selected the twelve items that elicited a range of strategy levels on problems appropriate for each grade level. The final grade-level forms were each composed of seven items, with some of the items administered to both grades 3 and 4 and grades 4 and 5, creating the conditions to vertically equate scores across grade levels.[5]

The pretest used for these analyses was a three-item assessment drawn from OGAP items that were removed from the OGAP item bank. These items were also grade-appropriate open-ended multiplication and division contextual problems. The treatment schools made copies of the assessment results and returned them to the research team and then kept the originals to use as part of the intervention as a preassessment of their students' understanding at the beginning of the year. Teachers in the control schools administered the pretest and returned them to the research team.

Scoring of the LTA Approximately twelve thousand LTA assessments were administered each year in 2014–2015 and 2015–2016, so scoring was a major undertaking. The assessments were scored in the summers following the school year. The research team developed rubrics for each item detailing characteristics of the elements of a response that would be scored at each level of accuracy (0–1) and sophistication (0–5). Multiple training sets of thirty responses drawn from the pilot data were used as practice to develop rater reliability on each item. During the second year of scoring, the training sets were supplemented with examples from the first year to better represent the nature of the student work being produced in the study schools.

About fifteen raters were hired each summer to score the student assessments. Most of the raters were recent graduates of a master's-level elementary teacher education program who had some previous experience analyzing student strategies in their mathematics methods course. Before beginning actual scoring, raters were required to reach 85 percent agreement with an expert's judgment on a set of thirty training items. If a rater failed to reach 85 percent agreement, they discussed their discrepancies with the project coordinator and then completed an additional training set. In almost all cases, raters reached 85 percent agreement after scoring the second training set. In a few instances, a third training set was required. This process was repeated for each distinct assessment item.

Scoring was conducted blindly; raters did not know whether students were in the treatment or control group. Additionally, raters were spot-checked for reliability to maintain 85 percent agreement with an expert rater on thirty items chosen at random. Scores on the pre- and posttests for both correctness and sophistication were derived from an evenly weighted average of the scores across the three-item pretest or seven-item posttest.

IMPACTS OF OGAP ON THE LEARNING TRAJECTORY ASSESSMENT

Figure 4.3 shows the average correctness scores for the "typical" student from both OGAP and control group schools with average size and percentage of free/reduced lunch assistance. As these numbers are on a 0–1 scale, they can be interpreted as the average percent correct for OGAP and control group students, after controlling for student and school demographics and baseline LTA performance. There are several important take-aways from this graph. First, OGAP students in all three grades (3–5) significantly outperformed students in the control schools. The results were stronger in the first year of OGAP than the second year, although the differences continued to be statistically significant. The stable sample, or the subset of matriculating third- and fourth-grade students who were in the OGAP and control school from 2014 to 2016 also showed consistent differences in favor of the OGAP schools. It is also important to note that, even though OGAP students consistently outperformed the comparison group students, there is substantial room for improvement, as students typically answered less than half of the items correctly.

Because OGAP emphasizes student developmental growth in their sophistication of solution approaches as they master content areas like multiplication, a particular emphasis of the project was to understand the extent to which students grew in the sophistication of their solution approaches, not just their ability to answer problems correctly. For example, on a multiplication problem a student could use a relatively inefficient additive strategy to solve the problem or a student could use a more sophisticated multiplicative strategy. Even though both students might answer the problem correctly, it is valuable to understand their differences in solution sophistication, as this has important implications as they progress to more complex mathematics, where low-level strategies are inefficient. To disentangle these differences, the LTA measured not only correctness, but sophistication.

Figure 4.3 Impacts of OGAP on LTA—correctness (all years reflect experimental results)

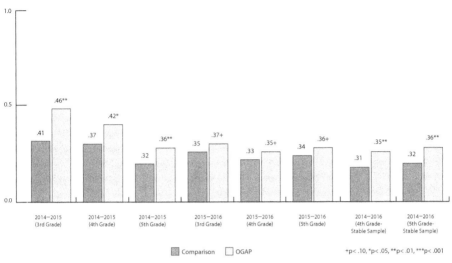

Note: The graph shows the predicted performance of a female regular education student (as opposed to a special education or ELL student) with average prior LTA performance from a school with average school size and average free/reduced lunch percentage.

Students' solution sophistication results across grades and years from 2014 to 2016 are shown in figure 4.4. Like the correctness results, OGAP students consistently and significantly outperformed the students in the comparison schools across years and grade levels. In 2014–2015, the typical third-, fourth-, and fifth-grade students all had significantly higher sophistication scores, on average, than the comparison students. These significant differences persisted in year 2 of the experiment. Those students who were present in their schools in both 2014–2015 and 2015–2016 (the stable sample) both significantly outperformed their comparison group counterparts and had higher average sophistication scores than those in the single-year results, suggesting that multiple years of experience of OGAP had a cumulative effect. Despite the fact that students in OGAP schools significantly outperformed students in the comparison schools, it

Figure 4.4 Impacts of OGAP on LTA—solution sophistication (all years reflect experimental results)

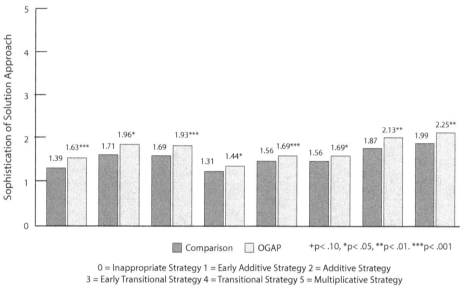

Note: The graph shows the predicted performance of a female regular education student (as opposed to a special education or ELL student) with average prior LTA performance from a school with average school size and average free/reduced lunch percentage.

is still important to note that students, on average, still used additive or early transitional multiplicative strategies, which indicates that all students had ample room for continued growth.

IMPACTS OF OGAP ON THE PENNSYLVANIA SYSTEM OF SCHOOL ASSESSMENT (PSSA)

Overview of the PSSA

The second assessment used to evaluate OGAP was the Pennsylvania state assessment in mathematics. The PSSA is administered each spring to students in grades 3–8 in English language arts and mathematics. The test is a standards-based, criterion-referenced assessment that provides students, parents, educators, and citizens with an understanding of student and school performance related to the attainment of proficiency of the academic standards. The PSSA was not vertically equated across grades, so average scores in one grade were not definitionally higher than those in the previous grade.

It is worth noting that Pennsylvania modified the PSSA in the summer of 2015 to align with changes in the Pennsylvania Core Standards, which produced a decline in year-over-year within-grade scores. According to the Pennsylvania Department of Education, the rigor of the test increased in 2015 due to changes in the standards that made proficient or advanced scores harder to achieve, which produced a downturn in student scores. All our analyses consisted of repeated cross-sections; therefore, we left the results in their original metric. Since this condition was present equally for schools in both the treatment and control conditions, we do not consider this to bias the experimental results.

It should also be noted that the PSSA was not perfectly aligned with OGAP's emphases, since only a portion of the assessment is focused on the area that OGAP emphasized in each grade (multiplication, division, and fractions in grades 3–5 and proportions in grades 6–8). For example, based on an examination of the content areas covered on the PSSA for grades 3–5 from publicly available items from the Pennsylvania Department of Education's webpage, we estimated that about 50–75 percent of the PSSA (depending on grade) covered multiplication and division.[6] However, the PSSA is the state test in Pennsylvania and therefore the most meaningful measure of student performance for school and district leaders.

The PSSA results can be seen in figure 4.5. We can see that in the first year of our experimental study of OGAP, the students of OGAP teachers significantly outperformed students in the comparison schools in each of the three grade levels we examined (3, 4, and 5) in the 2014–2015 school year. In the second year of the experiment, 2015–2016, the OGAP students scored higher on the PSSA in all three grades, but the differences were not statistically significant due to the wide variability in student scores. The stable sample, or third- and fourth-grade students who matriculated in their schools from year 1 to year 2 of the study and therefore

Figure 4.5 OGAP and comparison group student performance on the PSSA by grade and year

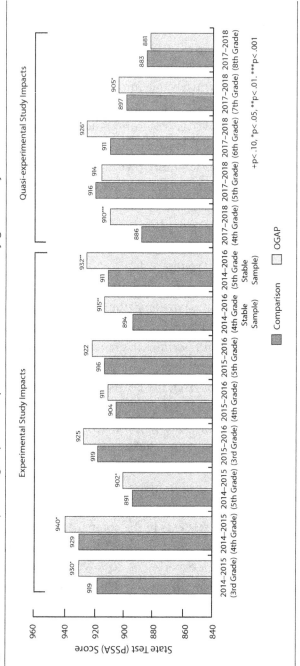

Note: The graph shows predicted performance of a Black female regular education student receiving lunch assistance in a school with average school size, average free/reduced lunch percentage, and average student ethnic composition.

received two years of OGAP-informed instruction, scored twenty-one points higher, on average, than students in the control group.

We replicated the PSSA analyses for grades 4–8 in 2017–2018, using the students of teachers in the OGAP and comparison schools. These analyses are quasi-experimental, since schools self-selected to participate in OGAP that year. The results indicate that student in grades where teachers were trained in OGAP significantly outperformed their peers in the comparison schools in fourth, sixth, and seventh grades, while there were no differences in performance between fifth-and eighth-grade students in the OGAP and comparison schools.

SUMMARY

In this chapter we examined the impacts of OGAP on teachers and students in different years and at different grade levels. Overall, we found consistent statistically significant and educationally meaningful impacts of OGAP on teachers' knowledge of formative assessments and student performance on different assessments. While OGAP teachers and students performed significantly better than their peers, it does not mean there is not substantial room for improvement.

To estimate the impacts on teachers, we used an assessment of teachers' formative assessment knowledge called the Teacher Assessment of Student Knowledge, or TASK. The TASK asked teachers to examine different grade-appropriate student work samples, comment on what they noticed about the work, order them by the sophistication of the student's solution strategies, and suggest appropriate instructional responses. The TASKs are highly aligned with what OGAP trains teachers to do in their classrooms. The results showed that teachers trained in OGAP had consistently higher TASK performance compared to teachers in a comparison set of schools that did not use OGAP. In 2016–2017 we had data on two different intensities of OGAP training. We found that teachers in schools with stronger levels of support had higher TASK scores than teachers with moderate support, and both groups had higher scores than teachers in the comparison group. The final year of analyses examined the persistent effects of OGAP. In these analyses we found evidence that teachers' knowledge of learning trajectory–oriented formative assessment persisted for both those whose schools continued to receive OGAP support and for those in schools that were no longer formally supported by OGAP. Taken together, these findings provide strong evidence that teachers retained their knowledge of learning trajectories and formative assessment practices.

We used two different kinds of assessments to assess the impact of OGAP on student learning. First, as part of our experimental study of OGAP, we developed an aligned assessment that examined both the accuracy (i.e., correctness) of students' math knowledge and the sophistication of their solution approaches. Assessing both correctness and sophistication was consistent with OGAP's emphasis on supporting students to both get the right answer and do so in an efficient way. We found that the students of teachers trained in OGAP's approach scored higher and had more advanced solution strategies compared to peers taught by teachers who had not received OGAP training. Finally, we examined student performance on the Pennsylvania state examination, the PSSA. Again, we found that the students of OGAP teachers scored significantly higher on the state test in most grades than comparable students in schools not using OGAP. These results are important to district policymakers who are focused on improving student performance on their state examination.

The consistently positive results chronicled in this chapter set up the rest of the chapters in the book by giving a bird's eye view of the outcomes of OGAP and PMLC's efforts. Average impacts like those presented in this chapter can mask the more complicated range of challenges faced by those on the ground and the efforts it takes to produce improvements. The next two chapters detail the micro-processes that it took to achieve these overall impacts and shows the wide variation in both school and teacher take-up as teachers and principals sought to implement OGAP's ambitious instructional reform.

CHAPTER 4 APPENDICES
Appendix A: TASK Models

	2014–2015	2015–2016	2015–2016	2014–2016	2014–2016
TASK subject	Multiplication	Multiplication	Fractions	Multiplication	Fractions
Sample	435 Teachers, 61 schools	147 Teachers, 51 schools	157 Teachers, 55 schools	129 Teachers, 50 schools	134 Teachers, 50 schools
Constant	1.10*** (0.15)	1.22*** (0.25)	1.37*** (0.26)	0.97*** (0.32)	1.44*** (0.33)
Pre-TASK	0.47*** (0.06)	0.56*** (0.07)	0.38*** (0.06)	0.53*** (0.08)	0.34** (0.11)
Treatment	0.34*** (0.05)	0.21** (0.08)	0.18* (0.09)	0.40*** (0.10)	0.29*** (0.08)
Teacher of English language learners	−0.01 (0.06)	−0.05 (0.16)	0.00 (0.09)	−0.06 (0.24)	0.13 (0.09)
Special education teacher	0.02 (0.06)	−0.16+ (0.09)	−0.24** (0.09)	−0.28* (0.11)	−0.08 (0.15)
Years experience	0.00 (0.01)	−0.01* (0.01)	−0.01 (0.01)	−0.01 (0.01)	−0.00 (0.01)
School size (hundreds)	−0.01 (0.01)	0.01 (0.02)	−0.01 (0.02)	0.01 (0.02)	−0.02 (0.02)
Free/reduced lunch %	0.07 (0.16)	−0.12 (0.32)	0.37 (0.51)	−0.03 (0.39)	0.29 (0.46)
School Black %	0.03 (0.11)	−0.15 (0.25)	−0.37 (0.49)	−0.02 (0.24)	−0.32 (0.36)
School Hispanic %	0.47 (0.17)	−0.15 (0.25)	−0.39 (0.54)	0.12 (0.33)	−0.28 (0.47)
School Asian %	0.66*** (0.18)	−0.16 (0.40)	−0.07 (0.71)	0.58 (0.55)	0.34 (0.50)
School Multirace %	−1.01 (0.63)	0.87 (1.38)	−1.08 (1.10)	0.95 (1.47)	−1.99+ (1.06)

Note: Effect estimates with standard errors in parentheses.
+ p<.10; * p<.05; ** p<.01 *** p<.001

Appendix A (continued): TASK Models

	2016–2017	2017–2018	2017–2018	2017–2018	Baseline–2019
TASK subject	Multiplication	Multiplication	Addition	Proportions	Multiplication
Sample	254 Teachers	94 Teachers, 33 schools	137 Teachers, 35 schools	49 Teachers, 25 schools	134 Teachers, 56 schools
Constant	0.84*** (0.15)	1.08* (0.52)	0.54 (0.40)	1.50** (0.47)	2.85** (0.95)
Pre-TASK	0.69*** (0.06)	0.47*** (0.07)	0.61*** (0.07)	0.51*** (0.08)	0.25** (0.09)
Treatment		0.49*** (0.09)	0.22** (0.07)	0.30+ (0.16)	
Intensive support treatment	0.43*** (0.09)				
Summer-only treatment	0.27*** (0.07)				
Dosage-treatment	0.11 (0.17)				
Treatment ongoing					0.20* (0.09)
Treatment ended					0.16 (0.10)
School started in 2014					0.17 (0.10)
School started in 2016					0.18* (0.09)

Appendix A (continued): TASK Models

	2016–2017	2017–2018	2017–2018	2017–2018	Baseline–2019
Teacher of English language learners	−0.016 (0.087)	0.25 (0.22)	−0.11 (0.16)	0.28* (0.13)	−0.07 (0.20)
Special education teacher	−0.140+ (0.081)	−0.23+ (0.13)	−0.13 (0.22)	−0.30* (0.15)	−0.12 (0.15)
Years experience	−0.006 (0.004)	−0.02** (0.01)	0.01 (0.01)	−0.02*** (0.01)	−0.01* (0.01)
Female teacher		−0.09 (0.15)	−0.09 (0.28)	0.26+ (0.14)	0.00 (0.14)
School size (hundreds)		0.00 (0.03)	−0.01 (0.02)	−0.04 (0.04)	0.02 (0.08)
School economic disadvantaged %		0.74* (0.29)	0.04 (0.16)	0.43 (0.29)	−0.01 (0.01)
School Black %		−0.51+ (0.27)	0.31 (0.23)	−0.76* (0.30)	−0.00 (0.01)
Hispanic %		−0.38 (0.32)	0.19 (0.26)	−0.82* (0.33)	0.00 (0.00)
Asian %		−0.97* (0.40)	0.20 (0.49)	−0.20 (0.94)	−0.01 (0.01)
Other ethnicity %		0.32 (1.55)	2.14 (1.51)	−1.00 (2.76)	−0.00 (0.02)

Note: Effect estimates with standard errors in parentheses.
+ p<.10; * p<.05; ** p<.01 *** p<.001

Appendix B: Learning Trajectory Assessment, Multiplicative Reasoning Models

	Correctness			Sophistication		
	2014–2015 (year 1)	2015–2016 (year 2)	Stable sample (2 years)	2014–2015 (year 1)	2015–2016 (year 2)	Stable sample (2 years)
Sample	9,099	7,162	4,508	9,069	7,162	4,508
Constant	0.51*** (0.04)	0.37*** (0.04)	0.49*** (0.04)	2.44*** (0.19)	2.03*** (0.21)	3.00*** (0.27)
Pretest	0.32*** (0.01)	0.45*** (0.02)	0.28*** (0.01)	0.46*** (0.02)	0.58*** (0.03)	0.47*** (0.03)
Treatment	0.05** (0.02)	0.02+ (0.01)	0.04** (0.02)	0.25*** (0.07)	0.13* (0.07)	0.26** (0.10)
Grade 3 student	0.04** (0.01)	0.02 (0.02)	—	−0.33*** (0.06)	−0.25*** (0.07)	—
Grade 5 student	−0.06*** (0.01)	0.01 (0.01)	0.01 (0.01)	−0.03 (0.07)	0.01 (0.07)	0.12+ (0.06)
Female student	−0.01* (0.01)	−0.01+ (0.01)	−0.03*** (0.01)	−0.10*** (0.02)	−0.05* (0.02)	−0.11*** (0.03)
Black student	−0.08*** (0.01)	−0.06*** (0.02)	−0.08*** (0.02)	−0.35*** (0.05)	−0.25*** (0.07)	−0.41*** (0.11)
Hispanic student	−0.04** (0.01)	−0.02 (0.02)	−0.04 (0.03)	−0.18** (0.07)	−0.12+ (0.07)	−0.15 (0.13)
Asian student	0.09*** (0.02)	0.09*** (0.02)	0.12*** (0.03)	0.39*** (0.08)	0.44*** (0.08)	0.62*** (0.14)

Appendix B: (continued)

	Correctness			Sophistication		
	2014–2015 (year 1)	2015–2016 (year 2)	Stable sample (2 years)	2014–2015 (year 1)	2015–2016 (year 2)	Stable sample (2 years)
Other ethnicity student	-0.02 (0.02)	-0.03+ (0.02)	-0.05* (0.02)	-0.13+ (0.07)	-0.13+ (0.07)	-0.29** (0.10)
Free/reduced lunch recipient	-0.02** (0.01)	-0.02** (0.01)	-0.02* (0.01)	-0.12*** (0.03)	-0.05+ (0.03)	-0.12* (0.05)
Student with disability	-0.13*** (0.01)	-0.07*** (0.01)	-0.1*** (0.01)	-0.58*** (0.04)	-0.39*** (0.06)	-0.59*** (0.08)
English language learner	-0.07*** (0.01)	-0.05*** (0.01)	-0.05*** (0.01)	-0.33*** (0.05)	-0.21*** (0.04)	-0.31*** (0.07)
School size (hundreds)	-0.01 (0.01)	-0.00 (0.00)	-0.01 (0.00)	-0.03 (0.02)	-0.03+ (0.02)	-0.04 (0.03)
School free/reduced lunch %	-0.17*** (0.03)	-0.17*** (0.04)	-0.18*** (0.03)	-0.68*** (0.15)	-0.77*** (0.17)	-1.10*** (0.20)
Charter school	-0.03+ (0.02)	-0.00 (0.01)	-0.01 (0.03)	-0.19* (0.07)	-0.06 (0.10)	-0.14 (0.13)
Upper Darby school	-0.04+ (0.02)	0.01 (0.02)	0.01 (0.02)	-0.17* (0.07)	0.07 (0.09)	0.03 (0.09)

Note: Effect estimates with standard errors in parentheses.

++ $p < .10$; * $p < .05$; ** $p < .01$ *** $p < .001$

Appendix C: Pennsylvania System of School Assessment Models, 2015–2016

	2014–2015 (year 1)	2015–2016 (year 2)	2015–2016 stable sample (2 years)
Sample	8,388 Students 61 Schools	5,891 Students 61 Schools	3,489 Students 61 Schools
Constant	1001.9*** (13.0)	962.0*** (22.9)	990.3*** (19.5)
Pretest	74.1*** (2.0)	102.3*** (5.5)	79.2*** (3.6)
Treatment	10.8* (5.5)	6.7 (8.3)	21.2** (8.1)
Grade 3 student	−10.0** (3.2)	14.4** (5.6)	—
Grade 5 student	−37.8*** (3.1)	11.7** (4.0)	17.0*** (3.8)
Female student	−5.76*** (1.4)	−10.2*** (2.3)	−9.8*** (2.9)
Black student	−30.9*** (5.2)	−32.7*** (6.3)	−40.4*** (8.8)
Hispanic student	−16.0*** (4.8)	−18.2*** (5.6)	−22.4* (9.3)
Asian student	36.8*** (5.9)	33.6*** (9.0)	41.6*** (10.5)
Other race student	−9.4+ (5.1)	−12.6* (5.9)	−15.2+ (8.6)
Free/reduced lunch recipient	−15.0*** (2.7)	−13.7*** (2.9)	−14.9*** (4.7)
Student with disability	−39.7*** (2.8)	−38.7*** (4.2)	−43.6*** (5.6)
English language learner	−38.1*** (3.4)	−37.3*** (4.8)	−34.4*** (5.4)
School size (hundreds)	−0.8 (1.1)	−1.5 (1.5)	−1.7 (1.7)
School free/reduced lunch %	−70.3*** (12.5)	−75.9*** (22.4)	−82.3*** (14.3)
Upper Darby school	9.0 (6.7)	21.5** (7.6)	19.7** (7.4)

Note: Effect estimates with standard errors in parentheses.
++ $p<.10$; * $p<.05$; ** $p<.01$ *** $p<.001$

Appendix C (continued): Pennsylvania System of School Assessment, 2017–2018

	Grade 4	Grade 5	Grade 6	Grade 7	Grade 8
Sample	2,673 Students 44 Schools	2,403 Students 42 Schools	1,661 Students 36 Schools	1,578 Students 33 Schools	1,174 Students 32 Schools
Constant	317.4*** (36.0)	271.0*** (23.7)	198.0*** (38.1)	78.3 (48.8)	189.8*** (34.2)
Pretest	0.7*** (0.1)	0.8*** (0.1)	0.8*** (0.01)	1.0*** (.03)	0.8*** (0.1)
Treatment	23.7*** (6.8)	−2.5 (5.8)	14.8* (6.6)	8.5* (3.5)	−2.2 (5.9)
Attended 4–5 days	−3.9 (6.7)	−1.4 (4.5)	−7.5 (5.7)	−4.8 (9.0)	−6.2 (5.8)
Attendance %	13.0 (11.9)	4.8 (13.9)	7.2 (−16.1)	1.2 (−17.4)	18.2 (−11.3)
Female student	−2.3 (2.5)	−0.5 (2.5)	8.9*** (2.2)	−1.9 (2.8)	8.2+ (3.3)
English language learner	−2.9 (3.6)	−9.9* (4.9)	−14.6*** (4.3)	−22.3*** (5.8)	−5.7 (4.6)
Special Education	−7.2* (3.2)	−13.4** (4.8)	−23.2*** (6.2)	−14.4** (5.5)	−19.0*** (4.4)
Black	11.4+ (6.0)	−10.3+ (5.7)	−7.0 (4.5)	−8.6 (8.2)	−3.0 (7.6)
Asian	17.5** (5.8)	19.3* (7.7)	21.2*** (5.2)	26.0** (9.4)	24.2+ (11.1)
Hispanic	−5.4 (5.3)	−6.4 (5.4)	0.6 (5.3)	−4.2 (8.5)	−0.7 (8.5)
Other ethnicity	−8.2 (5.2)	−3.1 (5.1)	2.8 (6.9)	5.7 (7.7)	−5.1 (11.6)
Free/reduced lunch	−11.1 (10.7)	−54.6*** (9.9)	−23.0+ (13.5)	−6.2 (14.2)	−56.3*** (10.1)
School size (hundreds)	−2.5+ (1.4)	−0.9 (.9)	1.0 (1.5)	−2.3 (2.2)	−0.3 (1.3)
Black%	−36.5*** (13.9)	−13.6 (13.8)	6.0 (14.8)	−44.8** (14.8)	14.7 (16.0)
Asian%	−14.8 (16.7)	34.8 (25.9)	36.8 (27.2)	28.3 (36.5)	−47.2+ (28.3)
Hispanic %	−58.8*** (15.9)	11.9 (18.2)	−35.5** (11.7)	−54.5** (21.2)	29.0* (14.7)
Other ethnicity %	20.8 (70.9)	−105.6 (87.9)	138.5 (142.6)	140.8 (145.5)	93.4 (96.5)

Note: Effect estimates with standard errors in parentheses.
+ p<.10; * p<.05; ** p<.01 *** p<.001

Appendix D: Average Values For Producing Graphs

Teacher Analysis of Student Knowledge (TASK)

	2014–2015	2015–2016	2016–2017	2017–2018	2018–2019
Avg teacher exp	12.75	12.93	13.52	16.20	17.72
Avg baseline TASK Multiplication (MR)	2.14	2.39	2.11	2.23	2.10
Avg baseline TASK Fractions (FR)	N/A	2.37	N/A	N/A	N/A
Avg baseline TASK Addition (AD)	N/A	N/A	N/A	2.25	N/A
Avg baseline TASK Proportions (PR)	N/A	N/A	N/A	2.17	N/A
Avg School Size	612	619	N/A	547	607
Avg lunch %	0.82	0.82	0.81	0.91	0.91
Avg Black %	0.52	0.47	0.41	0.50	0.43
Avg Hispanic %	0.14	0.16	0.23	0.17	0.24
Avg Asian %	0.10	0.13	0.11	0.07	0.09
Avg Multi-race %	0.05	0.05	0.08	0.08	0.07

Learning Trajectory Assessment (LTA)—Correctness/Sophistication

	2014–2015	2015–2016	Stable sample
Avg baseline TASK correctness	0.37	0.41	0.36
Avg baseline TASK sophistication	0.51	0.51	0.48
Avg school size	580	580	580
Avg lunch %	0.83	0.83	0.83

Appendix D (continued): Average Values For Producing Graphs

Pennsylvania System of School Assessment (PSSA)

	2014–2015	2015–2016	2017–2018 Grade 4	2017–2018 Grade 5	2017–2018 Grade 6	2017–2018 Grade 7	2017–2018 Grade 8
Avg baseline PSSA	509	610	933	910	914	908	889
Avg economic disadvantaged	0.83	0.83	0.93	0.93	0.92	0.91	0.93
Avg school size	560	550	666	667	626	641	586
Avg Black %	N/A	N/A	0.41	0.42	0.46	0.44	0.53
Avg Asian %	N/A	N/A	0.07	0.08	0.08	0.08	0.08
Avg Hispanic %	N/A	N/A	0.25	0.23	0.19	0.19	0.18
Avg other ethnicity %	N/A	N/A	0.09	0.09	0.08	0.08	0.08

5

Not so Fast

Expectations for First-Year School Implementation

Adrianne Flack, Brittan Hallar, Brittany L. Hess,
Katrina Morrison, Christian Kolouch,
and Jordan D'Olier

The first year of the School District of Philadelphia's summer Math-Counts Institute (MCI) for K–8 schools was 2016. The Institute marked a renewed effort in the district to prioritize mathematics, as well as the transition of OGAP from an external initiative to part of the district's mathematics improvement strategy (see chapter 3). At the MCI, OGAP led the summer training for teachers in grades 3–5, while another provider, Carnegie Learning, facilitated professional development for grades K–2 and 6–8.

The expansion of OGAP to a range of new schools offered the opportunity to examine implementation in grades 3–5 in a new model of training and support. Our chapter describes the modifications made to the OGAP model to accommodate structures in the district and how twelve schools responded to the invitation to implement OGAP, including analyses about the conditions that influenced OGAP adoption. Since Philadelphia is a city with many streets named after trees, we use tree names as pseudonyms for the twelve schools and follow this convention across the remainder of the book.

The research team based its assessment of OGAP implementation on three key elements of the OGAP model. First, we assessed teacher use of the OGAP framework for multiplicative reasoning. The OGAP framework incorporates information about problem contexts, solution approaches, and details the learning progressions that are the keys to teachers making sense of student work, which in turn, should inform their instructional responses. Hence, teacher facility with the OGAP framework is a central indicator of their fluency with OGAP formative assessment routines.

The second indicator of OGAP implementation that we examined was the regularity of professional learning communities (PLCs) within which teachers examine student work and plan instructional responses. OGAP's developers consider regular PLCs that employ the program routines to be an essential component of OGAP implementation because they are the place where teachers can regularly and collaboratively practice the routines of OGAP and gain familiarity with the approach.

The third implementation indicator was teachers' reported use of formative assessment practices in their regular planning and instruction. These practices included reducing the scope of summative assessments, increasing the frequency of formative assessments, and analyzing student work to understand student thinking as opposed to simply checking for correct or incorrect responses.

Based on the data we collected to assess these implementation indicators, we address two questions in this chapter. First, what was the influence of the initial OGAP training and differing levels of ongoing support on school and teacher adoption of key aspects of OGAP's reform strategy? Second, what conditions within schools and the district facilitated and impeded teachers' use of the OGAP model?

Our findings provide a reality check on the expectations of a one-year implementation cycle of reform measures. The district model for training and supporting teachers was focused on successive annual cohorts of schools, which would allow all schools to receive equitable resources over the course of four to five years. Yet our findings suggest that teachers and schools were just beginning to engage with implementation after one year. Foremost, teacher adoption of the core tools and principles of OGAP were uneven within schools, although schools with additional follow-up support showed slightly higher use of OGAP. In particular, changes to teacher meeting structures—a key routine of OGAP—were particularly difficult for schools to incorporate. This highlights that new reforms require full understanding and buy-in from school and district leaders if they are to thrive and have a chance at success. Even with more intensive support, integrating time for teachers to discuss student work proved challenging for schools to implement. For a new initiative to take hold, we highlight the need for commitment at all levels: district, school administration, school-based instructional leaders, and teachers. As a research team, we observed almost impenetrable barriers for OGAP to take root in many schools, despite school personnel's interest in the opportunity to transform student learning in mathematics. Finally, the findings of this investigation into the challenges that schools faced helped us understand the limitations of working with a subset of grades within a school, which led to fragmented support and paved the way for the expansion of OGAP to a K–8 model the following school year.

This chapter is composed of four sections. First, we describe the training and supports teachers and leaders received and changes that were made along the way as the Philadelphia Math Leadership Collaborative monitored school take-up. Second, we briefly describe our data collection and analysis plan. The bulk of the chapter presents our findings, in terms of both school implementation and school and district factors that influenced implementation. We close with a discussion of the findings and their implications.

SYSTEMIC SUPPORTS FOR OGAP IMPLEMENTATION

In June 2016 the School District of Philadelphia (SDP) sponsored its first annual MathCounts Institute for approximately forty K–8 elementary schools. This summer institute was an opportunity that all schools would eventually be asked to attend. However, because of resource constraints, schools' participation was phased in over the course of three years (from 2016 to 2018).

In the spring preceding the June institute, the district's director of mathematics sent invitations to principals to apply for admission to the Institute. A school's admission was based on several factors. The most important of which was that at least 65 percent of the relevant staff committed to attending, including the principal. Notably, schools' participation was incentivized with a $20,000 grant that schools could use to support math tutoring outside of normal school hours.

MCI took place over five consecutive days during the last week of June, just following the end of the academic year. While far from ideal for teachers to prepare for the next school year right after the completion of the previous one, the timing was due to district space and calendar constraints. Each morning began with a motivational speaker for an hour; this was followed by content-specific training from about 9 a.m. to 1 p.m. with a break for lunch and time at the end of each day for school faculties to come together to discuss and plan strategies for improving student achievement in math in the forthcoming academic year.

The institute was organized in two tracks: one track trained teachers of grades 3–5 on the OGAP model of formative assessment for multiplicative reasoning. The second track, which was facilitated by Carnegie Learning, Inc.—an independent, well-known educational training company—consisted of a variety of workshops featuring math strategies and classroom resources teachers could use to bolster mathematics instruction for students across grades K–12. The OGAP training offered was condensed to accommodate the time parameters of the Institute. Normally, OGAP provides approximately forty hours of initial OGAP training for teachers, which was condensed to thirty hours to fit into the planned schedule.

ONGOING SUPPORT FOR OGAP IN THE ACADEMIC YEAR

The SDP's initial plan for ongoing support for schools whose grades 3–5 teachers participated in OGAP during the MCI was three-fold. First, OGAP trainers were scheduled to train Carnegie math specialists (contracted school support personnel) on how to support grades 3–5 teachers to implement OGAP. These math specialists would support grades 3–5 OGAP teachers, along with the other teachers of math in their assigned schools, during their weekly school visits. Second, they planned to have school math lead teachers attend a half-day professional development in November 2016 to receive follow-up training on how to support OGAP in their schools. Third, the district funded an additional day of training for participants in March that focused on deepening multiplicative reasoning for third- and fourth-grade teachers and introducing fractional reasoning for fifth-grade teachers.

However, as things evolved, in the fall of 2016 OGAP leaders grew concerned about the extent to which this plan would provide sufficient support for implementation. Since math lead teachers were a linchpin of OGAP implementation and were responsible for supporting mathematics in their entire school, not just grades 3–5, they had to choose between attending the Carnegie or OGAP follow-up training in the November half-day professional developments. Consequently, the first OGAP half-day session for teacher leaders in November was unevenly attended.[1] In addition, questions emerged about the ability of Carnegie math specialists to adequately support OGAP without having attended the full initial training.

In response to these concerns, the Philadelphia Mathematics Leadership Collaborative (PMLC) reached out to approximately twenty-five of the forty schools that attended the Institute in June, inviting them to participate in a cohort of schools receiving ongoing OGAP support for the remainder of the school year. Schools were invited based on those who had reasonably high math teacher attendance at the Institute and those who had specifically requested additional support. Overall, sixteen of the invited schools volunteered to participate in PMLC's ongoing OGAP support across the 2016–2017 school year.

The ongoing support provided by PMLC was targeted to teachers, principals, and math leads, sometimes in combined sessions and other times for each audience separately. In sessions designed for principals, the principals sometimes sent in their place or brought along other school leaders, such as an assistant principal or the school-based teacher leader (SBTL).[2]

In other instances the math lead teacher attended in lieu of or with the principal. In addition to the series of supports provided by PMLC, OGAP was also contracted by the district to provide four separate trainings throughout the academic year, in coordination with the district's director of mathematics.

Ongoing PMLC support for the sixteen schools consisted of seven sessions across the 2016–2017 academic year. Three of the sessions were for teachers. Two of the teacher support sessions (in December and February) were customized half-day visits by OGAP trainers to schools to provide onsite training for teachers, small-group coaching, modeling of PLCs, and/or modeling classroom instruction, depending on the preference of the school. In addition, OGAP provided full-day regional training in January in several locations across the city, where teachers from schools in that region could come for additional training in OGAP.

Three of the PMLC support sessions (November, January, March) were specifically for school leaders and math leads and focused on school and leader supports for OGAP implementation. These sessions were geared toward developing the conditions needed to facilitate successful implementation of OGAP. One such condition was creating opportunities for teachers to examine and discuss students' math problem-solving strategies in a professional learning community format. The seventh and final session occurred in May 2017, which was for participants to celebrate the year and make plans for deeper implementation the following year.

INVESTIGATING OGAP IMPLEMENTATION

The creation of a small cohort of sixteen schools that volunteered to participate in the more intensive ongoing OGAP and leadership support created the opportunity to study the progress of OGAP in this cohort (which we refer to as *OGAP-A schools* going forward) in contrast to the schools that were introduced to OGAP at the summer institute and received less intensive OGAP follow-up support via the district's model (which we refer to as *OGAP-B schools*).

The sample for this qualitative study of OGAP implementation consisted of twelve Philadelphia elementary schools: eight were drawn from schools that elected to engage in ongoing OGAP support (OGAP-A schools), and four schools were selected from the pool of schools that declined the invitation to participate in ongoing OGAP support (OGAP-B schools). All of the schools in this sample sent at least 65 percent of their math teachers to the initial summer training.

Our data collection consisted of one visit to each school, which included interviews, field notes, and exit memos. Once schools confirmed their willingness to participate in the study, members of the research team worked in pairs to conduct interviews of teachers and leaders at each school. Our goal was to interview three to six teachers across the grades 3–5 band, each school principal, and the math lead teacher. The school visits were conducted between February and March 2017. Interviews ranged between thirty and sixty minutes. Through this process we collected interview data from twenty-seven OGAP-A teachers, fourteen OGAP-B teachers, eleven math lead teachers, three school-based teacher leaders, and ten of the twelve principals. Following the school visits, research team members completed exit memos at the end of school visits to note impressions of each school and how the staff appeared aligned or not in using OGAP.

Data analysis proceeded iteratively through several steps. First, the interviews were transcribed, cleaned, coded, and analyzed by the research team. Following the coding of the transcripts, the team constructed analytic memos for each school based on the coded data that aligned with our guiding research questions and the implementation indicators described below.

- **Criterion 1.** Teachers' reported uses of the OGAP framework (including problem contexts, structures, and progressions)
- **Criterion 2.** Teachers', math lead teachers', and principals' reported uses of PLCs to examine student work and plan instructional responses
- **Criterion 3.** Teachers' reported uses of additional formative assessment practices attributed to OGAP training (e.g., use of item bank problems, reducing the size of assessments and increasing the frequency of

formative assessment, analyzing student work to understand student thinking as opposed to simply checking for right or wrong responses)

To assess the degree to which these OGAP criteria were embedded in schools, we developed a rubric to denote OGAP uptake. The rubric, shown in table 5.1, used interview data to assess implementation of the first two dimensions of OGAP adoption. Our analytic memo, which focused on what teachers reported using from OGAP training mainly informed the third category of the rubric.

To examine the factors that facilitated or impeded OGAP progress, we used the qualitative data that produced the ratings and reanalyzed them looking for themes associated with facilitators and barriers to adoption.

FINDINGS

We first describe our findings for the first question regarding the degree of uptake of OGAP after one year across two categories of schools: those that participated in ongoing support (OGAP-A schools) and those that only attended the initial training (OGAP-B schools). This presentation of our findings utilizes the three criteria of our assessment scale (see table 5.1) as an organizational framework.

In the second section of the results, we present our findings in response to research question 2, which pertains to school-level and district-level conditions that impeded or facilitated OGAP adoption among teachers.

OGAP ADOPTION ACROSS THE TWO SETS OF SCHOOLS

Criterion 1: Use of the OGAP Multiplicative Framework

The OGAP framework encapsulates mathematics education research on how students develop an increased understanding of specific mathematics concepts. There are three main components of an OGAP multiplicative framework. The first two are problem contexts and structures. These are

Table 5.1 Assessment scale of OGAP use in schools

Rating	Criteria for OGAP framework use	Criteria for PLC use	Criteria for adoption of formative assessment practices and new instructional strategies
1—No use	Respondents spoke in generalities about the OGAP framework; little to no mention of its use in practice.	PLC focused on administrative tasks/student behaviors/generic data (i.e., not open-ended math items).	Teachers do not seem to understand or use any portion of the OGAP formative assessment cycle. They were unable to name any new math strategies that they have used in their instruction.
2—Low use	OGAP framework beginning to change mindset of teachers.	At least some of the PLC time focused on math instruction and strategies.	Teachers mentioned trying one to two new math strategies, but knowledge and use of the OGAP formative assessment cycle is weak or nonexistent.
3—Moderate use	OGAP framework use in analysis of student work.	Looking at student work was a regular component of PLCs.	Teachers engage in the formative assessment cycle, but do not utilize OGAP materials or resources. They may use some new math strategies learned in OGAP training; or teachers are engaging in parts of the OGAP formative assessment cycle (such as looking at student work) but not talking in detail about making instructional changes based on the data.
4—High use	OGAP framework use explicit in meetings and/or class.	PLCs had regular use of OGAP formative assessment cycle.	Teachers regularly engage in the OGAP formative assessment cycle both in their classrooms and together with colleagues. They are able to talk about new math strategies that they have learned through OGAP.

also reflected in the types of formative assessment problems provided in the OGAP item banks that teachers can use to match where they are in the curriculum or focus on a particular skill. Students who are strong multiplicative reasoners should be able to solve assessment items reflecting a range of different problem structures and contexts. The third component of the OGAP framework is the learning progression, which depicts a general pathway of increasing student fluency in a specific content area of mathematics. The schools that participated in the first year of the MCI focused on multiplicative reasoning, which includes both the multiplication and division learning progressions. These progressions demonstrate the strategies students may employ to solve problems as they gain multiplicative reasoning skills, giving teachers a roadmap to support students as they gain sophistication with problem solving in that content area.

OGAP-trained teachers are taught to use the progression to analyze their students' understanding of mathematical concepts using student work on formative assessment items. They learn to sort the work by strategy or strategy level as depicted on the OGAP Multiplicative Progression, taking note of any underlying issues (such as misconceptions or calculation errors). This is a significant change from the more typical practice of understanding student work based on correct or incorrect answers. Using the OGAP Multiplicative Progression, teachers can assess students' current levels of understanding and use this information to craft appropriate instructional next steps for students, even when they answer the problem correctly, to further develop students' multiplicative reasoning skills.

Overall, we found that teachers used the framework and were moving along in their use of it after several months of OGAP's introduction to schools. However, schools varied widely in their teachers' reported use of the framework as an instructional tool. As shown in figure 5.1, fewer schools had teachers who made moderate to high use of the framework—as defined by the levels in the rubric in table 5.1. None of the teachers we interviewed at OGAP-B schools used the framework beyond the low use category, suggesting that the ongoing school year training helped to deepen teachers' understanding and application of the concepts of the framework. The OGAP-A schools—those who received ongoing OGAP support across

Figure 5.1 OGAP framework use

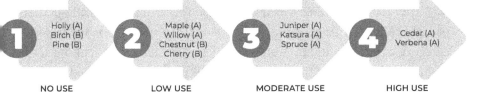

the school year—were stretched across the framework adoption ratings, but the majority exhibited moderate to high use at the time of our data collection in February/March 2017.

The OGAP framework was indeed a memorable aspect of OGAP among the majority of teachers we interviewed. Faculty members in all but one school made some reference to the OGAP framework influencing their beliefs and/or practices. Teachers' comments about their change in perspective generally spoke to the value they saw in the framework providing an understanding of how students actually come to learn and understand mathematical concepts. Often, interviewees described the framework as providing a "shift" in their thinking. Comments about a shift usually reflected teachers' new focus on students' developmental understanding as opposed to a binary, "right" or "wrong," perspective about children's knowledge and understanding of mathematics. Once exposed to the framework, many teachers reported realizing that students were on a developmental continuum, wherein correctness was only one aspect of student understanding.

The range of influence the framework had on teachers' practices varied widely both across and within schools. Most teachers' comments at low use schools were merely brief or general references to their *memory* of the framework and its impact on how they informally thought about student work. Conversely, in high use schools, teachers described explicit practices and actual use of the framework in classrooms and PLC meetings. Schools rated as having lower implementation of the OGAP framework was not necessarily due to a lack of mentioning the OGAP framework in comments but, rather, it was based on the faculty members' descriptions of its use.

At Birch (OGAP-B), for example, all interviewees referenced the OGAP framework, with one interviewee requiring a prompt to remember what it was. The teachers' comments at this school, however, described little actual use of the OGAP framework in practice. Thus, schools in this lowest category of our continuum were generally characterized as making referential rather than action- or change-based comments related to the framework.

Schools situated in the moderate use category were characterized as those in which teachers described making actual shifts in either mindset or practice following engagement with the OGAP framework. In these schools, grades 3–5 teachers moved beyond simply referencing the framework and credited it with changing their *thinking* about how students learn. Interviewees at these schools mentioned having "aha moments" that extended their thinking about how students learn mathematics. Teachers also cited changes they made toward becoming more careful analyzers of student work. In these schools, interviewees discussed how the framework informed the way they thought about the practice of teaching, assessment, and student work analysis.

In addition, teachers at schools categorized as having high use of the framework also described how it was having an impact on their students' learning. Additionally, high use schools went beyond one or two teachers simply rethinking their teaching practice and had multiple interviewees referencing active use of the OGAP framework in classrooms with students. One teacher in Cedar (OGAP-A), for example, described how he explicitly showed the framework to students to help them understand their own math progress: "It kind of turns on the lightbulb in their head, like, 'Oh, I should do it that way,' Then we kind of show them on the framework how we want them to keep moving up," he explained. In these schools, the OGAP framework had become an important enough tool that interviewees saw it as a fundamental part of the learning process. One interviewee from Verbena (OGAP-A) went so far as to say that she kept the framework with her on a regular basis. "I have it in my backpack," she reported. "Yes. I walk with it." This kind of high-level buy-in constituted a school being placed in category 4. Finally, and importantly, high use interviewees also described more of a schoolwide approach to OGAP adoption as opposed to the more fragmented, individual teacher attempts we heard about at many schools.

Criterion 2: Use of OGAP Professional Learning Communities

OGAP professional learning communities (PLCs) require the commitment of both teachers and school leaders, as they are a function of both school scheduling and teacher engagement. An OGAP PLC is a regular gathering of math teachers (ideally twice monthly) from a single grade level or grade span to examine their students' work on open-ended math problems using the OGAP formative assessment cycle (assess, analyze, respond) to plan instructional responses. Ideally, the PLCs are facilitated by a math instructional leader. Before the OGAP PLC, teachers from the same grade should administer a common item from the OGAP item bank of formative assessment questions. The student work from this item is sorted based on OGAP's Multiplicative Framework, which contains learning progressions for both multiplication and division. Depending on several factors, including the number of teachers, the time available, and the participants' level of confidence with OGAP, they might sort the work prior to the PLC or sort it as a part of the meeting. They then analyze the trends, looking for common strategies, errors, misconceptions, and any other evidence they can find of their students' understanding of the concept they were assessing. Using these patterns of evidence, they plan instructional responses based on these data. The instructional responses may be different from class to class, depending on what the student work reveals. At the end of the meeting, teachers decide what OGAP item they will administer and bring to their next PLC. Teachers are encouraged to complete this formative assessment cycle in their own classroom more frequently, but the opportunity for teachers to have collaborative discussions around student work and math instruction in PLCs is a key component of the OGAP formative assessment model, which is believed to bolster professional learning.

Overall, we found that most schools did not develop regular OGAP PLCs in grades 3–5. Even schools that received additional support struggled to enact this component of the OGAP model. As shown in figure 5.2, nine of the twelve schools were rated as falling within categories 1 (no use) or 2 (low use) on the

Figure 5.2 Implementation of OGAP PLCs in schools

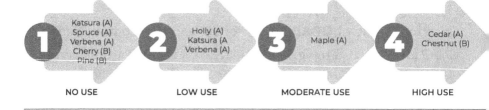

scale of PLC enactment, indicating that their grades 3–5 teachers reported having little to no experiences with OGAP PLCs. At these schools, teachers were meeting with their grade-level peers in weekly or biweekly meetings. However, teachers reported that meetings rarely focused on mathematics. Even when they did, interviewees mentioned a general focus on math strategies or an opportunity to have questions about the math curriculum answered, rather than the more systematic processes of analyzing student understanding in assessment items and discussing instructional responses. In these schools we found no evidence that they were using their PLCs to engage with mathematics formative assessment in any way.

Only one school, Maple (OGAP-A), was categorized in our third category of moderate use. In this school, grades 3–5 teachers reported bringing student work to their meetings. However, teachers who were interviewed did not feel that they were given time in these meetings to have professional conversations about math instruction with their colleagues. One teacher characterized the situation this way: "Although there are other teachers in the meeting, we're not collaborating. We are just sitting there; it's like a class lesson." For this school, it appeared that the leadership reinterpreted the PLCs as an opportunity for more direct training on OGAP, rather than providing teachers with practice in using the OGAP formative assessment cycle.

Two of the twelve in our sample reported operating PLC meetings consistently and in line with what OGAP teaches, which ends with teachers planning an instructional response after discussing student work. One of the two schools, Chestnut (OGAP-B), was from the group that had little OGAP follow-up after the initial summer training for teachers. The school's principal stated that they picked up ideas about formative assessment from the summer institute and were using them in their PLCs. The grades 3–5 teachers at Cedar (OGAP-A) were the only group that held regular OGAP PLCs and completed the full OGAP cycle.

Criterion 3: Adoption of Formative Assessment Practices

The third criterion in our assessment of teachers' uptake of OGAP was to identify what teachers reported they were using in practice as a result of exposure to OGAP training. During OGAP training, teachers are introduced to myriad concepts and instructional strategies that corresponded to the research-based OGAP Multiplicative Progression. Further, the OGAP model of formative assessment encouraged teachers to thoughtfully analyze students' work beyond the mere correctness of answers using the progression tool. OGAP also emphasized quick and frequent analyses of student work as well as collaborative analyses among grade-level teachers as a means of building teachers' instructional capacity. In this research, we hoped to gauge teachers' retention of OGAP beliefs and practices in the form of either knowledge or adopted practice.

Overall, we found that schools in their first year were just beginning to adopt OGAP formative assessment practices. As shown in figure 5.3, we found that the use of OGAP-inspired formative assessment practices varied widely across teachers in OGAP-A schools. There were examples on both ends of the spectrum—those schools where teachers reported consistently employing a wide variety of formative assessment practices and

Figure 5.3 Adoption of OGAP other formative assessment practices

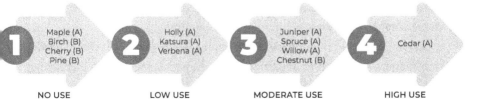

schools where teachers rarely used formative assessment practices. There was a large group of schools situated in the middle, where teachers adopted a few ideas learned from OGAP. In three of the four OGAP-B schools, OGAP practices were not evident.

Teachers in the schools on the upper end of formative assessment use (i.e., moderate or high use) reported employing a variety of the strategies we were looking for—often highlighting the OGAP Multiplicative Progression and OGAP item bank as particularly useful. Some school staff built weekly systems wherein teachers chose item bank problems, administered them to their students, and assessed them either on their own or as a teacher team at PLC meetings. The grades 3–5 teachers at Cedar (OGAP-A) were the highest implementing school in the sample. At Cedar, individual teachers not only expressed a good understanding of formative assessment generally and OGAP specifically, but collectively, leaders and teachers at the school created structures that would help them achieve both. Led by the school's math lead, and attended by the principal, the school held weekly PLC meetings in which they assigned OGAP item bank items for each teacher to use the following week, assessed the items from the week before, discussed what they saw as a group, and collaborated on potential instructional responses based on evidence provided in students' work. The teachers at Cedar indicated a consistent use of the OGAP framework both in these meetings and as individuals. Each teacher interviewed also expressly discussed his or her use of conversations with students as a means to teach mathematics. Further, teachers spoke of organizing students into mixed skill groups and letting them teach one another about how they approached assigned problems. Thus, children with different approaches got to share their approach with their peers. Apart from the PLC meetings, each grade group also met independently and analyzed and responded to item bank math problems chosen specifically to assess what the teachers were currently teaching.

At the lowest end of our OGAP adoption scale were schools where grades 3–5 teachers struggled to articulate what they took from OGAP training. These teachers showed little understanding of formative assessment in general and were unable to recall anything specific regarding OGAP. Most of the schools that fit this category were OGAP-B schools, which did not participate in ongoing professional development (PD) provided by PMLC. For instance, when one teacher at Cherry School (OGAP-B) was asked about her understanding of formative assessment or what she took from OAGP training, she stated, "At this point, very little, unfortunately. Just because it came at the beginning of the summer, and then we got thrown into a new math program . . . I've only had four days training with it."

The majority of the schools were in the middle of the rating scale. Teachers in these schools primarily focused on utilizing the OGAP framework in their teaching. This strategy/practice allowed teachers to triage students, delineate their strengths and needs, and provide them a means by which they could effectively differentiate instruction. Some used the framework when assessing their everyday assignments; others used item bank items and assessed student performance on the items, using the results to determine where to focus their instructional attention. Teachers at several schools, including those at the very top end of OGAP adoption, also discussed the use of area models. Some teachers mentioned this as being an entirely new method by which to teach math. They saw these as great ways to represent math, taking it from the abstract to the concrete, giving students a tangible example of multiplication concepts.

In some instances, we found that schools declined to give much credit to OGAP for the things they were doing to improve mathematics teaching and learning—highlighting that they had already been using formative assessment schoolwide (e.g., Birch and Chestnut, both OGAP-B schools). However, we noticed that many of the things they described were consistent with what OGAP would refer to as good formative assessment practice. The principal at Juniper (OGAP-A), for example, referred to their version of "item analysis," in which they sought to align particular open-ended items with the curriculum, which is consistent with OGAP's item bank organization. Another principal, at Brich (OGAP-B), discussed the use of a common problem teachers distributed to students, which the teaching team would later discuss. Ironically, the school declined to participate in ongoing support because OGAP was perceived to be a "heavy lift"—involving a significant shift in practice with regard to planning a response to student work. Hence, it was unclear how teachers actually approached addressing gaps in students' understandings of concepts. The principal at Chestnut (OGAP-B) similarly remarked that formative assessment wasn't something new for his school and that this was a practice his team began prior to their experience with OGAP. However, he recognized the sophistication of the OGAP model in building teachers' conceptual understanding of math and how the OGAP learning progressions approach provided a clear way to make sense of students' problem-solving strategies.

Supports for OGAP Implementation

In schools where teachers appeared to have moderate to high adoption of OGAP across the different rubric areas, we noted the following themes.

Principal prioritized math and made the commitment schoolwide. Principals articulated that improving math achievement was a high priority for their schools. Although their approaches to adopting OGAP occurred in different ways, buy-in from teachers and alignment between teachers' and leaders' responses about the vision for improving math education were apparent. Transforming the learning of mathematics had become a notable aspect of the school community.

Principals were not new to their roles and spent time cultivating the staff to be a cohesive team. In the higher implementation schools we noted that the principals appeared to have a positive working relationship with their teachers. The principal at Cedar (OGAP-A) made an administrative decision regarding OGAP adoption, whereas the principal at Chestnut (OGAP-B) made a decision in consultation with the teachers to individually adopt OGAP rather than "piling it on" amid so many other changes occurring in the district. Despite the lack of formal adoption occurring at Chestnut, the principal instituted elements of OGAP that he appreciated within his yearlong goal to improve student achievement in mathematics.

Released math leads were better able to support OGAP implementation. As part of the MathCounts Institute, each school was directed by district leadership to identify a lead teacher to support math instruction. We found no formal definition of "math lead teachers" on the school district's website. However, in an interview, the SDP's director of mathematics said that math leads, "can serve as an additional support for instruction, assessments, coaching, and professional development, and as a liaison between our office and the schools." We found that math lead teachers supported schools in these ways. Specifically, we found that at least half of the math leads in our sample (1) gave turnaround professional development, (2) provided ongoing teacher supports, (3) reviewed student assessment data, and (4) served additional roles.

Despite commonalities in duties, there were also notable ways that the role looked different depending on the school context. Although math leads across the eleven schools that had the position reported common responsibilities, we noted significant differences among math leads in terms of release time from teaching and the degree to which the teachers we talked to felt supported.[3] Not surprisingly, fully released math leads provided the strongest overall support for teachers.

A fully released math lead did not necessarily mean that teachers always felt fully supported. The math lead at Chestnut (OGAP-B), for example, was not able to fulfill their role, despite being fully released. In this case, the school's focus on literacy interfered with the math lead's math resource support. Math leads at Spruce and Cedar (both OGAP-A) shared that sometimes teachers were not receptive to their feedback. For example, the math lead at Spruce explained that teachers in higher grades resisted taking her suggestions. In Pine School (OGAP-B), a teacher blamed scheduling difficulties for the lack of math lead support.

CONDITIONS IMPEDING OGAP ADOPTION

Overwhelmingly, we heard more about barriers to OGAP adoption than we heard about supports for OGAP adoption. In our interviews with teachers and school leaders, several barriers were repeatedly identified as undermining the use of OGAP in both OGAP-A and OGAP-B schools. These factors are discussed thematically below.

Lack of structural support in schools. Contributing to our findings of low PLC enactment, teachers described that fundamental structural conditions did not exist in their schools to effectively support the use OGAP. A critical component of OGAP is teachers having protected time to collaboratively examine student work and subsequently plan a response to move students toward achieving specific learning goals. Teachers, instead, discussed an ongoing and pervasive lopsidedness in schools that emphasized a focus on reading achievement—thus revealing mathematics as a fragile, lower priority within the district and schools. In part, leaders framed their school's low attention toward mathematics as a result of not having a similar level of resources available as they do to support reading achievement. Schools were also prioritizing the discussion of school climate and safety, data, literacy, and the dissemination of a host of administrative tasks during grade-group meetings, which were supposed to be periodically replaced with OGAP PLCs. Further, principals and math leads told us that they found it difficult to support implementation in only grades 3–5 when they thought that OGAP would be valuable for teachers at other grade levels, which would made their support efforts more coherent.

Teachers feeling overburdened. Within our sample of OGAP-B schools, some administrators made the decision, often with feedback from their staff, not to push the use of OGAP, as teachers were already feeling taxed by a number of changes taking place within the district. Even among the OGAP-A schools, teachers and leaders attributed their challenges of adopting OGAP to being overburden by too many initiatives at once. For instance, all schools had to adjust to adopting a new curriculum for math and sometimes an additional new curriculum for reading. OGAP represented a significant investment of time and effort to incorporate into practice. And despite OGAP being applicable to any curriculum, some teachers misunderstood this fact and discounted OGAP as not being "aligned" with their curriculum and, consequently, something extraneous to other instructional priorities (e.g., benchmarks, Pennsylvania System of School Assessment [PSSA] testing).

Teacher buy-in. Related to feeling overburdened, we also noted that the teachers were in their fourth year without a new contract. Although teachers rarely discussed this with our research team directly, low morale and frustration was evident in how they spoke about their work. At one of our visits, school leadership discussed preparing for a teacher strike occurring the next day. In an interview at another school, the principal highlighted that the teachers' expired contract was having an impact on how they worked with administration, framing the issue as one of trust. Despite the high level of knowledge and use of OGAP that teachers reported at that school, we noted that only the principal attended the PMLC-provided trainings.

Time. Many teachers felt they did not have time to implement OGAP. Although many teachers reported seeing the value of using the model, they felt that the district simultaneously provided a competing or outright inconsistent message about the way in which they were to approach math instruction. Repeatedly, teachers described feeling as though they needed to plow through math topics because of the heavy emphasis on the district-provided pacing guide. Hence, topic coverage rather than actual student learning often oriented their instructional decision-making. Although some teachers reported resistance to this perceived expectation, they experienced tension in doing so. Most teachers we interviewed described themselves complying with pacing guide requirements, which they believed to be unrealistic given their students' gaps in mathematical knowledge. In essence, despite school leaders' emphasis on student achievement, teachers' interpretations of well-intentioned district- and school-provided supports undermined the establishment of a learning culture that made time for the type of iterative formative assessment process proposed by OGAP.

CONCLUSION

In this chapter we reported on a qualitative examination the experience of two sets of schools in 2016–2017, one receiving the district's model of training and support and the second getting additional attention for implementation from OGAP and PMLC across the school year. The findings point to some of the core challenges of teacher and school adoption of ambitious reforms like OGAP and helped us to suggest refinements for additional improvements to OGAP's implementation model and other supports.

First, the progress that teachers made in implementation indicates that a one-year training model is insufficient to bring about the type of sustained change that will substantially change teachers' practice, particularly in in the bustle of challenging urban schools. The premise of the SDP's model for improving math instruction in schools was that one year of summer professional development and ongoing support would be sufficient to bring about lasting improvement. Motivated by equitably maximizing limited resources, the district model was to provide a week of summer training for teachers and a weekly math coach to support all the different grade-level teachers in a school, as well as an additional day of math lead training. Even OGAP's more intensive and focused model of support for teachers and math leads and the enlistment and support of principals to support OGAP in their schools was inadequate. Looking at the degree of take-up in this sample of schools, we can see that they were just beginning to adopt OGAP practices. The OGAP framework, which immediately resonated with teachers in the summer training, was the most used element of the program taken up by teachers across the school year.

Second, we found that changing the meeting structures (i.e., integrating OGAP-focused PLCs) within the schools was difficult. All the schools had regular, weekly, or biweekly grade-level PLC meetings, but the use of those meetings and their prevailing structure was not the same as what OGAP hoped to use them for. In order to support OGAP, an appropriate grade-level open-ended item had to be chosen and administered in advance, teachers had to have administered the item and bring their students' work to the PLC, and the time in the PLC had to be used efficiently for teachers to sort and discuss their students' work and plan instructional next steps. Even if the PLC was allocated to this particular form, the time to do this amount of work was difficult and math leads had to effectively manage the process. The subgroup of schools where the math lead structured and organized the meetings for OGAP and where the principal sat in and reinforced this design were those that had the most engagement.

Third, we learned how difficult it was for school leaders—principals and math leads—to support OGAP in just grades 3–5. Principals and math leads who were charged with leading improvement across their school's grades found it difficult to make structural changes and communicate the importance of implementation to only a subset of teachers. Efforts to more deeply incorporate OGAP's instructional philosophy into schools exposed the weakness of only working with a subset of grades in the schools. This finding helped to pave the way for the transition of OGAP from a 3–5 to a K–8 model the following year.

6

Teachers' Understanding of Learning Trajectory–Oriented Formative Assessment in Theory and Practice

CAROLINE B. EBBY AND JORDAN D'OLIER

Educational leaders often assume that teachers will apply what they learn in professional development to their classroom instruction, ultimately leading to gains in student learning.[1] We know from cognitive science, however, that learning is not simply a process of absorbing or taking in new information but, rather, one of making sense of it through the lens of current understandings, at times resulting in the rejection, adaptation, or adoption of new ideas and approaches. Acknowledging this complexity, Clarke and Hollingsworth proposed an interconnected model of professional learning, where change in instructional practice is not only influenced by external professional development, but both influences and is influenced by teacher beliefs and student outcomes in the classroom context.[2] Thus,

The authors would like to acknowledge the contributions of Janine Remillard and Nicole Fletcher to the study design, data collection, and initial analysis.

as teachers try out new practices in the classroom and see positive changes in their student learning, they are more likely to continue implementing and refining those practices, and this may lead to changes in their beliefs.

This chapter focuses on what we learned about how teachers made sense of the Ongoing Assessment Project (OGAP) learning trajectory–oriented formative assessment system as reflected in both their beliefs and instructional practices. More specifically, we explored the following questions: How did teachers make sense of the OGAP formative assessment system in the context of their own mathematics instruction? How did they draw on this understanding to make sense of and respond to their own student work? How, if at all, did their understanding of formative assessment change over time?

OGAP professional development and follow-up support are designed to increase teacher capacity by building knowledge of (1) mathematics content, (2) research on children's mathematical thinking and developmental progressions of additive, multiplicative, fractional, and proportional thinking, and (3) formative assessment strategies that can be used to elicit and build on student thinking. Research on children's mathematical thinking and developmental learning progressions (or trajectories as they are commonly referred to in mathematics education), despite having a great deal of influence on both current K–8 mathematics standards and curriculum materials, are not typically a focus of either preservice or in-service teacher education, nor of the materials provided as guidance for teachers in adopting those standards or curriculum materials.

Formative assessment strategies that are designed to elicit and advance student thinking along a developmental progression, such as those introduced in OGAP professional development, rely on some important shifts in the focus and goals of assessment. First, this approach involves a shift from focusing on *performance goals* (measuring how well one performs) to *learning goals* (identifying the current level of understanding in relation to the development of proficiency). This in turn rests on an assumption that learning is a process of growth rather than achievement, and a shift from a focus on what the learner does not know or cannot yet do (a deficit lens) to a focus on what the learner does know and can do (an asset lens).[3] Given that most assessments that are used in schools to measure student learning are focused on performance rather than learning (e.g., quizzes, chapter tests, interim assessments, and year-end standardized assessments), this is a significant shift for teachers to make in school and classroom settings. We were therefore interested to learn not just whether teachers were using OGAP formative assessment items, but how they were making sense of them for their own instruction.

MAKING SENSE OF LEARNING TRAJECTORY FORMATIVE ASSESSMENT FOR INSTRUCTION

To understand how teachers were understanding learning trajectory-oriented formative assessment, we draw on sensemaking theory. From this perspective, people actively construct interpretations of phenomena by making meaning of information in the environment.[4] At the same time, new information is understood and used in relation to existing knowledge, beliefs, and expectations.[5] In conceptualizing how people attend to and interpret new information, sensemaking theorists focus on the role of *schemas*, or beliefs about what things are, and *mental models*, or theories about how things work. Mental models, often derived tacitly from experience, can act as filters for understanding new information[6] and are used to make predictions about what might happen in the future.[7] Importantly, people can have multiple mental models of the same situation: an *espoused model*, used when talking about the situation to others, and an *in-use model*, influencing actual behavior.[8] Furthermore, they may not be aware that these models are different.[9] We drew on these concepts to analyze and compare the way teachers talked about formative assessment practices, purpose, and value (their espoused models) and how they actually used formative assessment practices in the classroom (their in-use models).

The OGAP learning progressions provide a structure for teachers to both interpret student work and provide feedback or develop an instructional response. Once teachers identify a student's current level of understanding from evidence in their work, they can look to higher levels on the progression to think about models and strategies that would move the student's thinking forward. An underlying assumption is that intelligence and ability develop incrementally through effort, strategy development, and guidance.[10] Viewing learning as a process of development focuses the purpose of assessment on learning goals, or increasing depth of understanding over time, rather than performance goals, or documenting students' ability in relation to external judgements.[11] We were interested, therefore, in the degree to which teachers adopted learning goals, particularly given the fact that the performance logic is the dominant narrative in K–12 schools (see chapter 7). We suspected that teachers' sensemaking of formative assessment would be shaped not only by the OGAP training they received, but by the norms of the district, school, and grade-level contexts within which their work was situated.

RESEARCH DESIGN

The participants were K–5 teachers who attended the 2017–2018 district summer training and were implementing OGAP for the first time during the following school year. A purposeful sample was constructed from teachers who had attended the training, taken a survey given before training, and agreed to participate in a set of follow-up interviews. Acknowledging the importance of school context, we began by selecting a sample of sites that had at least two eligible teachers at each grade band and variation in terms of school size and student demographics (e.g., race/ethnicity, socioeconomic status, language proficiency). This strategy yielded thirty-two teachers from nine schools, with between one and six teachers at each school. The participating teachers had between two and thirty-six years of experience, with an average of fifteen years.

The summer training consisted of five full days of OGAP professional development by grade band that focused on conceptual understanding of the content area (additive reasoning for K–2, multiplicative reasoning for 3–5), research on student learning of the core concepts, problem structures, visual models, properties of operations, unpacking of grade-level standards, and practice using the OGAP learning progressions to sort and analyze student work for formative assessments. During the school year, participating schools also received follow-up support in the form of school visits by OGAP trainers and voluntary after-school workshops. Schools varied in the extent to which they took up these opportunities and in the approach of their school leaders in supporting implementation (see chapter 8).

Participating teachers were interviewed three times during the academic year: in the fall, winter, and spring. Each interview contained sections designed to help us understand aspects of how they were making sense of the formative assessment process at different time points. The first interview, which was conducted after the summer training but before schools had received follow-up support, focused on teachers' learning from the summer training and their use of formative assessment in mathematics instruction. The mid-year interview focused on teachers' use of OGAP tools and routines and their analysis and sensemaking of a set of their own students' work. Teachers selected a formative assessment item to bring to the interview and were asked to sort and analyze the student work as they normally would. By this time, OGAP trainers had visited all the schools to support the analysis of student work in grade-level professional learning communities (PLCs). The final interview, which was conducted toward the end of the year, focused on teachers' formative assessment use and overall understanding of the learning trajectory–based approach.

The interviews were analyzed with coding schemes that were developed both inductively and deductively to capture teachers' espoused and in-use models for formative assessment at both time points. We first developed a set of emerging codes to capture the variation in teacher explanations and then collapsed and categorized those codes in relation to whether they reflected a performance orientation (i.e., an overall focus on the degree to which students showed the desired or best solution) or a learning orientation (focusing on students' underlying thinking or understanding). Through this process we discovered that there were teacher responses that contained some aspects of both. For example, some teachers valued the process of seeing the different approaches students would use to solve a problem but ultimately compared these solutions to what they hoped or wanted to see in the work. We categorized these responses as a hybrid orientation, as shown in table 6.1.

To analyze teachers' analysis of student work (interview 2), or in-use models for formative assessment, we began by producing an analytic memo for each interview to document their categorization of student work and then looked across these memos to develop initial categories of sorting strategies. We then used a constant comparative approach to apply and continually refine these categories into a typology of five different approaches that captured the primary focus of the sorting (correctness of answer, multiple components of the response, or strategies) as well as the sensemaking framework that guided the interpretation and response (a binary judgment, continuum toward the desired response, or developmental progression). As shown in table 6.1, we then further collapsed those

Table 6.1 Coding schemes for espoused and in-use models for formative assessment

Espoused model, interviews 1 and 3 (purpose of formative assessment)		
Performance orientation	Hybrid orientation	Learning orientation
Defines where student performance should be and illuminates mastery of content, so that remediation or enrichment can be offered.	Illuminates multiple ways students are thinking and solving to inform instruction and tailor interventions to improve performance.	Illuminates student thinking so that instruction can build on and/or deepen and extend student understanding.
In-use model, interview 2 (sorting of student work)		
Performance orientation	Hybrid orientation	Learning orientation
The answer or solution is the primary indicator of student achievement in relation to a specific performance goal. May include consideration of multiple components or features of the response (e.g., explanation along with correct answer), but sorting results in binary distinctions (e.g., correct/incorrect, "gets it"/ "doesn't get it," proficient/not proficient).	Attention to qualitative differences in student work leads to viewing student performance on a spectrum of how close the response is to the desired response (e.g., more and less correct). May include assigning levels of performance (below basic, basic, proficient, advanced).	Primary attention paid to strategies students use to solve the problem resulting in multiple piles containing both correct and incorrect responses. Attempt is made to locate those strategies on a learning progression as evidence of current level of understanding.

approaches to characterize them in terms of whether they reflected an overall performance, hybrid, or learning orientation.

For the coding of both the espoused and in-use models, we established rater reliability by double-coding a subset of interviews while the coding scheme was being refined; once 80% agreement was reached, the remaining interviews were then coded by a single researcher and double-checked by an additional researcher. Coding all three interviews for each teacher allowed us to look at both change over time in the espoused models and the relationship between the espoused and in-use models in relation to underlying performance and learning orientations.

In the next phase of analysis, we added information on the teachers' reported frequency of administration of OGAP items per month at each of the three time points but found no discernable patterns by school, grade level, or reported frequency of OGAP use. Finally, to better understand the potential reasons behind changes (or lack of change) in teachers sensemaking around formative assessment over the year, we selected examples in each of the main patterns of stasis or change and constructed case studies, drawing from all three interviews as well as information about the school-level implementation to construct narratives of the teacher's sensemaking around formative assessment over time.

In the next section, we report the results of this analysis in three parts. First, we describe the overall patterns in changes in teacher's espoused models for formative assessment over the year. We then turn to examine the relationship between teachers' in-use models and their espoused models. The third section further explores change over time and sensemaking in theory and practice, and potential mechanisms behind these relationships, by presenting contrasting case studies of three teachers from the same school.

CHANGES IN ESPOUSED MODELS FOR FORMATIVE ASSESSMENT OVER THE YEAR

More than a third of the teachers (fourteen of thirty-two) held consistent orientations across all three interviews, but of the remaining eighteen cases, a significant number showed either a change in espoused orientations over the year or stable espoused orientations that did not match the orientation of their in-use models.

At the beginning of the year, over half of our sample of K–5 teachers (seventeen of thirty-two) held views of formative assessment that reflected a learning orientation. These teachers described formative assessment as a way to better understand student thinking and support their learning by helping them develop deeper understanding or more sophisticated strategies. In contrast, seven teachers held performance orientations, focusing on using formative assessment to more accurately identify those students who "got it" and those who needed more remediation around specific content or skills. The remaining group of eight teachers held hybrid views, embracing the idea that formative assessment could help them recognize and respond to different approaches that students might use, but in service of determining how close student work was to the desired performance.

Table 6.2 summarizes how the distribution of initial views either stayed stable or shifted by the end of the year. As shown by the bolded cells, the espoused views of the majority of the teachers (twenty-one of thirty-two) remained stable over the year. However, in eight of the remaining eleven cases, there was a shift toward a learning orientation by the end of the year, either from performance to hybrid or learning or from hybrid to learning,

Table 6.2 Change in espoused models from the beginning to end-of-year

		End of year		
		Performance (2)	Hybrid (12)	Learning (18)
Beginning of Year	Performance (7)	**2 (29%)**	4 (57%)	1 (14%)
	Hybrid (8)		**5 (63%)**	3 (37%)
	Learning (17)		3 (18%)	**14 (82%)**

shown by the shaded cells. This suggests that for a subset of teachers, the use of OGAP formative assessment items and/or additional follow-up training may have influenced their espoused views over time. Three of the seventeen teachers who held a learning orientation at the beginning of the year, however, shifted back to a hybrid orientation by the end of the year.

Before furthering exploring these shifts, the next section focuses on what happened in the middle of the year when we asked teachers to analyze their own student work and discuss the implications for their instruction.

IN-USE MODELS FOR FORMATIVE ASSESSMENT: ANALYZING AND RESPONDING TO STUDENT WORK

In the OGAP model of formative assessment, the analysis of student performance is focused first on the strategy the student uses to solve the problem in relation to the learning progression, and the correctness of the response is a secondary consideration. In OGAP training teachers are reminded to refrain from assigning scores or grades to student work and instead are asked to create piles or groupings for common strategies and understandings. These piles are then analyzed further to develop instructional responses to move student understanding along the progression. Figure 6.1

Figure 6.1 Sorting student work along a progression

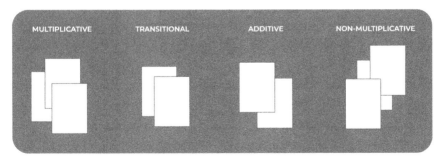

illustrates how student work in grades 3–5 might be sorted by strategy using labels from the multiplication or division progression.

Even though all the teachers in our study had attended five days of training and received at least some school-based follow-up training, our analysis of their sorting of student work showed variation in the approaches they used.[12] Moreover, the underlying orientation toward the analysis of student work influenced the instructional response that they generated from the evidence in the work.

Sorting into a Progression (Learning Orientation)

Nearly half of the teachers in our sample (fifteen out of thirty-two) demonstrated an in-use model of formative assessment that was aligned with a learning orientation. Teachers who sorted their student work from this orientation used the progression to identify the level of the strategies students were using, creating multiple piles that included both correct and incorrect answers. They paid attention to the process students were engaging in while solving the task as an indication of developing understanding. For example, for a problem that involved finding the total of two or more multidigit quantities, teachers in this category would look not only at whether the student recognized the need for addition, but also at how the student arrived at the sum: whether they counted by ones, tens, or multiples of ten, used visual models, number composition, base-10 understanding, and/or properties of operations to break apart and recombine the addends, or correctly used a standard algorithm. The focus of the teachers' analysis was on how students solved the problem, where that strategy fell on the OGAP progression, and what that suggested about students' developing understanding. One first-grade teacher explained the benefits of this approach: "It forces you to think about their way of thinking, rather than just right or wrong. What's their thought process? What strategy are they using? Who's higher on the thinking process, to be more efficient than everybody else . . . like rather than the specific black and white, right or wrong answer."

In thinking about instructional implications, teachers who sorted work from a learning orientation drew on their understanding of the development of additive or multiplicative reasoning to build upon what students knew and move their learning forward. One fourth-grade teacher talked about how he would respond to students who were solving a multiplication problem by drawing out equal groups and counting by ones: "Since they already feel comfortable drawing the circles, I would have them draw the same amount of circles if they want to in an organized array, and then once they understand the grouping of that array, I'd turn it into an area model and go from there." Like this teacher, teachers who understood the developmental progression often formulated instructional responses that focused on using specific visual models highlighted in professional development and on the progression, such as arrays, area models, or open number lines, that could be used to build on their current understanding to develop more advanced strategies. Several teachers talked about having students make sense of examples of other students' work from a range of levels on the progression, a "select and sequence" strategy for sharing student work that was emphasized in the OGAP training.

Teachers who sorted student work by strategy talked not only about how the use of the learning progression helped them determine which students needed extra support, but also about how to help all students continue to develop deeper understanding. They saw improvement, rather than ultimate performance, as the goal of the formative assessment process, and instructional differentiation as a way to benefit all students' learning rather than only those who weren't meeting the expectations.

Sorting by Proficiency (Performance Orientation)

Despite having been trained in the OGAP approach, a third of the teachers (eleven of thirty-two) demonstrated a performance orientation in their sorting of student work. For teachers in this group, the main objective of formative assessment was to determine if students were demonstrating proficiency on a skill or strategy recently taught, and they sorted their students' work by whether the solution met the desired criteria, regardless of the students' underlying understanding or the nature of errors in the response. In some cases, when the problem had more than one part, teachers sorted by whether the student obtained the correct answer on one or both parts of the problem, resulting in multiple piles, but then made binary distinctions within the piles between students who met the criteria and students who did not.

Teachers who sorted work from a performance orientation (typically by correctness of solution) tended to focus their instructional response on those students who were not demonstrating the desired performance. Getting the correct answer provided an indication that students were ready to move on to the next topic, while unsuccessful performance required intervention, most often in the form of reteaching through small-group instruction. One teacher explained, "If they totally didn't get it at all, I know that I'm going to have to reteach that skill in a small group." The teachers in this group were using OGAP formative assessment items as a way to measure and correct student performance, rather than to build on or extend student understanding.

Sorting into a Progression of Performance (Hybrid Model)

The remaining group of six teachers demonstrated a hybrid approach in sorting their students' work, drawing on both learning and performance models to attend to qualitative differences in student work and differentiate their instructional response. They often grouped student solutions by the type of instructional response needed to get them to the desired performance (e.g., learning foundational skills or concepts, being careful or checking their work, or using a more efficient strategy). These teachers maintained their performance goals while appropriating the levels on the learning progressions in their sorting, analysis, and response to student work. They viewed the formative assessment process as a way to tailor the focus of the instructional response to student needs but didn't always understand how to build on students' current levels of understanding to help them develop deeper understanding or procedural fluency.

In sum, even though the majority of teachers initially espoused views of formative assessment that were in line with a learning or hybrid orientation, their approaches to sorting and analyzing their student work in this mid-year interview were more evenly distributed among the learning (fifteen), hybrid (six), and performance (eleven) orientations.

RELATIONSHIPS BETWEEN TEACHERS' ESPOUSED AND IN-USE MODELS FOR FORMATIVE ASSESSMENT

Our analysis of individual teachers over time showed that their espoused models often, but not always, matched their in-use practices and that for some teachers, change in their espoused views may have been related to their in-use models. Table 6.3 summarizes three patterns that emerged

Table 6.3 Patterns in relationships between espoused and in-use models over time

No. of cases	Initial interview (espoused)	Mid-year interview (in-use)	End-of-year interview (espoused)
14 (44%)	Consistent models		
11	Learning	Learning	Learning
2	Hybrid	Hybrid	Hybrid
1	Performance	Performance	Performance
8 (25%)	Change in espoused model toward learning		
2	Hybrid	Learning	Learning
2	Performance	Performance	Hybrid
1	Hybrid	Performance	Learning
1	Performance	Hybrid	Hybrid
1	Performance	Learning	Hybrid
1	Performance	Learning	Learning
3 (9%)	Change in espoused model toward performance		
3	Learning	Performance	Hybrid
7 (22%)	Inconsistency in espoused and in-use models		
3	Hybrid	Performance	Hybrid
2	Learning	Hybrid	Learning
1	Learning	Performance	Learning
1	Performance	Hybrid	Performance

from this analysis, using increasing depth of shading to show changes from performance to learning over time. The first and most frequent pattern (44 percent of the cases) showed consistency in models across time and in both theory and practice; this was considerably more common for teachers who held views in line with a learning orientation.

The second pattern, which occurred in eleven cases, shows a change in the espoused model in both directions: toward learning in eight cases and toward performance in three cases. Moreover, in all but two of those cases, the in-use model matched the direction of the change. In other words, when the in-use model reflected a learning or hybrid orientation, the espoused model shifted in that direction as well. In at least one case, explored in more depth in the next section, the teacher's sorting by strategy in the context of school-based professional meetings may have served as a catalyst to shift not only her in-use models, but her espoused views over the course of the year.

In the five cases where the in-use model reflected a performance orientation, the espoused model shifted from either learning or performance to hybrid orientation. For example, a fourth-grade teacher stated at the beginning of the year that she could see the benefit of sorting student work with the progression to inform instruction, but by mid-year it was clear that she had received little support or practice in doing so, and she sorted her own work by correctness. At the end of the year, she described OGAP as a way to help her know how student learning progressed from year to year and what content needed to be retaught or reinforced, rather than as an approach to formative assessment. Taken together, these two patterns of change suggest that the in-use model may be associated with the change in espoused views over time. In other words, practice has an influence on theory.

The third pattern, however, suggests that some teachers continued to hold inconsistent views in theory and practice. In this category, only one teacher demonstrated more of a learning orientation in practice than in her espoused views. The other six teachers held espoused views that showed a stable hybrid or learning orientation while demonstrating a performance orientation in their practice. This may have been a result of not fully understanding how to use the progression and resorting to a tacit or more familiar model. For example, one teacher explained, "I was spending more time figuring out what level they were at and what that meant and it was frustrating to me.... So I just do it where, "Are they right? Are they wrong? What did they do right? What did they do wrong?" And that informs my instruction from there."

A second-grade teacher who expressed inconsistent espoused views and in-use practices described OGAP from a learning orientation, as an approach to formative assessment that could be used to "move students through the progression" and went on to describe her understanding of the development progression for addition and subtraction, moving from counting by ones to unitizing (making and using groups), using strategies based on place value and number composition, and then standard algorithms. Yet when she analyzed her student work on an addition problem, she sorted it by whether students had arrived at the correct sum and then looked through the piles to analyze their strategies. In her "correct" pile, she had examples of strategies from all levels of the progression, from drawing out circles and counting by ones to using a standard algorithm. She then drew on the learning progression to inform her expectations for students, stating that they should not be expected to "know how to regroup right away or do something that they're maybe not developmentally ready for," but did not use this progression to analyze the developing understanding represented by different strategies. In this case, she seemed to be fitting her understanding of the developmental progression into her usual practice of interpreting student work in terms of correctness of the answer.

VARIATION IN TEACHERS' ESPOUSED AND IN-USE MODELS OF FORMATIVE ASSESSMENT AT ONE SCHOOL

To further explore the different relationships between espoused and in-use models, and highlight some potential explanatory mechanisms, we now take a closer look at three contrasting cases of teachers in one school where OGAP was being supported by school leadership and implemented fairly consistently in grade-level meetings. Like many schools in the district at the time of the study, the approach to mathematics instruction that was being promoted involved the teacher presenting the content of the daily lesson, largely drawn from the textbook, followed by independent student practice and then differentiated small-group instruction.[13] The school had a designated math lead who went to OGAP training and facilitated regular grade-level "learning team meetings" that focused on analyzing student work on OGAP items. All three teachers agreed that there was a clear expectation from school leadership that they use OGAP items regularly.

The first case presents the example of Michelle, a teacher who had prior experience using formative assessment and demonstrated a consistent learning orientation in both her espoused and in-use models for sorting student work. In contrast, Julie consistently expressed and demonstrated a performance orientation and admitted that she did not fully understand how to use the progression to make sense of student work. The third case focuses on Sarah, an early-career teacher who initially expressed a performance view of formative assessment but at mid-year sorted her student work from a learning orientation. Notably, her espoused model shifted toward a learning orientation by the end of the year.

Michelle: Taking Up OGAP from a Learning Orientation

Michelle, who had twenty-six years of experience teaching multiple grade levels, was teaching third grade at the time of the study. Her interviews reflected a consistent learning orientation toward formative assessment over the year. She explained that prior to attending OGAP training, she had already been using exit slips to see if her students were understanding concepts she was teaching, but now she was using OGAP items weekly to collect evidence of student understanding to inform her instruction. "I will look and see where the children are, what their understanding is and then I'll put them into categories to see what their needs are, like where the gaps are in their learning, and then doing my lessons from there, to try to bring them where they need to be." In the fall interview, Michelle described the OGAP formative assessment system as being relatively easy to incorporate into her mathematics instruction and stated that she thought other teachers in her school were "making it harder than it had to be."

For the second interview, Michelle brought student work from an OGAP item that involved extending a multiplicative pattern (table 6.4). The task

Table 6.4 OGAP formative assessment item

Number of lollipops	Cost
3	$.15
4	$.20
5	$.25
6	$.30
7	$.35

showed a table for the cost of three, four, five, six, and seven lollipops and asked students to find the cost for nine lollipops as well as a rule for finding the cost of seventeen lollipops.

Table 6.4 shows the cost of lollipops at Brian's Candy Store.

A. What is the cost of 9 lollipops at Brian's Candy Store? Show your work.
B. Write a rule to find out the cost of 17 lollipops at Brian's Candy Store.

Michelle sorted her student work into separate piles according to the appropriate levels on the OGAP Multiplicative Progression,[14] paying attention not only to whether students could determine the cost of nine and seventeen lollipops, but whether they understood that multiplication by 5 could be used to find the cost (multiplicative), or had to repeatedly add increments of five cents (transitional), or were unsuccessful at extending the pattern (nonmultiplicative). There were correct answers in all piles, but she distinguished the students' underlying understanding in relation to the progression of multiplicative thinking. When she was asked to select an example from each pile and talk about what she would do next with each student, Michelle described questions she would ask or additional tasks that she could give to build on and extend each student's thinking.

At the end of the year, Michelle described how thinking about student learning as a progression was a shift away from her previous formative assessment practice: "Before I was like, either they understand it, or they don't. But there's like progression of the skills. . . . It's not black and white. There's a whole spectrum for where the students can fall." She admitted that she started using OGAP items because it was required at her school but then started to enjoy it. She drew an analogy to the character from a Dr. Suess story who only decides he likes green eggs and ham after trying it. "I guess everyone has done something before like okay, I gotta do this, another thing I have to do on my day. And then it's kinda like, wow. Like *Green Eggs and Ham.* I really do like this. It's pretty cool. So I realized that it was really beneficial to me and the students. Not just something that I had to do." Michelle reflected that the most important part of OGAP was the fact that it was focused on continuously deepening student understanding, and she explained how this had impacted both her own and her students' orientations toward learning and assessment:

> It's not one test and you're done. That's what helped me break through the mindset with the children. "You may not have done how you wanted to on this one, but let's talk about where you may have gone wrong, and then we can try another one . . ." So it's just ongoing, and they see that math is not static, that it's ongoing, and that we just keep working through it. You don't have to wait until the final test to see if there's growth. You don't have to wait a month and say, "Oh, they got it now."

In contrast to Michelle, both Julie and Sarah began the year with an espoused model of formative assessment that reflected a performance orientation. However, the paths their implementation of OGAP took over the year diverged.

Julie: Consistent Performance Orientation

Julie had been teaching second grade for fifteen years and described mathematics as her favorite subject to teach. At the beginning of the year, she explained that after she introduced a new strategy or concept, she would have students come up to the board to work through some examples, and then have them work on their own for a few minutes while she walked around with a checklist. As she explained, "I'll see who is struggling, [and] who doesn't get it." This helped her determine who needed to be "pulled on the rug" with her for intervention while the rest of students would work on the computer, playing a game that involved the strategy or concept from the lesson. In the first interview, there were sixteen instances where she referred to student learning in binary categories (e.g., "getting it" or "not getting it").

When asked about her use of OGAP, Julie explained that every two weeks, she was choosing an OGAP item to align with the content she was teaching and attempting to use the progression to sort her student work. Notably, she referred to the progression as a rubric, and though she named some of the levels (transitional, additive), she described not fully understanding how to use it:

> What I do is I have the kids complete a problem and then I go back into and try my best using this rubric, because some of it I don't understand, like trying to use the rubric to put them into certain stages. If the kids are counting, if they're transitional, if they're in the additive, and then moving them one step forward at least. . . . I mean, I know in my head like who's struggling, who didn't get that adding, who needs the extra help, but then I didn't know how to group them according to the OGAP progression. I didn't know how. I was so confused.

Julie seemed to understand that the progression could be used to identify levels of student thinking to support their development, but she found it hard to apply to her own student work. In the face of that difficulty, she reverted to her tacit knowledge about which students were struggling.

In the second interview, Julie brought student work on a two-part OGAP item that was designed to assess students' understanding of counting by fives onto a two-digit number to make a prediction. She explained that they were working on using an open number line and counting by five and tens and would be moving into two- and three-digit numbers. "So, we chose this one to start off on the easier end. Then we want to give [another item] this week that starts with bigger numbers."

The first part of the task asked students to count by fives nine times starting from 25, and the second part asked "If you kept counting by 5's, would you say the number 185? Show or explain how you know." Julie sorted her student work on this problem into three piles in relation to her students' proficiency with counting by fives and showing their work: whether they counted correctly in both parts of the problem or only on the first part. For students in the latter category, she separated out those who she felt did not understand what the problem was asking from those who counted incorrectly by fives to 185. She used labels from the levels on the OGAP Base-Ten Progression,[15] assigning the higher level to the work that had both parts correct and the transitional level to the work that had only one part correct, rather than the underlying thinking. In general, she focused on whether they could skip count correctly, but not on whether they were noticing or using patterns to make a prediction.

In the end-of-year interview, Julie described initially using OGAP because it was expected, stating "We were kind of like, forced into it." But she explained that she found it useful because it "helps me see who gets the concept in class, and who doesn't get the concepts in class, who I need to work with, what small group." She added that having students show their work gave her more accurate evidence on which to base these decisions. When asked how she would describe OGAP to someone who wasn't familiar with it, Julie responded, "We have an item bank, and we match it with what the kids are learning in math that week. And we have the kids figure out the problem. And from there, we group them into groups and see who's getting it and who's not getting it. Or who's getting it, who could be pushed forward to another strategy."

Julie's explanation of how OGAP formative assessment informed her instruction suggests that both her espoused and in-use models were based on a performance orientation and a binary "get it or don't get it" conception of learning. Although she used OGAP items when required and attempted to use the OGAP progressions to make sense of her students' work, this performance orientation remained largely unchanged over the course of the year. Without a full understanding of how to use the progressions to make sense of student thinking and understanding, she appropriated OGAP into her existing practice for using formative assessment to inform her small-group instruction.

Sarah: Shifting to a Learning Orientation

Sarah, a first-grade teacher in the same school, had been teaching for a year and a half when she went to OGAP summer training. When interviewed at the beginning of the school year, she described using small-group instruction in a way similar to Julie, basing her decisions on what she noticed from observing her students: "I get a good sense when we're starting a new material who is completely lost and who understands it." She admitted, however, that it was "a lot of the same kids" who she ended up identifying as needing extra support through small-group instruction. She also described giving an OGAP assessment and interpreting the results by doing a "quick sort" from a performance orientation: "just like who got it right, who was close, who was completely off the mark."

However, when talking about what she learned from the OGAP training, Sarah embraced the idea of focusing on strategy rather than "just a solution": "I think so often, we just look for the right answer and we forget about, well, this kid did everything, but this kid just got lucky and got the right answer. So, I think that emphasis is so important because we're all about right and wrong. Sometimes, it's easy to get caught up in that grading." Sarah concluded that this perspective had helped her to "be more positive with the students and give them more specific feedback" around what they were doing right, rather than only what was wrong.

In the second interview, Sarah brought student work on a task that asked students to determine the number represented by a collection of base-ten blocks (two groups of ten and twelve ones). She sorted the work into three groups based not only on whether they solved it correctly and got the answer of thirty-two, but also whether their solutions showed evidence of base-ten understanding (e.g., understanding that twelve ones are equivalent to one ten and two ones). However, while she looked for underlying understanding in the work rather than only correctness of answer, she did not pay attention the strategy students were using to determine the total (counting by ones or by groups of ten), an important distinction on the OGAP Base-Ten Progression. Thus, her sorting reflected a hybrid orientation in that she was using the students' strategies as a window into their understanding but was not yet fully understanding the developmental progression of that understanding.

At the end of the year, Sarah explained that she had given the same item to her students again a few weeks after the interview and was surprised to see how much their understanding had grown. She reflected that having the comparison helped to shift her thinking away from grading. She went on to talk about how valuable OGAP was in terms of shifting her mindset, which she was initially skeptical about: "At first, after the Summer Institute, I was like "Oh no, we're gonna get something and then not grade it. What's the point of doing that?" However, she admitted that over time she found this approach to be quite influential in helping her focus on growth:

> When I have a kid that bombs an assessment, I'm like, "Oh. What did I do wrong?" But here, I'm like, "Okay, what can we do to fix it?" Because there isn't that, there's nothing attached to it. So I think that has been the biggest thing for me. It's made it more enjoyable than sitting at home and marking a task, when I can just say, "Okay, well say this group they're getting there, they have some understanding. And this group's got it so we can move on with this group. And this group doesn't get it." I think that's made the biggest difference for me.

She also explained that it was not until the second or third time they were asked to bring work to a grade-group meeting that "it kind of clicked" and she thought, "Well, this was actually, really useful information." As the year went on, she began to give formative assessment items on her own, rather than only when it was required for grade-level meetings.

Looking across these three teachers, all who went to the summer training and were expected to give OGAP items regularly, provides a window into different ways teachers made sense of the formative assessment system in their espoused and in-use models and the relationship between the two. For Michelle, OGAP fit into the way she was already thinking about formative assessment, a way for her to gauge student understanding on a regular basis to inform her instruction that was different from summative assessments. Bolstering her in-use model was a view of learning as a progression that could be supported by instruction. Julie, however, did not fully understand the progressions and used OGAP in a way that fit with her prior performance orientation, providing a more accurate and systematic way to determine who was "getting it" and who needed extra support to reach the desired performance. Finally, Sarah began to shift away from a performance orientation after using OGAP items and sorting with the progression, seeing what she could learn about her students and their growth when she refrained from assigning a grade.

CONCLUSION

Mental models are important to the sensemaking process because they influence both what gets attended to and how evidence is interpreted and used.[16] This chapter illustrates that teachers came away from OGAP professional development with different mental models for how formative assessment works that can be located on a continuum from performance to learning orientations. OGAP has an explicit focus on learning goals, and while more than half of the teachers in our sample also embraced that focus, in theory and/or practice, some teachers held onto their performance orientations and fit their analysis of student work into that orientation. The evidence of hybrid orientations suggests that some teachers may have layered OGAP on top of their existing or more familiar assessment approaches, a common finding in studies that look at sensemaking around policy implementation.[17] As Cohen states, "As teachers and students try to find their way from familiar practices to new ones, they cobble new ideas onto familiar practices."[18] For some teachers, sorting student work into different categories by strategy seems to have been layered on top of the more familiar practice of categorizing student work in terms of "getting it" or "not getting it," resulting in a progression of different degrees of "getting it."

It is encouraging that over half of the teachers embraced the learning orientation in their espoused models after participating in the summer training, and a considerable number maintained those models in practice and over time. Our study design did not allow us to determine how many of those teachers already embraced a learning orientation before the training. Many of those teachers with an initial performance or hybrid orientation, however, eventually took up a learning orientation in their end-of-year espoused models, and those shifts were associated with similar shifts in their in-use models. In cases like Sarah's, sorting student work appeared to shift and deepen teachers' orientation toward learning goals.

The inconsistencies in the way some teachers understood the OGAP formative assessment system in theory, or through their espoused models, and the way they used it to make sense of their own student work also suggests the need for more opportunities to put their ideas into practice. As Spillane and Miele, state, "evidence is of little practical benefit if it is not incorporated into practitioners' in-use models of how things work within an educational context."[19] As others have found, many teachers appeared to hold different mental models for formative assessment depending on whether they were talking to someone else about it or actually using it in practice.[20] Some teachers initially embraced the learning orientation, either as a result of new learning or because they came in with that orientation, and yet the performance orientation still came out in their actual practices.

Taken together, these findings point to the importance of engaging in day-to-day practices and routines that provide repeated opportunities to encounter and practice interpreting student work in relation to learning goals rather than only performance goals. Although this study focused on how individual teachers were making sense of formative assessment, it is important to note that sensemaking is not only an individual process. Sensemaking around formative assessment in school is often a social process, and in the case of OGAP, is supported by more experienced others in professional learning communities (PLCs). This study provides some evidence that supported implementation can lead to both consistency and change in espoused views. Both Michelle and Sarah admitted that they only used the OGAP progression to analyze student work because they were asked to do so in their PLCs and over time began to see evidence that it was useful for their instruction. In Sarah's case, it was giving the same assessment twice that helped her see how her students' understanding was growing over time. In Clarke and Hollingsworth's model for professional growth, these teachers were seeing "salient outcomes" in student learning that influenced both their beliefs and practice.[21] This may help to explain why the direction of change in espoused models matched the orientation of in-use models, and why continuing to use an in-use model with a performance orientation could have the opposite effect.

Finally, the depth of teachers' understanding of the progression seemed to play an important role in how teachers used it and thought about using it to inform instruction. Michelle found the OGAP Multiplicative Framework easy to understand and use, and described how being expected to use it regularly shifted her conceptualization of student learning as "black and white" to seeing it on a "spectrum" which she found to be impactful for both her and her students. Julie struggled to make sense of the conceptual development represented by the OGAP Additive Framework and continued to rely on correct or incorrect answers as the primary indicator of her students' learning. Sarah's understanding of the OGAP Additive Framework, while not fully developed, supported her attention to students' strategy, and she began to see learning as more than a dichotomy between knowing and not knowing. Seeing learning as a process of continual growth helped her shift away from "What did I do wrong?" to "What can I do to fix this?"

The results of this study offer an important reminder that what we know about student learning is also true for teachers who are learning a new approach to formative assessment. A central tenet of OGAP and other learning trajectories is the notion that there are a variety of strategies that students can use to solve problems and that the strategies students choose to use will reflect their underlying understanding. Likewise in this study, teachers exhibited a variety of strategies as they implemented new ideas about formative assessment in their classroom instruction, and those strategies reflected their developing understanding of a learning orientation. Learning to use OGAP to inform instruction is not simply a matter of teachers "getting it" or not (a performance) but, rather, a more complex and gradual process of making sense of a new approach, not in a vacuum, but in relation to their existing models and past experiences. It is important, therefore, to take a learning orientation toward teachers' professional growth, in the same way that we are asking them to take on that orientation toward their own students.

Finally, this chapter and others in this volume also suggest that the learning orientation needs to be supported over time and across different levels of the system if it is going to have any impact on classroom practice.

The OGAP system represents a significant shift in ways of thinking about learners, learning goals, and assessment practices, and teachers need both extended time and practice along with continual support and reinforcement. This could include providing additional and ongoing learning opportunities, consistent school-wide expectations, and routines to administer and analyze formative assessment items for the purpose of informing instruction, and having a more knowledgeable other present to support teachers as they learn to analyze their student work with the learning progression.

7

The Logic of Benchmark Assessments

JONATHAN A. SUPOVITZ AND JORDAN D'OLIER

One of the themes of this book is the internal contradictions that reside within education systems that can impede instructional improvement efforts. These incongruities are often manifested in systems intended to support teaching and learning but actually have substantial limitations and carry assumptions and beliefs about how learning occurs. In this chapter we encapsulate this contradiction in the distinction between a learning logic and a performance logic and how education systems often blur their difference. As introduced in chapter 1, learning is the process that students go through with the guidance of teachers to master particular domains, and performance is an indicator of the degree of their mastery. Teachers, as the key facilitators of learning, need tools and resources that enhance their ability to foster learning. System leaders, seeking to provide teachers with tools for learning, often mistake performance tools for learning tools, and in doing so limit the resources teachers have to do their jobs. While performance tools provide some utility to teachers, because of their composition they are limited tools for enhancing learning. Moreover, they convey powerful signals about how learning occurs, which can perpetuate the confusion. The extent to which leaders distinguish between learning and performance is manifested in the ways in which they construct a range of instructional support systems.

In this chapter we examine the design and utility of benchmark, or interim, assessment systems for different consumers of their data, including teachers and school and district leaders. Benchmarks are particularly relevant because they are a bridge between district support systems and classroom instruction whose central purpose is to provide formative information for teachers while also informing other stakeholders. In addition, they act as signaling mechanism to teachers and school leaders about both the priorities of the district and how learning occurs, and therefore what teachers should focus on.

This chapter begins by situating benchmark assessments within the array of testing that is typically done in districts. We then define two "logics" or sets of operating principles underlying benchmark tests, which are the learning logic to inform the process of learning and the performance logic to inform the product or outcome of learning. Third, we briefly review the design of the benchmark system in the School District of Philadelphia (SDP) at the time of our investigation. Fourth, in the heart of the chapter, we report how district leaders, school principals, and teachers viewed the purpose and utility of the SDP's benchmark system. We conclude the chapter with a discussion of the consequences of the different stakeholder views about the benchmarks.

HOW BENCHMARK ASSESSMENTS FIT INTO DISTRICT ASSESSMENT SYSTEMS

An assessment "system" can be thought of as a series of complementary assessment types that seek to measure student understanding at different points in time to provide information to different constituencies. One way to distinguish between the types and purposes of assessment is by considering their frequency, composition, and utility for different audiences, as

Table 7.1 Central components of a typical assessment system

	Short cycle	Medium cycle	Interim cycle	Long cycle
Type	Classroom informal assessments	Classroom formal assessments	Interim/ benchmark assessments	Annual (often high-stakes) assessments
Timing	Within lesson	Across lesson, within unit	Across units	Annual
Common instruments	Informal techniques ranging from questioning to observation of student interactions, to quick checks of student work	Teacher- or externally constructed measures, including homework, writing assignments, end-of unit tests, portfolios	Externally constructed tests, performance tasks, benchmark assessments	State assessments
Primary use and audience	Feedback to teachers	Feedback to teachers and students	Feedback to teachers and school and district leaders	Feedback to leaders and community about student and system status
Proximity to place in the curriculum	Close	Close	Removed	Distant
Orientation	Learning	Learning	Performance	Performance

Source: Based on Jonathan A. Supovitz, "Getting at Student Understanding: The Key to Teachers' Use of Test Data," *Teachers College Record* 114, no. 11 (2012): 1–29.

shown in table 7.1. These assessment types are organized by frequency, ranging from short cycle, which occur within lessons and are tightly connected with the curriculum, to long cycle, which are annual and only generically connected to any particular curriculum. The ways that district leaders design and employ their benchmark assessment systems, and advocate for the use of the resulting data, are one of the major ways in which they signal their relative emphasis on learning and performance.

From the perspective of assessment for learning purposes relative to assessment for performance purposes, short- and medium-cycle assessments most clearly fall into the learning category, as they are classroom-based and tightly aligned with what teachers are covering, and their primary objective is to give feedback to teachers and students about students' learning relative to the standard or expectation. Ongoing Assessment Project (OGAP) assessments, with their emphasis on instructional feedback to teachers, fit into the short-cycle category. Long-cycle assessments are most clearly assessments of performance, since they are infrequent and their form (mostly multiple choice or numerically scored short answer) provides little insight to teachers about how students are understanding content that would provide teachers with information from which to make instructional adjustments.

Benchmark assessments are particularly incisive because they sit at the crux of the learning–performance continuum. While end-of-year state standardized tests have become the commonly accepted indicators of educational performance, there is little consensus about how to support teachers and students to achieve these performance goals. One major movement in education has been the increasing use of benchmark, or interim, assessments to provide information to teachers to assist students to reach summative outcome goals.[1] Benchmark assessments typically mimic the form and structure of end-of-year tests, using multiple-choice items to assess student knowledge of the content and standards that teachers are expected to cover during a specific time period and report numeric data back to teachers on the percentage of items students answer correctly in standards-aligned domains. Benchmarks are typically given three to four times a year, covering about ten to twelve weeks of instruction and are designed to be predictive of annual tests.[2]

Benchmark systems are intended to provide feedback to multiple stakeholders, including teachers, school leaders, and district administrators, about student understanding at a point in the year. The central question that we examine in this chapter is how key actors—teachers, principals, and district leaders—view benchmarks and the extent to which they see them as instruments for learning and/or performance. If benchmarks are useful as learning devices, then they should be giving useful feedback to teachers that can help them to make informed instructional adjustments to facilitate the learning of their students. If they are largely assessments of performance, then they are essentially another way to capture the end product of learning.

THE DIFFERENT LOGICS OF LEARNING AND PERFORMANCE

Underlying the relative utility of interim assessments to improve instruction are two competing logics about the most effective way to prepare students to perform well on end-of-year tests. Each logic contains at least four components, including the purpose of the interim assessment, the form of data and how they support learning, the underlying view of how learning occurs, and the belief system that the assessment implicitly conveys about student capability.

The first logic, which we call *the performance logic*, views the purpose of interim assessments as providing a series of aligned precursors to end-of-year tests to help teachers prepare students for the ultimate high-stakes exam. As such, pacing and content coverage are prioritized. Under this logic, learning is viewed as the process whereby students are introduced to curricular content at a regular pace and the instructional experience transfers understanding from the teacher to the learner. Rooted largely in the tenets of behaviorism, learning from this perspective is conceived of largely as a linear process of transferring knowledge and skills from the teacher to the learner.[3] The role of assessment under the performance logic focuses on providing feedback to teachers about what students can and cannot demonstrate to identify who needs remediation, done through reteaching the same content. Since learning is viewed as the relatively straightforward transfer of knowledge, reteaching the content is a rational remedial approach. The purpose of data in such a system is to distinguish between which areas of content students do and do not understand so that teachers may fill in those gaps of understanding. While some may view this as an outdated and overly simplified notion of the complex process of teaching and learning, it is nonetheless the dominant experience provided in the vast majority of schools in America.[4] Under this logic the results of assessment data are represented by numerical percentages of correct answers organized by content area or standard, to group and reteach the same content to students who answered incorrectly. Finally, because of the binary nature of the assessment results and the repetition of the remediation process, which tends to group the same students together repeatedly, scholars believe this process reifies a fixed mindset about fundamental limitations of student capability in both teachers and students.[5]

The second way of thinking, which we call *the learning logic*, distinguishes between the learning processes that students experience, largely facilitated by teachers, and the outcomes of their learning, which are represented by their ultimate performance. Under this logic, the formative purpose of the interim assessment is to give teachers feedback on *how* students understand subject matter content to inform instruction to facilitate continued growth in understanding. The learning logic views learning as a more fitful developmental process whereby student understanding is bumpy and dependent on the solidity and depth of their understanding of curricular concepts in different contexts. Rather than a binary switch, understanding is on a continuum that is influenced by multiple factors, including problem context and depth of learner understanding. More closely aligned with a constructivist theory of how learning occurs, learning happens along a developmental progression toward mastery or fluency.[6] The role of assessment under the learning logic is to provide instructors with feedback on student thinking processes to inform instructional decision-making, with the premise that information about how students are thinking about problems, just as important as their ultimate answer, provides the necessary information for targeted instructional responses. Teaching under the learning logic depends on gaining insight into how students are thinking and building upon or modifying that thinking to move students along in their understanding, which will enhance their eventual performance. Due to the developmental nature of these notions of learning and the belief that student understanding can grow in more incremental ways that may not be evident on assessments of performance, the learning logic is more associated with beliefs about growth mindsets.[7]

If we agree for the moment that the academic goals of education are performance goals, the question is which logic—performance or learning—is most likely to help teachers get more students to reach performance goals? Further, as we document in this chapter, these two logics are conveyed through organizational systems and send important messages to teachers, students, and leaders about the ways that students learn and how educators can support that process.

STUDY OVERVIEW

To shed light on the extent to which benchmarks are perceived of as learning or performance measures, we interviewed Philadelphia district leaders, school principals, and teachers about how they understood the purpose and utility of the district's benchmark testing system in the 2016–2017 school year. In that year, the SDP benchmarks were electronically administered to students four times and provided quick turnaround data on students' knowledge of standards in relation to the district's pacing guidelines and curricular expectations. In general, the results indicate that district leaders, and to a lesser extent principals, felt the information produced was for the instructional benefit of teachers, while teachers felt the benchmark assessment data provided some information about content coverage and student grouping possibilities but were less useful for providing actionable instructional feedback and were used by administrators for accountability purposes.

By analyzing the structure of SDP's benchmark assessment system, as well as how teachers, school leaders, and district leaders talk about, advocate for, and the use the resulting data, we argue that this, and similarly constructed, interim-cycle assessment systems align more with the performance logic than with the learning logic. This exposes a major disconnect among educators about the way that district leaders construct external support systems for teachers and the field's growing understanding of the learning processes that produce performance.

Despite the limitations discussed by teachers, from a system leadership perspective, interim assessments have important components that can help teachers prepare students for the end-of-year high-stakes test. These include signals of appropriate content pacing and information about student performance organized by grade-appropriate standards, as well as giving students opportunities to gain practice with timed assessments of similar form to those that will count at the end of the year.

In the rest of this chapter we briefly describe the SDP benchmark system at the time of the study, the structure of our investigation into how teachers and school and district leaders view the purpose and affordances of the benchmark system, and what we found were the common and divergent views among these stakeholders. We conclude the chapter with a discussion of the implications for an educational system when performance outcomes are introduced as learning assistance indicators for teachers.

THE DESIGN OF THE BENCHMARK SYSTEM IN PHILADELPHIA

In 2016–2017, benchmark tests in English language arts and mathematics were administered four times: early November, early February, mid-April, and mid-May, after the state test was completed. Thus, there were about eight to ten weeks of instruction before each benchmark, except the final one, which was separated from the third benchmark by only a month. They were administered to students online in primarily a multiple-choice format where teachers and administrators could see the results, organized by standard for student, class, grade level, school, and district, within twenty-four hours.

According to the SDP's Benchmark Information Sheet[8] the benchmark is "designed to be low-stakes, formative assessments" that correspond to the content of the district's scope and sequence for that quarter for each grade/subject or course. In mathematics, there were approximately twenty-five multiple-choice items and two constructed-response items. The constructed-response items were to be completed on separate paper and scored by the individual teacher. Students used their IDs to log into the testing system and take the benchmark online.

THE LOGIC OF BENCHMARK ASSESSMENTS   163

The results of benchmarks are rapidly provided to teachers in an electronic format. Teachers can log in the day after the administration and see the multiple-choice results organized into an array of representations, allowing teachers and school and district leaders to organize performance by students, classes, grade levels, or schools, as well as by standards and content areas (mathematics, English language arts [ELA]). Users can quickly see what percentage of students scored correctly in a range of ways, including overall, by item, by domain/standard, as well as growth over the school year.

Several teachers in the study marveled at the advantages of quick turnaround. For example, a fourth-grade teacher noted, "So, the kids take the benchmark and they input them on the computer . . . you will know what score they get right when they input it, but then, the following day it will break it down, what questions they got correct, what kinds of questions they got incorrect based on the standards." Another teacher similarly reported that the quick turnaround of the assessment gave her immediate feedback on student performance. "I think they're very informative . . .'cause once the students take the benchmarks you see that feedback right away and it's like, 'Wow! They really got this' or, 'Wow! They really didn't understand that concept' and it shows me what I have to go back and reteach."

Teachers were encouraged to analyze their benchmark data in grade-group meetings, professional learning communities, or common planning time, guided by the academic office's benchmark data protocol.[9] The protocol was intended to be used for math and ELA and was organized into three phases. The first phase of the protocol asked teachers to look at their class averages in performance organized by content/standards and organize performance into those areas with the highest aptitude, moderate aptitude, and lowest aptitude and discuss what trends they see in the data, how the content/standards were taught and differentiated, what teachers might attribute the performance to, and what are barriers to mastery. (Note that the levels of aptitude are relative, which means that the highest relative performance could be high, moderate or low in absolute terms).

The benchmark protocol's second phase focused on the standards/ content that demonstrated moderate and low student performance. It asked teachers to identify activities, resources, and additional assessments to improve student progress. The third phase of the benchmark protocol focused on the constructed response items in ELA, but not mathematics, asking teachers to identify the Pennsylvania standards assessed by the question, score student responses on four-point scale, and identify student knowledge and misconceptions on the standards, what strategies can be used to address the gaps in understanding, and what materials could be used to address the gaps.

INVESTIGATING THE USE OF THE DISTRICT'S BENCHMARK SYSTEM

Our investigation of the benchmark assessment system was organized around three questions. First, how did teachers, school leaders, and district leaders describe the purpose of the benchmark system? Second, what utility did they see in the benchmarks and for which audiences? And third, which logic (performance/learning) did their views reflect and why?

The data for this chapter come from two primary data sources. First, we used interview data from the year 3 (2016–2017) study of twelve schools implementing OGAP that was reported in chapter 5. In the winter and spring interviews, teachers and school leaders were asked about the purpose of the benchmarks, how the resulting data were used, and in what ways and to what extent the interviewees found the benchmarks useful for improving teaching and learning and for district support. In the fall of 2017, we also interviewed six district leaders about their support for mathematics teachers, including their views of the purpose of the benchmarks and how they thought teachers should be using the results. Overall, thirty-seven teachers, ten principals, and six district leaders were interviewed for the study.

To analyze the data, we read the full interview transcripts from the twelve schools and pulled out the relevant sections that discussed the benchmark descriptions for each respondent. We then inductively developed a coding system from these excerpts as well as the district leader interview data. Our coding scheme focused on beliefs about the purposes of the benchmarks and specific ways that teachers might use them and their benefits. We then looked across the different stakeholder groups (district leaders, principals, teachers) for commonalities and divergences by theme. Once these data were coded and analyzed, we reexamined them to see the extent to which they reflected either the performance or learning logic and how so. These analyses became the basis for writing the results.

RESULTS

Through our interviews with teachers, principals, and district leaders, we heard about four major uses for benchmark results. All three constituencies discussed the potential of grouping and reteaching students based upon the benchmark results, as shown in table 7.2, although teachers had a more nuanced view of the limitations of these strategies. Both teachers and district leaders pointed out the feedback on the extent of content coverage, yet teachers expressed this more in accountability terms than did district leaders. Third, both principals and district leaders acknowledged that the benchmark data provided information to a broader range of stakeholders, illustrating the multiple purposes of the benchmark data. Finally, a few principals discussed the ways in which the form of the benchmarks modeled for teachers and students the format of the state test, while this was not mentioned by the other groups.

Table 7.2 Uses of benchmark data described by respondents

| | Role | | |
Benchmark use	Teachers	Principals	District leaders
Grouping/reteaching	✓	✓	✓
Content coverage	✓		✓
System feedback		✓	✓
Modeling the state test		✓	

In the following sections we describe these uses and analyze how they reflect the performance or learning logic emphasis expressed by members of each role.

GROUPING AND RETEACHING

The theme of using the benchmark results as guidance for grouping and reteaching students was the most prominent explanation of the application of the benchmark results across all three role groups. This was not surprising since it was the response advocated in the district protocols and other messaging and shows a clear transmission of the policy of how the benchmarks should be used by teachers.

The district leaders we interviewed thought that the benchmark data provided important formative feedback to teachers to adjust their instruction. "The benchmarks are designed to be formative and a tool for the teachers to reteach or provide opportunities to reteach really specific skills," said one of the district's regional superintendents, voicing the commonly held view of the central administration about the primary purpose of the benchmarks. Another central office member of the curriculum and instruction department similarly explained that "the benchmarks are formative. It's really, 'this is how I taught this. This is how they're doing on the standards. These are the standards I need to reteach for whatever reason.' That is the adjustment of instruction that they [the benchmarks] should inform." This comment stresses the content (i.e., the standard) that teachers should reteach based on what students got wrong. The seemingly tossed in statement "for whatever reason" suggests that the respondent recognizes that the benchmark results do not contain guidance about *why* students did not respond correctly, which is one of the keys to adjusted instruction under the learning logic.

Grouping and reteaching were also the primary instructional responses to the benchmark data advocated by principals. A principal of a K–5 school, for example, explained the ways that teachers should use the protocols that the district disseminated to help them make use of the benchmark results. The protocol created a structure for teachers to group students by their benchmark scores in particular areas. As the principal described the process:

> They [the benchmark results] serve the purpose of letting you know where you are, what are the lowest skills that your students are performing at, where you need to reteach, but reteach with an action plan. So my teachers after they give the benchmark and they get the results back they also get a benchmark protocol which says how many students are in the green, red and yellow areas. And then you have to decide what you are going to do for those students that performed in this skill versus this skill? How is your guided math session going to go now? What groups you are going to have? Who is going to be in the groups? And what is this skill for the group to focus on to make sure that afterwards they are able now to answer those questions?

This principal laid out the procedure advocated by the district in the benchmark protocol, which provides a structured format for teachers to use low performance on subsets of the benchmark results to groups students and to identify what skills they should reteach. This kind of decontextualized skill-based teaching reinforces the instructional approach of the performance logic because it emphasizes the product of learning rather than its process. Also notably absent is any information to inform how teachers might reteach differently to produce a different result the first time, which is a central tenet of the learning logic.

Examining the structure of the benchmark data and the advocated application of the results for grouping and reteaching also surfaced different conceptions of the meaning of *formative* from the perspectives of the performance logic and the learning logic. Under the performance logic, *formative* means learning about which students are not understanding which content and using this information to group and reteach. If students learn from a repetition of the same content, then this is an appropriate response. But from the perspective of the learning logic, as we shall see from teachers, these data are not sufficiently informative to guide improved understanding because they lack the crucial insight into why students got the answers wrong.

Other principals expressed a slightly more nuanced understanding of the grouping and reteaching tasks that teachers were asked to do based on the benchmark results. For example, a K–8 principal explained about the purpose of the benchmarks and the approach to using the data derived from them:

> Teachers should use the benchmarks to look at what was taught to inform instruction. Also, to group our students based on particular scores. And then also to address misconceptions as well, too. As we look at analyzing student responses. We do an item analysis. We do a standards analysis, too. Within the standard analysis, we begin to group our students and outline how it should be taught and whether it should be whole group or whether it should be a small group, depending on how many students still need support in a certain area.

This principal expressed a formulaic approach to grouping and reteaching students based on student responses on the standards similar to that of the previous principal but added a more detailed approach to item analysis, which included trying to understand student misconceptions. Focusing on misconceptions gives teachers some insight into how students are thinking about the content areas represented on the benchmarks because these are at least patterns of misunderstanding that provide an entry point for more informed teacher adjustments.

Through their interviews, teachers demonstrated that they had absorbed the district's advocated approach about how to use the benchmark data. Teachers from different grades and schools also told us that their most common instructional response based on the benchmark data was grouping and reteaching students:

> How do I use the benchmarks? If there's something that I noticed a lot of kids didn't do well on, that's something I'll try and approach differently, either in whole group or in small groups. [third-grade teacher]

> The intention of the benchmark is to analyze the results and look at exactly what standards they [students] are doing well on and what kinds of

teaching methods I used and then look at the lowest questions—the questions they did not do well on—and how am I going to reteach that, how am I going to regroup students. [fourth-grade teacher)

The benchmarks are supposed to be used to assess the standards that the kids learned ... and as an item analysis that breaks down each question by standard. What percentage got it wrong? So, there's a lot of data you could use to reteach and there's a lot of data you could use for small groups, kids that struggle with the same problem. [fifth-grade teacher]

These descriptions by teachers concerning the use of the benchmarks indicate that many teachers have integrated the district's advocated approaches into their practice. All these teachers discussed thinking about how to teach differently but didn't describe any guidance about how they might do so. This suggests that the benchmarks can identify which students were struggling but provided less information to guide how teachers might respond.

Although we did not specifically ask teachers to critique the benchmarks, several teachers took the opportunity to point out their constraints, which reflects a recognition of the distinction between the learning process that produces performance and the limits of the use of performance data to improve student understanding. Since the sample came from teachers trained in formative assessment practices by OGAP, this may be an indicator of the influence of OGAP's philosophy on their conceptions of the instructional utility of the benchmarks. For example, according to one fifth-grade teacher:

The problem is the translation. . . . Okay, the students score 45% on inference. Alright, so, how does that work? Now what do you need to do with them now in your classroom? Is it about teaching more inference? . . . I understand that looking at the data should inform what to teach, but the benchmarks should be more than just simply a general number or to be minimally—again say 45%, what does that mean? I don't think we have that yet. I don't think you can sit with me, look at my number and tell me okay, this is what this means, and this is how you should teach next that we can improve their performance."

As this teacher points out, the scores on the benchmark lack depth of meaning because they don't provide any information about what produced their students' performance. This gets at the crucial difference between the learning logic and performance logic and the confusion between learning data and performance data. There are multiple reasons that a student might answer an assessment item incorrectly, and a refined instructional response requires that teachers have some data on students' thinking processes that produced their answers. Even the premise of multiple items producing a more stable representation of student understanding of a domain (or standard) is true from the summative perspective of the performance logic but does not produce actionable information for an informed instructional response.

Another fourth-grade teacher pointed out how the benchmark data raised a host of questions that it did not have the information to address:

> Specifically, for math you might have the same skill, multiplication, but it could be a small multiplication equation of three times seven and fill in the blank or it could be a question that has parentheses, different operations in it and it's the same standard. So, to me the level of questioning, kids might get the same standard correct on one question, but they might get that same standard incorrect on another question. So, then the teacher is left to wonder, I taught the standard, they know it. So I might have to create more rigorous questions from them because some questions are easier than others and they understand the standard in a certain form but they don't understand the standard when it's written as a different question. So, I mean there's confusion on how to reteach because the question has the standard assigned to it but the same question five questions later has the same standard but all the kids got that wrong. So, reteach the standard or reteach how to take a test, what do you do?

Reteaching implies that a replication of the same instructional strategy as before would produce a different result. Groupings based on incorrect responses are likely to mix together students with different levels of understanding. Neither of these approaches is predicated upon any more information about the learners, which is the missing ingredient, other than that the students did not respond correctly to the items. In essence, the stock responses of grouping and reteaching are acknowledgements of the limited information provided by a performance-oriented data system that cannot go beneath correct/incorrect to understanding the student thinking that produced the response.

From a learning perspective, this is useful but ultimately insufficient data to inform the flexible grouping of students and the reteaching of concepts. This is because groups based on the benchmark data may include students who scored similarly, but the reasons for their scores may be very different, leading to groups of students with very different instructional needs. One student could have understood and made a simple reading error. Another student could have a fundamental conceptual misunderstanding. Another student could have understood the concept and made a procedural error. Reteaching them all in the same way is inefficient and likely to help some in the group and frustrate others.

Lacking information to address the range of underlying reasons for one or a series of incorrect responses gives a teacher very little information by which to adjust instruction to the whole or small groups. As a consequence, the instructional response in whole and small groups may be fairly similar. Reteaching the areas where students had lower understanding is a relatively crude strategy absent information about why students answered incorrectly. In these ways, the responses to the benchmark results advocated by system leaders promote approaches that teachers steeped in OGAP formative assessment techniques found underinformed.

CONTENT COVERAGE

A second use of the benchmarks discussed by district leaders and teachers, but not principals, was as a gauge of content coverage. District leaders viewed this as formative feedback to teachers about the extent to which they had covered the material they were expected to teach up to the time of each benchmark. Teachers, on the other hand, tended to view this as a monitoring purpose, since they knew how far they have gotten in the pacing guidelines at the time of each benchmark, and therefore viewed the information as redundant.

From the district leaders' perspective, the benchmarks were a way for teachers to assess their coverage relative to district expectations. A central office leader explained how the benchmarks were intended to be used by teachers as information about instruction, and specifically as a means of assessing their pacing. "Benchmark assessments are for teachers to learn about their own practices and the work that they've done with students. They're meant to be used for teachers to gain formative assessment data to be able to make adaptations to suit students' needs, and to adjust their pacing if they've discovered they're maybe a little bit behind. So they're definitely designed for teachers to make instructional decisions, and nothing beyond that." Like earlier district leaders' views, this leader puts an emphasis on the benchmarks as formative.

A regional superintendent had a somewhat different understanding of the purposes for assessing content coverage based on benchmark performance. He focused on alignment with the state test in terms of what material needed to be covered in preparation for the state test. "They [the benchmarks] are aligned to the scope and sequence so they [teachers] are able to drill down into what we call the eligible content, which is the most granular assessment we have." By "eligible content" the district leader explained that he was referring to the content that was covered on the state assessment. He explained that teachers sometimes taught material that preceded the expectations for that grade because they felt this was a necessary precursor to the eligible content, and the district leaders wanted to be sure that teachers were not spending too much of their time covering the content from prior grades.

The contrast between these two district leader statements and the signals they send reveals a core tension between the performance logic and learning logic. The central office leader expressed a learning perspective when he talked about the benchmarks. He recognized that the instructional priority is to meet students' learning needs, which often requires a developmental approach to teaching to where students currently are as opposed to where they should be based on the pacing guidelines aligned with the state test. The second leader's comment reflected more of a performance perspective. His focus on the eligible content urged teachers to emphasize what was covered by the state test, regardless of teachers' recognition of students' developmental learning needs.

For their part, the teachers we interviewed also reported that the benchmark acted as a gauge of their content coverage. "When I look at my classes results, I can immediately tell what they expect me to cover that I haven't covered yet," said a third-grade teacher. Interestingly, this teacher relied on the benchmark results rather than the pacing guides to identify content coverage expectations. In this way, the timing and content of the benchmarks sent a signal to teachers about the expectations for their instructional pacing and what content should be covered at the time of each benchmark assessment.

Relatedly, teachers reported that the benchmarks provided them with a general sense of where their students were, but this was not really so much to inform instruction as it was a general indication of student performance at different times of the year. "They are [the benchmark results] kind of just seeing where the kids are at, and to also help me as a teacher understand like okay, so this is what the kids are still—this is what they seem to have mastered or they do well at, but this is what they still need some more practice on," said a third-grade teachers.

Several teachers reported how they felt pressed to make sure that students were exposed to all the topics covered on the benchmark. "I feel a ton of pressure to teach it all [the content covered by the benchmark]. I feel pressure to get to a certain point," said a fourth-grade teacher. "The students are supposed to have understood so much content within that time and then they take an assessment on all the things that were meant to be taught in that time period," said a fifth-grade teacher. "But it doesn't always happen that way," she continued. "It depends on the kids you have and what's going on. So then if I haven't gotten to fractions yet and the benchmark is on fractions, my students' scores will reflect that, and will show poorly that we haven't gotten to fractions yet and haven't mastered any of that yet which will bring their scores down, obviously. So, I kind of have to keep up with that because of the benchmark assessments," she said.

For some teachers, the press to cover content by the time of the benchmark had a negative effect on their instruction. One fourth-grade teacher described how she covered content shallowly when she got close to a benchmark "just so they are exposed to it." A fifth-grade teacher said, "I never—and I work as hard as I can—I never cover everything that they want us to cover in that time period. My kids are always like—when they take that benchmark—'we didn't learn this. . . . I feel I failed my kids because I didn't get them there, but, in reality, we just have to go at a certain pace," she said.

So which logic does an emphasis on content coverage reflect? The benchmark data are providing teachers with feedback on the extent to which they covered the content relative to district expectations, which can be found on the district pacing guides as well. At the most basic level, for students to perform on an end-of-year assessment, they must be exposed to the content, and in this sense the benchmark data are formative for teachers. But beyond initial exposure, the resulting data are not particularly insightful to guide instructional strategies. In addition, the signal of the basic connection between content coverage and performance reifies the performance logic in that it reinforces the assumption that learning is a product of a straightforward connection between what teachers teach and what students are expected to understand.

SYSTEM FEEDBACK

Both school and district leaders recognized that the benchmarks provided strategic feedback for system leaders. Several district-level leaders pointed out how the benchmarks could be aggregated to different levels, providing information not just for teachers, but also for school and district leaders. One of the regional superintendents, for example, viewed the benchmarks as primarily informative for teachers, but also noted that the resulting data could also be used by principals and district administrators for system planning: "The primary purpose of the benchmarks is to provide information about the weaknesses of the children and watch the coverage of the statewide standards," she said. "But they can also provide action planning for principals at the grade and school level."

Another regional superintendent explained that he used the benchmark data to give him a sense of how the schools in his region were getting ready for the end-of-year tests, so that he could provide talk with principals about progress and provide supports. "There's a lot that's provided in the benchmarks that we can use to inform systematic things like particular supports for a school or a particular grade, or even particular to a classroom," he said.

When discussing system feedback, a few principals talked about them in terms of a unique common metric. "Many of my teachers and even colleagues that I talk to, they say that they don't see the purpose of it. But you've got to have a common assessment to gauge whether children are making progress or not. The one thing that I see as the purpose of it is that. If it's not going to be this benchmark, what benchmark are we going to use? Because I do think that we need something to identify—that's across the district—to identify whether kids are making progress or not."

MODELING THE FORM OF THE STATE TEST

Finally, a fourth way that a few principals in the interview sample reported that the benchmark was used was as a practice test that modeled the form of the state test. In their views, the benchmark was a way of preparing students for the *form* and *language* of the end-of-year test. Interestingly, these benchmark uses were mentioned by principals rather than teachers or district leaders. One principal, for example, told about the practice at her school of trying to model the benchmark question structure in other tests at the school. "We take a look at those types of questions and kind of mimic those kinds of questions through performance tests that we give students," she said.

A principal from another school emphasized how he was encouraging his teachers to focus on the language of the assessment:

> We have used quarterly benchmarks since I have been in the district.... but what we never did was focus on what type of questions they were asking our kids and how the language of the questions is what students need to hear that on a regular basis. So you need to use that rich language. Your instruction has to be around that language so that when kids see it [on the test] this is nothing new to them and I think that was the eye opener. We went back and we looked at some old benchmarks and said, oh this is how they are asking the question now how would you say it, see the difference? It's just wording.

For these principals, a key component of the benchmarks was to prepare students for the end-of-year test. These actions are less about teaching students the skills represented in the standards as they are about test preparation, which conforms to the performance logic. It is also interesting to note that these uses were identified by school leaders rather than teachers, which might indicate that school leaders, who are situated between teachers and district administrators, and therefore have less visibility of the learning needs of children and more access to the exigency of performance, identify these approaches more readily.

CONCLUSION

Almost any assessment can be called "formative" if the definition of formative is that the data can be used by some actor as information to guide future performance. In this vein, end-of-year assessments are formative in that they can inform district and school leaders and even teachers about the emphasis of future professional development or areas for more teaching attention. So debating differences between formative and summative assessments can be a distraction, because one stakeholder's formative assessment can be another stakeholder's summative assessment. The key question becomes this: formative for whom, in what ways, and to what extent?

In this chapter we examined the ways in which teachers, principals, and district leaders understood the purposes and utility of the district's benchmark assessments, with a particular focus on their formative instructional benefits for teachers. All three groups reported that the benchmark results should be used by teachers to group and reteach students. While teachers recognized this use, they tended to see this purpose as instructionally limited because grouping students based on the proportion of test items they answered correctly, or even by groups of questions, still resulted in a range of understanding within the subgroup of students, because there are many reasons students could answer questions incorrectly. Teachers and district leaders also reported that the benchmarks results were a way for teachers to take stock of their content coverage by comparing what was covered on the benchmark to the pacing guides aligned with the curriculum. This was broadly informative to teachers, but somewhat redundant in that they already know where they were in the curriculum relative to the pacing guides. Principals and district leaders also viewed the benchmark data as feedback to system leaders for strategic decision-making and resource allocation. Finally, principals reported that benchmarks were designed mimic the form and structure of the end-of-year exam and thereby help students prepare for the high-stakes end-of-year exams. Ironically, district leaders, who are most removed from the classroom, were most likely to view the benchmarks as formative for teachers, while teachers—who are primary intended users—were least likely to view the results as useful instructional feedback due to their lack of both timeliness (related to when things were actually taught) and limited information about student thinking, which is the source of guidance for more precise instructional responses.

We also used this examination of the benchmark assessments to introduce two competing logics about knowledge acquisition that we argue course through education systems: a learning logic and a performance logic. Each logic carries with it views about how learning occurs, how teachers can best support learning, and the form and structure of data to inform teachers. The learning logic assumes that learning is an uneven developmental process of acquiring content fluency through repeated exposure to subject matter in different forms and contexts, while learning under the performance logic is more linear, whereby exposure to subject matter catalyzes a binary switch from nonunderstanding to understanding. The teacher's role under the learning logic is to figure out the levels of student understanding of content and align instruction to move students toward deeper understanding (much like Vygotsky's paradigm of proximal development). In the performance logic, teachers need to reteach to turn on understanding. Instructionally useful data from the perspective of the learning logic provide insight into students' thinking processes to inform subsequent instruction, while from the perspective of the performance logic, data focus on the product of learning to reiterate what is not understood. Both of these logics have deep roots in education systems, and formative assessment systems are just one way in which they manifest.

Table 7.3 Logics represented in the benchmark assessment uses

Benchmark use	Formative for whom?	Logic represented
Grouping/reteaching	Teachers, with limitations	Learning
Content coverage	Teachers/school leaders/district leaders	Learning/performance
System leaders' feedback	School and district leaders	Performance
Modeling the state test	Not formative	Performance

The results of this investigation show how both the learning and performance logic play out in the enactment of benchmark or interim assessments. When we use the lenses of the two logics to view the different stakeholder reports of the purpose and use of the benchmarks, we can see how they are manifested. Table 7.3 encapsulates the different uses of the benchmarks reported by stakeholders in these analyses, for whom these uses provided formative feedback, and the logic represented in that use.

Grouping and reteaching were the most often mentioned applications of the benchmark results by all three stakeholder groups. This use was focused on teachers and reflects the learning logic in that the data were intended to help teachers provide additional learning opportunities for students. Teachers used the results to inform instruction, although the focus of the data on the product of learning rather than the process of learning limited their instructional insights and, therefore, the utility for teachers.

A gauge of content coverage was the second use mentioned by teachers and district leaders as a use of the benchmark data. Most teachers reported that they knew where they were in the curriculum sequence, so getting feedback on what they had covered to the point of the benchmark administration was not new information to them and gave them relatively little useful instructional feedback. By contrast, content coverage was information that school and district leaders could use to assess where teachers were in the curriculum, but this was more for performance purposes than for learning purposes. Therefore, we ascribe this more for administrators, and it reflects the performance logic, as it was primarily feedback on helping teachers cover the content needed for students to perform on the end-of-year assessment.

The third use reported was feedback to system leaders. This use fits into the performance logic, in that it does not help teachers to inform instruction but, rather, to inform leaders to plan ways to improve end-of-year performance. Similarly, the fourth use, modeling the form and structure of the state test, fits squarely with the performance logic, in that this use can help students perform on the high-stakes exam but is not a learning activity. Overall, the benchmarks reify the performance logic more than the learning logic.

Additionally, the benchmarks send important signals about how learning occurs through the timing and form of the benchmark data and how leaders advocate using the results. The underlying premise is that content coverage and general reteaching strategies are sufficient instructional responses to raise student performance to meet end-of-year learning goals. This blurs the distinction between learning and performance and suggests that the elements associated with the performance logic are sufficient to produce performance, when all evidence indicates the contrary. Thus, the design and application of the benchmarks have more in common with the performance logic than they do with the learning logic.

All of this is not to say that benchmark or interim assessments have no place in a system of assessments that serve different purposes for different education stakeholders. However, instead of rethinking how different forms and kinds of student data might be more useful to teachers, system leaders have chosen to recreate the form and structure of the summative tests. From the leadership perspective (as opposed to the classroom perspective), this makes sense because it builds on existing data and structures, rather than taking on the more difficult task of rethinking the kinds of data and systems that might be useful to teachers for classroom guidance. The current incarnation of benchmark assessments seems poorly designed to provide valuable feedback for teachers to enhance learning.

8

Leadership Moves

How Two School Leaders Organized the Schools for Deeper Implementation

ADRIANNE FLACK AND BRITTANY L. HESS

INTRODUCTION

In this chapter, we discuss the role of school leaders in OGAP implementation at two schools during the 2017–2018 year, the fourth year of the overall project. The Philadelphia Math Leadership Collaborative's (PMLC) theory of action informing this iteration of OGAP implementation focused on two areas: (1) establishing buy-in from school principals and (2) tailoring a portfolio of tools, resources, and supports to facilitate OGAP implementation in the School District of Philadelphia context. The two schools that are the focus of this chapter were chosen because of their relatively high level of principal support, allowing us an opportunity to examine more closely this aspect of the PMLC theory of action.

This phase of the project marked the expansion of OGAP to grades K–8. Previously, implementation solely focused on grades 3–5 in multiplication and fractions. Although there was much enthusiasm about the prospect of bringing OGAP to scale across entire K–8 schools, the project team faced new challenges in serving a wider range of grade levels.

Using our findings from the 2014–2016 randomized controlled trial (RCT) investigation of OGAP and PMLC's year 3 research in winter 2017, year 4's implementation plan was modified to better facilitate schools' implementation experiences. Key changes to PMLC's implementation support included adjusting the school year OGAP professional development sessions and creating the OGAP Connections website to assist grades 3–5 teachers with easily aligning OGAP items with the content in their new math curriculum (see chapter 3). Principal information sessions were also embedded into the district's summer professional development schedule (i.e., the MathCounts Institute), and the content of the school year principal PD sessions were modified.

Our discussion in this chapter makes use of the three-phase implementation framework of Berman and McLaughlin and other scholars (e.g., Waugh and Punch), consisting of support/adoption, implementation, and incorporation/continuation.[1] The support or adoption phase is described as the period in which a new program or initiative is considered for implementation by the district or school leadership. This phase includes determinations of need, evaluations of the right timing, as well as assessments of "costs" and "benefits."[2] The implementation phase is the period in which a program or initiative is actually implemented for the first time, and incorporation/continuation marks the period where a program or initiative "loses it special project status" and becomes part of the organization's norm—often in the absence of incentives and supports that were present in the introductory phases of implementation (i.e., support/adoption and implementation). Specifically, our research speaks to the first two phases: support and implementation, whereas chapter 9 explores the third phase: incorporation or continuation.

This chapter focuses on the role principals played in the two schools' experience of implementing OGAP. We begin with a narration of the principals' rationales for adopting OGAP and the vision they had for its adoption in their respective schools. We also highlight the way in which principals constructed implementation plans for their respective schools in response to the implementation tools, resources, and supports provided by PMLC, and what subsequently unfolded across the school year in the execution of those plans. Further, we discuss our own assessment of OGAP implementation regarding the unique contextual factors we saw shaping the process at each school. Then we highlight teachers' experiences of this process and present both teachers' and principals' interpretations of implementation success from their first-year engagement with OGAP. We end with a discussion of the way in which principals' leadership approaches in these cases shaped their school's implementation experience and identify unexpected areas, in addition to principal support, which emerged as influential to implementation.

With regard to OGAP's introduction to the School District of Philadelphia, we view the support/adoption phase as having two parts, the first of which entails the district agreeing to make OGAP training available to teachers as a district-sponsored initiative, and second, principals' individual decisions to select OGAP training at the summer institute and then subsequently adopt OGAP at their respective schools afterward. Hence, this chapter picks up on the adoption phase at the school level. The two schools selected for this chapter were chosen because we believe they represented strong cases of school leadership in spearheading OGAP implementation. A critical factor pertaining to their selection was the fact that these principals clearly communicated expectations for teachers to engage with OGAP that echoed throughout our interviews with teachers. The principals, however, demonstrated different approaches in how they pursued this initiative to improve teachers' instructional capacity in mathematics, which serves as the focal point in our analysis and interpretation of school implementation outcomes.

Data Informing This Study

Data collection occurred across several points throughout the 2017–2018 school year. We visited the two schools, Fern and Rosewood, three times across the year to conduct on-site interviews with teachers and school leaders (fall, winter, and spring).[3] The first round of interviews consisted of individual interviews with school leaders and primarily focus group interviews with teachers.[4] We also visited the schools between the interviews to observe OGAP professional learning community (PLC)

Table 8.1 Characteristics of Fern and Rosewood Schools

	Fern	Rosewood
Grades	K–8	K–8
Number of total math teachers	~15	~25
Number of teachers attending OGAP training	15 teachers 2 school leaders	9 teachers[a] 2 school leaders
School size	~500	~700
Free/reduced lunch %	100	100

[a] Five teachers who attended the summer MathCounts Institute from Rosewood were not general classroom math teachers. Three were English for Speakers of Other Language (ESOL) teachers, one was an art teacher, and one taught computer technology.

meetings, which often coincided with in-school professional development (PD) sessions conducted by the OGAP trainers. As this research sought to understand implementation of OGAP from a schoolwide perspective, our study included interviews with teachers who had not been formally trained in OGAP but who were expected to participate in the implementation per the expectations of their school leadership. As participation in the summer OGAP training was voluntary, this was an implementation challenge we knew existed and were interested in following. In total, we interviewed ten people at Fern; three of these individuals were in leadership roles, and the remaining seven were teachers with responsibilities to teach mathematics. Eight of this group, including two of the school leaders and six teachers, attended OGAP training. At Rosewood, we interviewed eleven people, of which two were administrators and nine were teachers. At Rosewood, both administrators and only three teachers in our sample attended OGAP training. In both schools, we had participants represented across all three OGAP content areas (i.e., additive reasoning, multiplicative reasoning, and proportional reasoning). See table 8.1 for further demographic information about the two schools.

THE SCHOOLS

Fern

Fern is located in one of the most economically depressed regions in the city.[5] There were approximately 500 students enrolled at the school, almost all of whom identified as African American. Additionally, approximately 10 percent of the students reportedly had a disability, and fewer than 10 percent of students scored at proficient or advanced levels on Pennsylvania's yearly state mathematics test, the Pennsylvania System of School Assessment (PSSA) in 2017.

Both teachers and administrators described the students as having disrupted educational histories that contributed to many being severely behind academically, and especially in mathematics. Some students were characterized as coping with severe cases of trauma and other struggles that interfered with their academic development. Staff who had roots in the area were particularly empathetic about the students' situations. They reported that parent/guardian involvement with the school was very low.

During our visits to the school, members of the research team assessed the general climate as being a challenging one. Amid the typical school hallway sights of kids smiling and playing with their friends on the way to class, we also at times observed middle schoolers running unsupervised through the hallways and students on the verge of fighting. We also noted the principal and other staff working diligently to calm down distressed students—and sometimes their families. As we became more familiar with the staff, they spoke at length about students' behaviors as a "challenge" toward improving their academic achievement. One teacher expressed frustration with the principal's perceived lack of consequences for students' negative behavior. She felt that the principal failed to set consequences at the administrative level yet expected teachers to have established consequences in their classrooms. This interpretation was a common one uncovered in the Consortium for Policy Research in Education's (CPRE) research on district and suspension policy modifications in the School District of Philadelphia.[6] Despite this, we observed the staff interacting collegially. Despite there being frustrations about aspects of their work lives, there was a positive rapport among and across grade-level teachers.

Starting in 2016, the school received additional resources from the district because of its students' persistently low test scores. These resources included additional teacher PD, additional administrative support, and a math lead teacher who received targeted PD. In addition, Fern teachers were mandated to follow a protocol that structured conversations around reviewing student work, planning instructional responses, and reflecting on the effectiveness of those responses. Through the use of this protocol, teachers were already beginning to employ a formative assessment cycle similar to OGAP.

The principal was a veteran in her tenure with the district and had been at Fern for several years prior to initiating OGAP adoption. She reported having more than ten years of school leadership experience following more than a decade of experience as an elementary education teacher. A member of the research team encountered this principal at the first PMLC principals' session, at which she spoke enthusiastically about incorporating OGAP at her school because it appeared to align with her regional network's instructional priorities, as well as her own goals to improve student achievement in mathematics. When asked if she'd allow us to study her school's implementation experience over the school year, she graciously agreed and later sent a copy of the protocol her teachers were presently using to analyze and discuss student work.

Rosewood

Rosewood is a large K–8 school situated in a diverse and thriving area of the city. Within its enrollment of over 700 students, many cultures are represented. Consequently, Rosewood offers various special programs to support its diverse learners as well as their families. In addition to these programs, the school also has a strong portfolio of other supports and services enacted through the school to address academic, social, and community needs. Aside from implementing OGAP during the 2017–2018 school year, Rosewood also instituted a nationally known literacy intervention and a federally funded after-school program.

Rosewood was overseen by a veteran principal who was highly motivated to raise the achievement scores of his students. He had been at Rosewood for several years and shared that one of his crowning achievements to date was that the school had made significant improvements in students' English Language Arts scores on the state assessment.

A member of our research team who spoke to him at the first leadership meeting described the principal as seemingly very goal-oriented and competitive. Still basking in the glow of his students' raised reading scores, the principal's positive experience at OGAP training resulted in him feeling enthusiastic about attacking students' low achievement in mathematics. A disparity between literacy and math scores was reflected on the state assessment, with about 30 percent of students scoring proficient or advanced in reading, while less than half that many performed as well in math.

We had an opportunity to sit in on the end-of-day planning sessions for this school at the summer OGAP training and noted early on that one of this school's challenges might be instituting the PLC meetings advocated by OGAP. None of the teachers present had experience participating in one, and they expressed initial concerns about frequent schedule interruptions that made existing grade-group meetings challenging to maintain. Further, the teachers seemed unclear about who would lead this initiative during the school year. The principal was not present at this meeting, and although the math lead teacher was in attendance, he remained silent through most of the conversation.

THE OGAP IMPLEMENTATION STORIES OF FERN AND ROSEWOOD

In what follows, we present the individual stories of the OGAP implementation experience of the two schools, beginning with the "adoption phase," in which we present the decision-making and interests that factored into the two principals bringing OGAP to their respective schools. This aligns with Berman and McLaughlin's "support/adoption" phase, which has been framed as a potential early indicator of how strongly implementation of an educational innovation might be taken up. Second, we describe the implementation plans principals devised with the tools, resources, and supports provided through PMLC. Third, we situate the school within our broader analysis of school implementation. Fourth, we discuss what differentiates school personnel's interpretations of implementation from our own. We conclude with a discussion in which we identify five lessons that cut across the experiences of the two schools.

Adoption Decision-Making at Fern

In the case of Fern, the principal was drawn to OGAP because it was aligned to the priorities articulated by her regional superintendent to analyze students' work. The district had adopted a protocol that had parallels to OGAP's formative assessment approach. However, OGAP came with tools, resources, and training supports that seemed less well-represented in the protocol her network provided. From the principal's standpoint, OGAP was a valuable resource in that it provided teachers with a meaningful structure and set of tools to analyze students' work more effectively. Further, OGAP came with the promise of ongoing training, which she believed was an essential component to improve teacher effectiveness. Thus, one-time training—i.e., the summer OGAP training alone—would have been less of a draw for her to introduce OGAP to her school.

The principal described receiving an email invitation to send her teachers to OGAP training and jumped at the opportunity to get them free ongoing support with mathematics—noting that students, especially middle school students, had not performed well on the math portion of the annual state test in the past. She was further motivated by the fact that students' already low state test scores had recently dropped even further. Thus, a "free program" with the potential to boost their math achievement was welcome. As described in the quote below, she attributed low achievement in math to *teacher capacity* as opposed to student capacity: "I think the bigger challenge is teachers can't teach math. I don't think they know math. Me, personally, I will own up to it. Anything beyond 5th grade, forget it. I can't do it. But, I see they can't do it either. . . . I see that a lot of them lack the skills to teach it because they can't do it. If you can't do it, how can you be expected to teach it? That is a big dilemma."

The assistant principal similarly echoed the desire to build teachers' instructional capacity in mathematics: "One of the influencers is mainly the scores, the achievement scores. So, that's always—you'd always start with the data. Our principal sort of came across [OGAP] and she felt as though it coincided with some of the work that we were doing already. So, I think the more effective practices we can bring into the school, the better off our students' knowledge and achievements are going to be."

The math lead teacher added that a goal of participating in OGAP was to improve teachers' content knowledge for teaching math. She noted that the teachers at her school were skilled as teachers, but were not all proficient with math content: "Most of them can teach. It's whether they feel that they have the resources and, you know, in order to be able to teach the subject, and how familiar are they with the content. So what we're finding out now is that some of them aren't as familiar with the content, and we're trying to figure out how to get them to own being able to pull those resources themselves."

Thus, all three leaders of the school had somewhat different, but complementary, reasons for adopting OGAP. The principal wanted to build teachers' capacity to teach mathematics, the assistant principal was particularly encouraged by the promise of improving math achievement, and the math lead wanted to build teachers' content knowledge. All three of these components were important motivating factors for adopting OGAP.

Fern Principal's Implementation Plan

The principal's approach to emphasizing OGAP implementation entailed communicating to the leadership team and her teachers that OGAP was a priority. Teacher buy-in was facilitated by OGAP's alignment with their regional network's goals. And although teachers' participation at OGAP training was voluntary, their attendance was greatly aided by the fact that teachers would be paid to attend in addition to their principal's encouragement to go. Fern sent fifteen teachers and two leaders to the summer OGAP training, exceeding the district's participation criteria of schools having at least 65 percent of the teaching staff represented at training.

Although the principal maintained an active, visible role in supporting teachers' engagement with OGAP, she assigned the day-to-day supervision of implementation to a fully released math lead teacher in whom she had great confidence. The math lead teacher was a former middle school mathematics teacher who also attended the summer OGAP training. According to the math lead teacher, the minimum expectation was that teachers would issue an OGAP item at least biweekly in preparation for discussing the evidence in students' work at OGAP PLC meetings held on an alternating basis with their literacy meetings. Essentially, the OGAP PLC meetings would take place during already scheduled grade-group meetings at least twice per month.

The principal expressed early on her enthusiasm about the opportunity to receive ongoing in-school mathematic instructional support through OGAP and committed to allocating time for these to occur. Unlike some schools in our sample, all grades were initially expected to participate in the OGAP initiative.

The Reality of OGAP Implementation at Fern According to Our Research

We tracked implementation progress by evaluating the frequency of teachers' administration of OGAP items, their use of the OGAP framework, and how often they had PLC meetings to collaboratively analyze and discuss the evidence in students' work, in addition to the quality of those conversations. From the research team's perspective, implementation of OGAP at Fern was a case of modest success. The principal demonstrated important signs of follow-through in her implementation intentions by appointing the school's math lead teacher to oversee the initiative and carving out time for OGAP PLC meetings to occur. She was also a visible and vocal supporter of OGAP within the school, which appeared key for most teachers to try it. Across all teachers interviewed, the math lead teacher was repeatedly credited for facilitating their ongoing engagement with OGAP throughout the year. Without the expectation being set at the top, OGAP would have easily faded given the number of expectations thrust upon the school's staff.

The principal and math lead teacher diligently tried to follow the basic recommendations of implementing OGAP, which called for teachers giving an item once or twice per week. The reality, though, was that in onboarding this practice, setting the expectation for an item to be given at least twice per month would at least enable teachers to participate in two OGAP PLCs each month to build their familiarity with the OGAP cycle. Hence this became the goal that teachers spoke of in implementing OGAP. Very early on, it became clear to the math lead teacher that teachers needed a push to administer the items, so she took the initiative in selecting the items for teachers to administer to their students based upon the premise of "eligible content" according to the district's scope and sequence for grade-level instruction. Over time, we heard teachers grow in their use of OGAP items, which served as a basic step toward implementation. Toward the end of the year, a couple of teachers began selecting these on their own rather than the math lead teacher choosing them. Others felt overwhelmed by other school priorities, and welcomed the math lead teacher's provision of preselected items, even if they didn't appear to align exactly with what they were teaching at the time. Although we found the lack of teacher ownership in selecting problems from the OGAP item bank troubling, administration of the items appeared to be the most notable effort toward implementation.

In the early fall, the teachers began participating in OGAP PLC meetings, with the math lead teacher serving as facilitator. We learned that these meetings were difficult to maintain regularly despite the best intentions to have them. Teachers shared two major complaints about these meetings: one, that they more often occurred once per month rather than twice per month and, two, the math lead teacher was not able to provide the support needed to use the OGAP progressions in the same way as the OGAP trainers, which made the analysis of student work difficult and seemingly weakened the potential of teachers' instructional responses. The math lead teacher agreed with this assessment, voicing that she felt unprepared to support grades covered by the OGAP content areas that she hadn't attended at the summer training. Subsequently, teachers shared that the most meaningful PLC meetings occurred when the OGAP trainers facilitated them during the in-school PD sessions, as they possessed the expertise to speak to the OGAP learning progression for their particular content area.

OGAP use at Fern started off slow but steady and peaked by the time we completed our second round of interviews in January 2018. In the latter half of the school year, statewide testing provided an interruption to the implementation plan for some yet facilitated use of OGAP items for others. In one instance, a fifth-grade teacher found value in administering the OGAP items more frequently to help her students prepare for the statewide test. Other teachers reported struggling to administer the items, as they were typically overwhelmed with other priorities (i.e., literacy instruction, making sure students completed required time on the network-mandated online program, and covering "eligible content" in a timely manner). Another challenge occurred in the middle grades (i.e., 6–8). A permanent middle-years math teacher was not in place at Fern until mid-year. As a result, the sixth-grade math teacher had no colleagues to meet with in OGAP PLCs. Additionally, the math lead teacher discontinued supplying the sixth-grade teacher with OGAP items in the early fall because network leadership instituted yet another expectation of administering "math maintenance problems" to improve students' long-term retention of earlier taught content.

Overall, OGAP implementation was faced with a range of challenges that often emanated from competing priorities communicated from regional network leadership, which undermined time to focus on OGAP. Implementation fell short in that the OGAP cycle remained incomplete for many teachers. We saw various elements of OGAP in use, but not necessarily well-coordinated in the execution of the full OGAP cycle. The OGAP framework, for instance, was the most underutilized component of the cycle, which has significant implications for the type of instructional responses that would follow the analysis of students' work on item bank problems. Despite this, we saw valuable traces of OGAP's influence on the teaching and learning of mathematics at Fern. Teachers embraced the idea of looking more closely at students' work beyond the mere correctness or incorrectness of responses. Figuring out what students could do already, or knew, became a new lens in evaluating students' work. Some teachers also reported finding helpful a myriad of teaching strategies they learned from OGAP training. A few spoke to finding value in the OGAP progressions in making sense of students' problem-solving strategies and in thinking about other ways to support students' learning via visual models.

Fern Leaders' and Teachers' Perceptions of Implementation Success

At the conclusion of the year, the principal perceived that OGAP implementation had been successful and envisioned that teachers would become better practitioners of the formative assessment cycle in year 2. She credited the competency of her math lead teacher in leading the implementation effort. She communicated that OGAP provided a way for her to assess teachers' strengths and weaknesses as well, which she attributed to the conversations teachers had about student work. The PLCs were viewed as valuable in that they got teachers talking about an instructional area that was rarely discussed before OGAP. Further, the principal saw the OGAP PLCs as an opportunity to break teachers out of their silos to cross-talk and think collaboratively about the challenges of math teaching and learning. In talking with the math lead teacher, she too, counted the teachers' OGAP implementation experience as successful in that 100 percent of teachers met the goal of issuing an OGAP item to their students in preparation for the PLC meetings and that at least 50 percent of the teachers made use of OGAP instructionally outside of their required use. Overall, teachers at Fern were credited by the principal and math lead teacher as being very receptive of OGAP despite the time limitations they experienced to regularly integrate it into practice.

Teachers, however, varied in their perceptions of implementation success. OGAP-trained teachers felt that exposure to OGAP professional development was extremely valuable in helping them to personally understand mathematics better, yet they lamented the degree of ongoing support they received to develop their capacity as independent users of OGAP. Repeatedly, teachers stated that much more in-school training was needed to support their proficient use of OGAP. Although they got the general premise of what OGAP was about, teachers largely remained unconfident about using the framework, which we surmised weakened the instructional responses teachers made. Aside from use of the OGAP cycle, some teachers spoke about the teaching strategies they learned at OGAP training as the real takeaway they got from OGAP. Most of all, teachers found value in looking at student work beyond mere correctness and incorrectness. Aside from desiring more individual time with the OGAP trainers, some teachers spoke about the limitations of the math lead teacher supporting their specific OGAP content area. Nonetheless, they very much appreciated the work the math lead teacher did to support them with math instruction throughout the year.

Adoption Decision-Making at Rosewood

At the time of our research, the principal was starting his fifth year at Rosewood. Prior to his tenure, the school had gone through multiple principals over the course of twelve years. In his view, this led to a vacuum of leadership, a revolving door of programs and initiatives, and a lack of motivation within the staff to give any new things a real shot. He viewed himself as bringing both consistency and hope to the school. And he felt that their recent assessment data confirmed that they were moving in the right direction under his leadership.

One of the changes he had begun to implement was a focus on formative assessment in both reading and math, starting the prior school year. After attending a two-year principal fellowship program, he had become convinced of the importance of formative assessment to instruction. He instituted a weekly assessment that was not graded but was instead used to help teachers effectively reteach where needed.

The timing of the Summer Math Institute for Rosewood was incidental; it was simply their school's turn to attend. However, it did coincide with an internal decision to focus on math instruction. Their reading scores had gone up after a sustained focus, but math state test scores had dipped slightly. After several years of concentrating mostly on literacy, he felt it was time to have a real push for math. Specifically, he believed that a strong foundation was needed, which would come from giving K–2 math the same attention that early literacy had received from the district in recent years in the form of funding, staff to train and support teachers, and ongoing professional development.

When a middle-grade math teacher brought OGAP to the principal's attention, he was not initially interested. Perhaps because he is stubborn, as he described, and doesn't like to deviate from the plans he has already set. However, when he heard that OGAP was not only focused on formative assessment, but also included a bank of items, he was sold. OGAP fit in with their existing focus, and the item bank would save the teachers time because they wouldn't need to create their own assessments. Hence, the principal enthusiastically selected OGAP training at the math institute for his school.

Rosewood Principal's Implementation Plan

The principal described himself as "micromanaging" OGAP at Rosewood. For other school initiatives, he felt as though he had strong support within his school team to lead them. With OGAP, however, there were not many people whom he felt understood the program well enough to lead it, so he took it upon himself to be in charge. When the principal was unable to attend OGAP PLCs, the school-based teacher leader (SBTL) who had also attended the math institute would run them. Perhaps due to the SBTL's role as a literacy leader, she expressed that she didn't feel completely prepared to support or teach others how to use OGAP.

One of the biggest challenges faced by Rosewood was the lack of teachers who attended the initial summer training. Five days were spent giving teachers the opportunity to gain knowledge and experience in using OGAP's tools and method of formative assessment at the MCI. Only four of about twenty-five general education math teachers made it to the training. The rest of those in attendance were school leaders, ESOL teachers, and specialist teachers. Throughout our interviews with teachers over the course of the year, the message that they didn't feel prepared to use OGAP, or needed more support and training, was echoed many times.

Rosewood had an initial plan for how they would implement OGAP to support their existing school goals. The principal had identified a problem in math instruction. During observations, he often noticed teachers sitting at their desks during the independent practice portion of the lesson, which he found to be a waste of instructional time. In response, he decided that everyone would do "guided math," which meant meeting with small groups of students while the rest of the class was working independently or in centers. OGAP was perceived as a method to form these groups as well as to set their instructional focus.

Starting from the beginning of the year, each grade team was asked to pick a common weekly OGAP item. They were then expected to use the data from that formative assessment to create their daily guided math groups. The OGAP learning progressions were to be used as a way for teachers to see what students were lacking, and they could then utilize the small-group time as an opportunity to fill in those gaps. They were not expected to teach grade-level content in the guided groups, although the principal acknowledged that this was a controversial area and some people only believed in spending instructional time for the tested grade-level content.

In addition to using items weekly within their classrooms, grade teams also met monthly in PLCs to go over their OGAP data. These meetings were one class period, thirty-nine minutes long, which the principal felt was not enough time. He was committed at the beginning of the year to attending all of the OGAP PLCs as the leader of this initiative.

The Reality of OGAP Implementation in Rosewood According to Our Research

As with the Fern school, we tracked implementation progress by evaluating the frequency of teachers' administration of OGAP items, their use of the OGAP framework, and how often they had PLC meetings to collaboratively analyze and discuss the evidence in students' work, in addition to the quality of those conversations. Overall, Rosewood represents a case of moderate take-up after one year. Undoubtedly, the principal was the number one driver of OGAP implementation at the school. The principal asked for additional school-based professional development and carved out PLC time for teachers to talk about OGAP. Additionally, the principal attended teacher and leadership trainings so that he could be an effective instructional leader in math and OGAP—a role he took rather seriously. Most importantly, he required that his teachers use OGAP items at least once per week, which we found was indeed the case for most teachers throughout the school year.

At the beginning of the year many teachers expressed confusion about aspects of using OGAP items and the OGAP formative assessment cycle. Specifically, some teachers found it difficult to find OGAP items that matched their curriculum content during certain parts of the school year, and others wanted to adapt the items for struggling students, such as those newly learning English. Several teachers said that OGAP did not line up with what they were supposed to be teaching. It was difficult for teachers to feel comfortable with giving students some of the OGAP items when they felt it wasn't helping them instructionally given what they were covering in the curriculum at that time. This issue was exacerbated by the principal's insistence that every week an OGAP item had to be chosen and used as a basis for the guided math section of the math block. Teachers could have been given more flexibility to choose a separate formative assessment item some weeks or to use their OGAP item as a preassessment and not necessarily as the topic of their guided math groups.

As the year progressed, most teachers gained understanding, and their use became more sophisticated. However, use fell off for a few teachers toward the end of the school year due to competing priorities, especially state-wide testing. The middle-year teacher, who was a strong proponent of OGAP and initially brought it to the principal's attention, lamented the lack of time to implement it weekly alongside the demanding middle school curriculum and grading responsibilities for a large number of students.

About half of the teachers we interviewed felt that their understanding of how to use OGAP for formative assessment improved over the course of the year. This was highly correlated to teachers who attended the summer institute or OGAP workshops that were offered during the school year. PLCs were planned to focus on OGAP monthly. This happened more during the beginning half of the year. Teachers reported that other issues would sometimes take up a significant portion of the time for the PLC, which was already limited to about thirty minutes. After sorting the work and talking about it, they often ran out of time to discuss next instructional steps, which was an area several teachers expressed confusion around. The principal and school-based teacher leader exhibited strong OGAP support for the first half of the year, but they waned in their active monitoring of OGAP due to other priorities, such as standardized testing and the district's emphasis on early literacy instruction.

Rosewood Leaders' and Teachers' Perceptions of Implementation Success

The principal was open about the immense pressures faced by teachers, especially those in grades K–5, who taught both literacy and math. He knew that the accountability from the district came down on literacy more strongly and so that was where people tended to focus their efforts. In addition, they also had a number of community initiatives within the school, which frequently took up time. There was very little room to fit another program onto teachers' plates. The initial plan and the expectations that went along with it were a way get teachers regularly using and practicing the OGAP formative assessment cycle. The principal stated several times that they were in this for the long haul and that he saw OGAP implementation as a process that would take several years to take root. The principal at Rosewood expected that over time and with additional practice and training, OGAP would be become easier to implement and even something that was a part of their school's culture.

Early on, the principal was very aware that many teachers were using OGAP for compliance only. He viewed this as procedural use without really understanding the purpose. Taking the long view, he stated that giving OGAP items and meeting with guided math groups was enough for the first year. If he could get all of his teachers doing that much, he felt as though he could build on that usage in subsequent years. He never spoke much about any opposition to OGAP and described himself as "patient" with inconsistent implementation. He seemed confident that he would be able to convince teachers to buy in to his ideas through consistent, enforced use. By the end of the year, only two of the teachers we interviewed expressed that they were using OGAP solely because of the principal's mandate. While it certainly increased regular usage at Rosewood, teachers also personally found value in OGAP for their students and their instructional capacity.

By the end of the school year, the principal viewed engagement with OGAP school-wide as "moderate." Some grades had more challenges with using it, such as the kindergarten teachers. He believed that they had taken a first step toward building a school culture around using OGAP and formative assessment that would continue to grow in subsequent years.

The teachers that we talked to were varied in their assessment of the success of OGAP implementation in the first year. Seven out of the eight teachers we interviewed agreed that they had used OGAP items either weekly or biweekly due to a mandate from their principal. Some stressed the challenges more than the successes of implementation. These included perceived misalignment with the math curriculum, lack of understanding of the framework, and not enough time to fit regular OGAP use in. Four teachers mentioned that the support of their colleagues was important to implementation. Many grades chose the items together and some even looked at and discussed student work in between PLC meetings. Three teachers felt that the framework was something they were beginning to internalize and that this helped them to understand their students' mathematical knowledge in a deeper way.

Principals' Role in Supporting Implementation

In the sections above, we provided an overview of two schools' OGAP implementation experiences that we viewed as moderately successful based on regular item usage, instituting OGAP PLCs, and school leaders' plans to continue with the program the following school year. In revisiting our earlier stated goals about exploring the principal component of PMLC's theory of action, this section presents a comparative look at each principal's role and approach to supporting OGAP implementation and how this shaped teachers' engagements with OGAP. In this way, we respond to scholars' observations about contextual factors that contribute to the varying levels of implementation despite the strength and quality of the program to be implemented. We also approach this section from a lessons-learned perspective in offering recommendations for similar districts and school contexts seeking to implement new instructional initiatives generally. Our discussion focuses on the following areas:

- principals' enacted roles in leading OGAP implementation
- availability of internal capacity to support implementation
- leadership beliefs about the implementation process
- protecting opportunities for teacher collaboration
- principals' perceptions of teacher professionalism

Principals' Enacted Roles in Leading OGAP Implementation

In the case of Fern, the principal described herself as the driver of mandates that seemingly came from her network administration rather than her own ideas about what should be done to improve students' achievement. Leading a school in which educational failure was considered extreme appeared to thus remove a lot of decision-making from her hands and in many ways positioned her as merely a driver of a multitude of top-down mandates that resulted in her acting as an enforcer. When asked about her perspective of successfully implementing programs and initiatives in Philadelphia, she replied, "What doesn't get monitored doesn't get done." This fundamental belief showed itself to be a cornerstone of her implementation approach, which involved appointing someone other than herself to take the lead in monitoring. In this regard, the principal counted herself as fortunate to have a highly competent, fully released math lead teacher at her school who could lead implementation. The math lead teacher had also attended OGAP training, which was considered a big plus. The principal perceived herself as not being strong in mathematics beyond the elementary level and thus removed herself as an expert in this area, although she clearly took initiative to understand the basics of OGAP and the expectations for learning mathematics as defined by district leadership. The principal also appeared well informed about the wide variety of assessments that were used to monitor students' achievement and provide clues to teachers' instructional practices.

OGAP at Rosewood was led by the principal because he had come to believe both in its value as well as in its usefulness to helping achieve the school's math goals. Because he didn't have anyone else that he felt was able to take control of OGAP implementation, it became the principal's pet project. This focus supported implementation to a certain extent because it compelled compliance with regular engagement from most teachers. The principal checked their lesson plans for OGAP, attended their monthly PLCs, and asked to see completed OGAP items during classroom observations. However, as the school year went on and other priorities arose, his attention to OGAP waned. He believed that without his attention on teacher use, some of them reverted back to their old ways of doing things and engagement with OGAP declined.

In comparing our two principals, there are parallels in their perspectives in that teachers require applied pressure—or in other words, must be forced to learn and use new practices in order for change to occur. Despite this less positive framing of teachers as being self-propelled pursuers of innovative practices, both principals highlighted the contextual realities of their schools, in which teachers were inundated with multiple priorities vying for their attention. In fact, we found evidence of both principals expressing empathy for teachers in how they must juggle so many competing demands. Hence, their tactics of "monitoring" and applying administrative pressure to implement OGAP were strategies employed to earnestly push the initiative amid a crowded field of demands. This stance also resonates with the Theory of Action undergirding this research, which positions principal engagement as a critical lever of implementing OGAP. In comparison to other schools using OGAP during this same time period, these principals' administrative engagements seemed to create a more noticeable difference in the implementation culture in that PLC meetings were prioritized beyond the OGAP trainer visit sessions. Because teachers were pushed to administer OGAP items and had opportunities to discuss student work at PLC meetings, this led to more frequent engagement with OGAP than what we found in schools where administrative oversight was not as forceful.

Availability of Internal Capacity to Support Implementation

One of the prominent things we noticed in this research was the issue of internal capacity to lead OGAP implementation. This was made visible in really substantive ways in the two cases profiled in this chapter. In the context of Rosewood, the principal's approach was explicitly framed from the perspective that no one other than himself was really prepared to lead OGAP implementation. This route was unsustainable given the myriad responsibilities embedded in the principal's role, so implementation slowed as his attention understandably shifted to other areas.

In the case of Fern, the principal had someone to whom to delegate this role to who not only had knowledge of teaching mathematics, but also had release time to oversee the day-to-day mechanics of implementation. It was also immensely helpful that the math lead teacher at Fern had attended OGAP training, which made her familiar with the general premise of OGAP. The challenge, however, came in the math lead teacher's unfamiliarity with *all the OGAP content areas*, which made it difficult for her to maximize her support across grade levels beyond her own training in the proportional content area of OGAP. This was one of the major challenges that came with the pursuit of our schoolwide implementation approach: the person responsible for spearheading OGAP was usually limited to being knowledgeable about only one content area.

The math lead as well as the teachers cited the difficulties this posed to implementing OGAP at a high level. This condition was further complicated by the way in which the math lead position was often appointed to a middle-year math-certified teacher, who was rarely knowledgeable about teaching lower grades (or vice versa in some other cases). Relatedly, the gaps in knowledge about the other OGAP content areas made the task of onboarding untrained teachers even more challenging. Hence, this led to teachers' perceptions of the OGAP trainers as the best implementation resource during the course of the year. Because of budget constraints, however, OGAP trainers were limited in the amount of ongoing support they could provide. And although two district teachers were sent to OGAP facilitator training with the hopes of building some in-house expertise within the district, these teachers were rarely utilized to support other teachers in implementing OGAP. Going forward, the district should evaluate its capacity to provide the ongoing support needed to get an initiative off the ground completely rather than partially. Some of these challenges, however, were not initially anticipated on the side of PMLC, making this a hole in our implementation theory of action.

Leadership Beliefs About the Implementation Process

At Rosewood, the principal believed that implementation was a several-year-long process, which was led by his vision. He had a plan that saw each year as building on the next until a practice became a part of their school's culture. Buy-in didn't seem particularly important to him initially; he was happy for people to be using the program purely out of compliance. He believed that regular use would lead to developing understanding of the value, which in turn would increase buy-in as time went on.

At Fern, the principal repeatedly expressed a strong belief in that improving teachers' practices was a matter of them having opportunities to receive ongoing professional development. Early on she highlighted that her attraction to adopting OGAP was that it came with the promise of ongoing in-school professional development. This was, in fact, a huge selling point, and she explicitly critiqued one-time professional developments as an ineffective strategy of improving teachers' instructional practices, which she noted was common in the district. Hence, the principal was very receptive to the in-school trainer visits, although we sometimes noted the PD environment as not appearing very conducive to learning. Similar to the Rosewood principal, the Fern principal and the Fern math lead teacher believed the first year went well and anticipated that teachers would grow in their practice of OGAP over time.

Opportunities for Teacher Collaboration

Creating opportunities for teacher collaboration was also found to be an important aspect of our principals' implementation successes. Both schools started off with good intentions but reported finding it challenging to consistently maintain these meetings because of so many other demands and competing priorities. Yet, in both sites, collaboration appeared to provide opportunities for teachers to discuss math in ways that were not common prior to OGAP's introduction. Teachers in both schools found these meetings desirable in trying to become OGAP users, and we also heard appreciation for the focused attention mathematics was getting through this opportunity. At Rosewood, collaboration was identified as a strongly instituted norm of practice among grade teams that supported implementation. Teachers planned lessons together, which also incorporated the selection of an OGAP item, which helped with initiating implementation.

Fern's principal spoke of finding PLC meetings meaningful in her own ability to monitor what teachers knew and didn't know, which could lead to further targeted support. In this way, OGAP was serving as a vehicle for the principal and math lead teacher to formatively assess teachers' instructional strengths and challenges. Both school leaders were excited about the potential of the PLC meetings and made sincere efforts to protect these meetings as much as they could. Fundamentally, this structural support served as an important sign that OGAP was a movement in the school.

Principals' Perceptions of Teacher Professionalism

A noticeable difference we observed between our two principals was the way in which they positioned the teachers under their charge. In Fern, we came to know these teachers early on as lacking, whereas the teachers at Rosewood were more positively positioned as capable. Both school leaders had concerns about raising students' achievement scores on the state assessment test and largely framed students as capable learners who could achieve if their teachers were provided with the right professional opportunities to develop their expertise as mathematics educators. Despite this difference in how they viewed teachers, both principals' theory of action for instituting change included the mindset of forcing teachers to engage with OGAP-prescribed practices, with the anticipation that these practices would eventually take hold and lead to improvements in math achievement for students. By the end of the year, the principal at Fern continued to lament about the lack of teacher quality present in her school but believed opportunities such as OGAP training were crucial to being able to cultivate the teachers available to her. Rosewood's principal, in contrast, projected a stance in which teachers were perceived as professionals who were capable of teaching in ways that veered away from the reliance on specific curricular resources and other rigid protocols. Despite this stance, the principal at Rosewood held specific beliefs about the types of instructional practices he wanted implemented; therefore, in action, teachers were not afforded complete autonomy in what took place in their classrooms.

CONCLUSION: LESSONS LEARNED FROM THIS ITERATION OF OGAP

This research was informed by a theory of action that in part hypothesized the role of principals as being pivotal to OGAP's successful implementation. Our investigation of OGAP implementation across five schools during the 2017–2018 school year provided us an opportunity to consider the ways in which this hypothesis would play out. Out of the five cases, we identified two of the strongest cases of principal buy-in to explore the ways in which principal's support enabled teacher take-up of OGAP. Our research in the context of Philadelphia revealed that leadership buy-in was necessary beyond the scope of principals, whom we encountered feeling less autonomous about what got prioritized in their respective schools. As we moved through all phases of the PMLC research, we noted that OGAP was hopelessly buried by numerous other district-led initiatives that carried greater urgency, highlighting that buy-in must also be inclusive of district-level administrators who really set the agenda for most schools—especially those in which low achievement appears chronic. Despite our takeaway about the need for district-level administrative buy-in, principals nonetheless served as important figures in communicating OGAP as a schoolwide priority. Their vocalized support of OGAP *in addition* to the provision of *structural* and *resource* supports of OGAP were found to be key for implementation to have a chance at even taking root. Finally, our research identified a critical gap in preparing schools to carry out OGAP implementation on their own due to leadership capacity constraints in the form of either time or knowledge of OGAP.

9

Persisting with OGAP

Why Educators Valued the Reform, and How One School Organized for Persistence

JILL C. PIERCE, ADRIANNE FLACK, AND BRITTANY L. HESS

Persisting with the Ongoing Assessment Project (OGAP) was a choice made by teachers and schools who found high value in this way of teaching mathematics. Initially, Philadelphia schools signed on to receive thirty hours of base summer training as well as follow-up professional development and supports for the ensuing school year. Beyond this, school leaders and teachers made choices about how long and how much they engaged with the project. Some discontinued their use of OGAP after one year, while others persisted with OGAP implementation and engaged more deeply with the project. In this chapter, we examine why many teachers and schools continued to work with OGAP and why they found value in persevering. First, we focus on why individual educators persisted in using OGAP. Second, we take an in-depth look at one school's engagement, where a mass of teachers incorporated OGAP into their instructional repertoire.

Our intent is for this chapter to offer readers a sense of the elements implementers valued about this educational reform, that they carried beyond the stage of initial professional development and into their continued use of the project (with help from ongoing professional learning opportunities). Reform designers may find lessons in these elements, which relate to fundamental shifts in teaching and learning. Core facets of OGAP that had staying power could be replicable in other reforms aimed at strengthening teaching and deepening learning. These elements have the potential to shift classroom practices, a notoriously challenging task.[1]

We also hope that reading about factors that facilitated schoolwide use in one context helps reform designers and reform implementers (especially district/school leaders) to think about concrete steps they can take to facilitate deep project ownership. At the conclusions of sections I and II of this chapter, we discuss the key takeaways of this study for those stakeholders.

DESIGN OF THE CHAPTER

We conducted fifty-three interviews with school leaders and teachers, primarily in 2018–2019, OGAP's fifth year in Philadelphia. Our inquiry was designed to help us understand how and why persisters were using and adapting OGAP to make it their own, and the individual and institutional factors that impacted their implementation. In addition, we interviewed three "nonpersisters," to add to our understanding of implementation challenges gained in our previous studies, as well as two OGAP trainers, to triangulate our understanding of institutional factors that impacted implementation.

The educators in our sample came from fifteen schools across Philadelphia where some or all of the teachers continued to use OGAP beyond the first year of training and support. Using our database of OGAP participants, we sent out a request for interviews with teachers and leaders who continued to use OGAP. At the majority of the schools, fewer than four educators volunteered to participate in interviews. Therefore, our ability to characterize schoolwide use of OGAP was limited. However, through our study, we gained the general impression that schoolwide use fell on a continuum: from a few OGAP users in a school, to pockets of use throughout a building, to something closer to whole-school use. One school in our sample stood out because of where it appeared to fit on this continuum. Educators at Cedar Elementary volunteered for our interviews en masse, and they appeared to be persisting with OGAP as a school.[2] While data from the fifteen interviews we conducted at Cedar are part of the study of individual persistence we present in section I of this chapter, Cedar-related data are the sole focus of section II, where we examine institutional factors that facilitated whole-school persistence with OGAP and deep ownership of the reform. The findings presented in sections I and II are the results of thematic analyses of our data.[3] We honed and strengthened these analyses over time through regular meetings of our four-person research team and with the Philadelphia Mathematics Leadership Collaborative (PMLC) leaders.

I: WHY EDUCATORS VALUED OGAP

Across our interviews with teachers and leaders, we heard a common set of elements that educators valued about OGAP. These elements included what educators learned from the project and how the reform guided teachers' examination of student thinking and impacted their math instruction. Specifically, interviewees shared the following:

1. OGAP enhanced educators' understandings of math learning. The project made teachers more comfortable with math and helped them to foster positive math learning environments in their classrooms.
2. OGAP pushed teachers to look beyond correctness and focus on students' problem-solving strategies. Teachers valued the information that OGAP student work gave them.
3. OGAP emphasized the importance of noticing and building on *strengths* in student understanding.
4. OGAP gave teachers tools to teach math differently. These included visual models, hands-on activities, and ways to form small groups.
5. OGAP encouraged teachers to facilitate student discussions of math.
6. OGAP helped teachers understand how to use their curricula better.

Educators' descriptions of what they valued about OGAP overlapped with their descriptions of how OGAP changed their beliefs and practices. We largely accept self-reported changes as facts, as we did not independently observe teachers' practices to look for evidence of these changes. We did, however, ask a targeted set of questions that gave us insight into how teachers engaged specifically in the OGAP formative assessment cycle of *assess–analyze–respond*.

1. OGAP enhanced educators' understandings of math learning. The project made teachers more comfortable with math and helped them to foster positive math learning environments in their classrooms.
Educators valued OGAP because it enhanced their understandings of math learning—their own and their students' learning. Many stated that through training and continued work with OGAP, they had come to think critically of the ways in which they had previously been taught to problem-solve (or to teach math). A first-grade teacher commented, "I'm an older teacher, and I would say [OGAP is] a realistic approach to math that was never taught to us, being from the older generation. It's really, in my opinion, the kids really are grasping and getting a firm understanding of what math is, how it looks, how we use it, and why we use it. Not just memorizing it and doing it because we said you have to" (Ms. I, first grade, Cedar).

OGAP helped teachers to move beyond a focus on rote memorization. Many commented that they and their colleagues had never learned math deeply enough to teach it well and that they had relied on very procedural approaches in math learning and teaching. One teacher described her eye-opening experience learning mental math strategies in OGAP training and noted, "I never was taught to learn math that way. I didn't learn math that way. I think, for the kids growing up now, that's the way that they need to be taught math. They need to have that mathematical thinking... [OGAP is] a different way to look at math" (Ms. T, kindergarten, Fern).

Teacher leaders and principals valued that OGAP was built on a solid foundation of research. The project provided adults with the conceptual building blocks they needed to help children learn increasingly sophisticated problem-solving strategies. The math teacher leader at Fern School shared this observation of her teacher colleagues: "In terms of the teaching itself and that conceptual understanding of math, I think they [teachers] like OGAP because it helps them to better understand what they're teaching, or again, giving them research to help with their teaching; that it's like 'Okay, I get this, because somebody has spent a week explaining it'" (Ms. J, math teacher leader, Fern).

The math teacher leader at Katsura shared that at OGAP training, "I really felt like there was a good marriage between the research and the theory level and the actual applications in your classroom and what that truly means, which is super powerful for me."

Interviewees stated that their own comfort with math increased as a result of training, and they sensed that students felt more comfortable with math as they worked with OGAP over time. Some teachers said that OGAP-related practices helped students to fear math less, and they valued the learning environments that OGAP helped them to create. As a math teacher leader noted, "It's helped with the whole math structure of the classroom because we say that mistakes are okay and that we look at where our learning is and we can analyze our learning and it's been a better overall feel about math instruction." (Ms. G, math teacher leader, Ivy)

2. OGAP pushed teachers to look beyond correctness and focus on students' problem-solving strategies. Educators valued the information that OGAP student work gave them.

Looking Beyond Correctness While OGAP does not ask teachers to *ignore* the correctness or incorrectness of students' answers to problems, the process of sorting student work should be driven primarily by an examination of student strategies, rather than a simple assessment of correctness. Again and again, interviewees said that they appreciated that OGAP moved them beyond just looking for whether students got problems right or wrong.

A teacher leader at one school described that OGAP had prompted a facultywide shift among teachers, who were moving from a focus on correctness to an analysis of other information that student work provided: "I do think that they're all really starting to think about, 'What does the work tell us?' Because that's a huge shift. Before math teachers would say, 'Is the answer right or is the answer wrong?' Now it's like, 'Whether or not the answer's right or wrong, what is the process this kid is going through? What are they thinking about? How are they thinking about it?' I think it's pretty school-wide that people are [doing that]" (teacher leader, Oak).

Another teacher took up the theme of looking beyond correctness, describing that "prior to OGAP, I would have been like, 'Okay, good job. Move on.' That was the end of my job, right? They got the right answer. And now I realize it's not the end of my job" (Ms. K, third grade, Katsura). While this teacher emphasized the shift from product to process in *her teaching*, another teacher noted that "OGAP is a way for *students* [emphasis added] to think about the process, not so much the end result" (Ms. D, kindergarten, Ivy). So what did it mean to pay attention to "process"?

Understanding "Where Students Are" in Mathematical Thinking and Problem-Solving Interviewees from nearly all of the schools in our sample framed OGAP as a tool that encouraged teachers to look closely at students' work and pay attention to students' problem-solving strategies. OGAP offered a way of "really looking at students' work to direct your next level of instruction": looking specifically at "how they're attacking a problem" (Ms. R, math teacher leader, Poplar). A third-grade teacher offered an example of what this looked like: "If I notice one child is still making bubbles for a very large number, like 18×3, and I notice they are making 18 bubbles with three dots in each, that makes me feel like I need to interject and do something to push them to the next level" (Mr. C, third grade, Holly).

A teacher at Ulmus shared that OGAP was a "good resource to really hone in on what my students know, and how I can help them progress and develop more. . . . It kind of helped me narrow in on the developmental stages of my students" (Ms. T, first grade, Ulmus). This kind of explicit reference to understanding students developmentally was relatively rare in our data. In fact, a few teachers reported that they encouraged students to use whatever strategies they preferred, without attending to sophistication at all. More frequently, interviewees offered relatively vague statements about how OGAP helped teachers to focus on strategies and engage in a process of looking at where students were and where they needed to go. While teachers appeared to have different definitions of what it meant to examine where students were in mathematical thinking and problem-solving, it is promising that they found value in OGAP's emphasis on examining work for more than just correctness.

Seeing Evidence of Student Growth Interviewees saw other value in what they learned from OGAP's emphasis on student work. This included an increase in students' understanding of word problems and mathematical concepts, more frequent use of sophisticated problem-solving strategies, and an enrichment of students' math vocabularies, explanations, and discussions. Teachers reported that the focus on student work helped students understand math concepts more deeply. As one teacher explained, "It makes the students understand the concepts with much more depth than learning how to carry the one or whatever, you know what I mean? They understand value so much more" (Ms. F, fourth grade, Ivy).

Other teachers felt that OGAP helped students prepare for the state test. As a teacher leader from Yarrow said, "I think that the teachers that are using it have discovered the value in it. And because the [state math test] is so heavily weighted on word problems and mathematical reasoning and explanations, I feel that OGAP ties right into that with supporting that. So having a bank of problems that they could go to has been really helpful." A special education teacher from Juniper valued OGAP because it focused on examining items and skills "in depth." In looking at responses to benchmarks and summative assessments, she engaged in a process that she associated with OGAP analysis, of examining patterns in misconceptions and deciding what to reteach. Miscomprehensions are critical for teachers to note; as this teacher describes, they guide instructional next steps.

3. OGAP emphasized the importance of noticing and building on strengths in student understanding.

When analyzing student work, OGAP trainers instruct teachers to ask, "What's the good news?" The good news, according to OGAP, is evidence of developing understanding that can be built upon. Teachers and leaders valued OGAP's emphasis on good news: on *strengths* in students' understanding. In the words of one of our interviewees, OGAP involves "actually looking for what [students] know instead of what they don't know" (Ms. C, third grade, Cedar). As a math teacher leader put it,

> It was a big change for me, and I have used that for working with other teachers . . . being able to see children as being successful in math thinking and understanding, instead of just assuming that student just doesn't get it at all. And trying to focus on what they do know instead of always focusing on what they don't know. . . . It makes them feel successful because you can tell them what they're doing well and give them something to build upon. (Ms. G, math teacher leader, Ivy)

OGAP helped to shift some teachers' mindsets. These teachers moved away from deficit models of thinking about student understanding and instead focused on examining what students knew and then capitalizing on that knowledge: "Now, I'm always looking at children with what they know and how we can build from what they actually know. Because, they all know a lot. They all know a lot. It's like, how do you take what they know and understand what they know and build from there, you know? They do have a foundation. Before I would look at kids and be like, 'I have no idea,' you know?" (Ms. H, fifth grade, Juniper).

While a growth orientation was not ubiquitous, we heard several math teacher leaders and principals frame OGAP as a tool that helped their schools' teachers to see students positively.

4. OGAP gave teachers tools to teach math differently. These included visual models, hands-on activities, and ways to form small groups

Tools and Activities OGAP showed teachers how to teach math content differently. They leveraged what they learned from learning progressions, shared visual models with students, and used hands-on materials.

Nearly half the teachers in our sample spoke about using their knowledge of OGAP learning progressions and the strategies within them to make instructional shifts. Learning about the transitional stage of the learning progressions, which includes visual models, affected the way some teachers thought about teaching concepts to students. This was especially true with the area model in multiplication and the number line in addition and subtraction. These visual models can provide a bridge between concrete and abstract methods of solving problems and help students truly understand an algorithm, rather than memorize a series of steps. One teacher described her experience learning about the area model as a tool to teach conceptual understanding of multiplication:

> Until I taught fourth grade, I hadn't seen multiplication taught through the area model, and then one person from OGAP came in and talked to us about the area model. And at first I was like, "That doesn't make any sense." But then the more I did it, I realized that's how you kind of do it in your head anyway. So it was helpful to have someone break it down, and I do that with my kids all the time now. We do it that way and the students really do well with it. (Ms. Z, fourth grade, Verbena)

Two principals even stated that learning the area model in OGAP training shifted how they solved multiplication problems in their lives beyond school.

A second-grade teacher at Dogwood described how she used a visual model as a steppingstone to support students in getting to an algorithm: "I give them the number line so that kids who aren't as quick to succeed in the traditional method have another lifeline to go to. They know, 'Okay, if I can do it on a number line, then I'll be able to figure it out no matter what.'

So I feel it gives them that perseverance that they need to get it after a lot of practice" (Ms. B, second grade, Dogwood).

Some tools and activities that teachers referenced, including number lines, were not created or owned by OGAP. But teachers were first exposed to them and learned of their potential instructional uses in OGAP training. Often, teachers spoke about using one or more of these tools or activities to create engaging, hands-on learning experiences for their students. "Kids love it [concrete number line]. I felt like they thought it was tangible. They grasped the concept. Kids did really well with number lines" (Ms. E, second grade, Cedar).

For some teachers, these new tools and activities went beyond simply engaging students; teachers linked them to other concepts being learned in class. One kindergarten teacher found that the activity "Math Hands" helped students to develop the conceptual understanding needed to decompose numbers in a variety of configurations, and she said she wove the activity into her math instruction repeatedly.

Small-Group Formation   Interviewees from a third of the schools in the sample framed OGAP as a valuable teaching tool because it helped them organize students into groups. Only some teachers said that the strategies students used to solve individual OGAP items drove their decisions about how to group students. A small subset of those teachers described that they no longer predetermined which students were in which of their small groups. Rather, these teachers now flexibly grouped their students, which they formed after examining the strategies students used in response to individual OGAP items. This practice not only allows a teacher to target more specific skills within their small groups, but ideally, also gets away from the practice of having groups comprising students perceived as "low" or "high" performing. The Tamarack math teacher leader shared:

> The best thing is, OGAP got me out of me pre-determining who's going to be in that group until I had the data come. . . . I can do a heterogeneous or a homogeneous [grouping]. I can have a reason for it, and all of my reasons are connected to data. I make no pre-decision before that. It's not like

this student does well and this student [doesn't]. . . . You have the same strategy, you made the same mistake. You're going to be in the same group. Or I want one person to read these, I want one student to do each strategy in each group.

This teacher leader offered an understanding that data from each item administered provided *new* information about individual students' strategies, and that these data should shape immediate decisions about how to group students.

In persisters' classrooms, small groups were one place where students talked to one another about math. As we discuss next, educators deeply valued that OGAP encouraged teachers to facilitate such discussions.

5. OGAP encouraged teachers to facilitate student discussions of math.

Educators appreciated that OGAP led teachers to incorporate more student discussion of math into their classes, including conversations about the strategies students used to solve problems and why they chose those strategies. One teacher called this "math talk" and described her approach of "allowing the kids to talk, come up and do the problem, and then say how they did it" (Ms. T, kindergarten, Fern). Another teacher noted that this was a way of focusing on the process of mathematics, rather than the product (Ms. I, seventh grade special education, Juniper). This teacher learned how to have students "model their thinking" for each other and felt that it helped students to be more accountable for their learning. A fourth-grade teacher at Verbena noted, "I'm seeing this year their math language increasing, which is also helping with their math responses. Like when they have to do a written response, they're better at explaining it because they've talked through it before."

At Locust, a third-grade grade teacher stated that sharing student work on a document camera and having students explain their thinking helped students to learn math because "they're seeing it through different perspectives" (Ms. L, third grade, Locust). OGAP encourages exchanges such as these; students can learn from each other by looking for commonalities and differences between the different methods they use to solve problems, from the most concrete to the more abstract. The ultimate goal is for students to use increasingly sophisticated—or efficient—strategies. In the words of one teacher, "I think that some the best math lessons that I've had have been just putting an OGAP item, putting some student work up on the board and having kids analyze that work and talk about how that strategy was powerful or not effective" (Ms. P, second grade, Oak).

Having students share and discuss their perspectives and processes was also powerful for some teachers because it disrupted their norms of teacher-led discussions. As one teacher described, in discussions, "It's more them than me talking" (Ms. Z, fourth grade, Verbena).

6. OGAP helped teachers understand how to use their curricula better.

Some interviewees—math teacher leaders in particular—stated that OGAP helped them to become better users of their curricula and become more precise in addressing students' problem-solving challenges. Verbena's math teacher leader felt that OGAP had made him more "deliberate": "I'm not just doing it because enVision [the math curriculum] says to use this step, but I'm also thinking, 'Why this step? And why does this step work?' I'm thinking more like the background about the mathematical conceptual knowledge that is behind all these facts. [I'm a] more critical consumer of curriculum."

The math teacher leader at Poplar shared that she was trying to help teachers use OGAP formative assessment items to make their instruction in general more responsive.

She and other interviewees framed OGAP as helping teachers to engage in more authentic and responsive instruction than teachers' curricula alone would lead them to do. This framing was prevalent at Cedar. A teacher from Cedar also found value in OGAP's developmental focus, as it clarified grade-level expectations for students in math:

> OGAP allows teachers to understand what is the expectation that the student needs to have in each level. OGAP allows you to understand that

kindergarteners can recognize numbers from one to five. First graders [are] expected to add numbers from one to 10. They made the connections. What they're supposed to know before they go to the next level. OGAP refreshed us with that understanding. Because sometimes if you don't, you're just hitting in the air, you know? (Mr. Y, second grade, Cedar)

Some educators suggested that there had been schoolwide shifts in instructional practices and that, institutionally, teachers had refined, abandoned, expanded, or better learned instructional materials, strategies, or processes as a result of working with OGAP.

Some persisters found it valuable that OGAP could be used with any curriculum; others appreciated that the formative assessment cycle could be applied to non-OGAP problem-solving prompts. The Tamarack math teacher leader liked being able to pick and choose elements he wanted to use from OGAP. The adaptability of OGAP was a positive for many OGAP persisters.

Implications Part I

- *Persisters brought valued elements of OGAP with them beyond their initial professional development. Reformers within and beyond math can learn from what teachers and leaders valued about OGAP—what stuck with them.* Educators appreciated professional learning opportunities that allowed them to deepen their mathematical content knowledge. Teachers learned to better navigate their curricula, and they gained tools to support students' learning. They valued the emphasis on examining students' thinking in detail, not just assessing whether students answered questions correctly. OGAP encouraged interviewees to view students positively—to focus on students' strengths—and the project fostered positive classroom learning environments. These environments placed students at the center of math talk and facilitated increased comfort with the subject area. *Overall, OGAP called for educators to make profound shifts in their approaches to teaching and learning. The persisters who spoke with us valued having opportunities to engage in challenging work: to relearn*

how to teach content and deepen their understanding of how to assess and facilitate student learning.
- *Persisters adapted the project.* Those in charge of reform design and implementation should consider how projects can be adapted, as adaptations will facilitate teachers' integration of a project into their classrooms. We heard of many adaptations that persisters made to OGAP while implementing the project. These adaptations appeared to allow teachers, who faced more demands than they had time to address one-by-one, to work strategically. For example, folding OGAP instructional responses within requirements from school and district leaders to facilitate small groups, teachers succeeded in threading the needle. They worked within a system that exerted multiple (sometimes-contradictory) pressures (see chapter 7), successfully incorporating pieces of an instructional reform that called for significant shifts in approaches to teaching and learning; even adaptations of OGAP that may not have been ideal, appeared to facilitate their use of the project within a district context that largely was not calling for such ambitious shifts. Reform designers and implementers working in similar district contexts may need to pay special attention to how projects can be adapted to fit within such contexts. We revisit a similar theme about the need for coherence and alignment in section II as we tell the story of a school that organized for persistence.

II: HOW A SCHOOL ORGANIZED FOR PERSISTENCE

As we just discussed, there was variation in how individual persisters engaged in OGAP. There also appeared to be wide variation in how schools engaged in OGAP—in how they structured supports for the project and in how widespread OGAP use was across their teaching bodies. While our analysis was focused on individual users of OGAP, the data we collected suggested that at some schools only a few teachers were persisting in using OGAP. As stated earlier, we hesitate to make generalizations about school-wide engagement because we interviewed only a few individuals from most schools. However, at a school such as Holly, the few interviewees who spoke with us painted a similar portrait of limited OGAP use across the school. The Holly principal described use as "sporadic" and lamented that he had no math coach to support OGAP efforts at his school. Holly teachers described their school as lacking in the areas of math leadership, follow-up OGAP professional development supports, and OGAP-focused professional learning community (PLC) meetings.

These challenges closely matched those we heard about in our study of five schools' OGAP implementation during project year 4.[4] In section II, rather than return to factors that may have impeded schoolwide use in a context such as Holly's, we shift to a discussion of learnings from a school where a mass of teachers continued to use OGAP. While section I featured reasons for individuals' persistence with OGAP, it did not address institutional factors that might facilitate such persistence across a school.

Individual persisters we cited in section I did reference strong leadership for OGAP, time for collaboration with colleagues, and enriching professional development experiences as contextual elements that helped them to understand and use OGAP. Yet only from educators at Cedar—where fourteen educators participated in our interviews—did we get the sense that supports were painstakingly planned, enacted in conjunction with one another, and successful in creating a mutually reinforcing system that facilitated widespread OGAP understanding and use. We hypothesize that deep ownership of an ambitious instructional reform such as OGAP comes only from enacting such supports in concert—a hypothesis we revisit in "Implications Part II," later in this chapter.

OGAP at Cedar: How a School Organized for Persistence

At Cedar, more than at any other school in our research, interviewees described OGAP use as entrenched. OGAP had become "a routine for us . . . not even a directive anymore as much as it's what we do" (Ms. U, first grade, Cedar). The principal agreed: "OGAP is like saying our ABCs. It's part of our structure" (Principal Z). While teachers engaged in the project differently from classroom to classroom, baseline OGAP use (giving an OGAP problem to students in advance of a PLC meeting and bringing student work on the problem to the meeting for analysis) was widespread, and many teachers regularly incorporated OGAP problems into their classes multiple times per week. The OGAP trainer who worked closely with Cedar staff confirmed to us that the school engaged deeply with OGAP and supported the project in a "systemic" way. The trainer herself was part of that system; she provided on-demand expertise to the school as it implemented the project.

Factors that appeared to facilitate schoolwide use of OGAP included the following:

1. Cedar's principal engaged in OGAP trainings that built her understanding, enthusiasm, and commitment.
2. OGAP leadership was distributed.
3. Faculty engaged (repeatedly) in trainings.
4. Cedar protected "sacred" spaces of professional learning.
5. Cedar's teachers had time and space to collaboratively plan instruction.
6. Cedar faculty understood how the project aligned with existing work and could be integrated into instruction.

In the pages that follow, we offer details about what each of these factors looked like at Cedar.

1. Cedar's principal engaged in OGAP trainings that built her understanding, enthusiasm, and commitment.

At Cedar, the principal had profoundly eye-opening experiences at her first OGAP training. At the weeklong professional development session, Principal Z said she "learned that the way I had learned [math] was all wrong." The training shifted her understanding of how adults and children develop mathematical reasoning and how teachers can facilitate math learning. She especially appreciated OGAP's emphasis on strengths—rather than just deficits—in students' understanding. The training helped Principal Z to understand how teachers could move students toward greater sophistication of problem-solving strategies by building on what students already knew.

After her initial professional development experience, the principal continued to attend trainings alongside her faculty in order to expand her understanding of the content and pedagogy underlying OGAP and to display her passion for the project: "I've given up many of my summers . . . to get the training *with* them [the teachers], because I think part of my excitement rubs off on them. I'm learning with them; I'm struggling with them; I'm asking the same questions they're asking. I've learned. I feel I've grown a lot as a leader, being there learning with teachers."

The principal's commitment and enthusiasm had an impact on teachers. They frequently mentioned her as one of the project's fundamental supports: "She gets really, really excited. Like when we do the training, she comes to the trainings with us. She's all in, she's totally invested. It's not like—we don't have one of those atmospheres where the principal says, 'Go do this. I want results, and that's it'" (Ms. O, kindergarten to fourth grade, Cedar).

The Cedar faculty related that the principal tended to grab hold of new initiatives early, eagerly welcoming professional learning opportunities for her faculty. When an initiative appeared to work for teachers and facilitate student learning, she strategically carved out space for it, sending teachers to professional development sessions and bringing trainers and other resources into her school. It was at her initial week of summer training that the Cedar principal began to form relationships with OGAP trainers, including a very close connection to the trainer who provided Cedar with years of ongoing support. This off-site trainer made herself widely available beyond professional development sessions: "We know we can call her. . . . It's kind of like she built a relationship with the school, they built a relationship that goes further than, 'Here's your training. One and done'" (Ms. U, first grade, Cedar).

The principal and her teacher leaders reached out to the trainer regularly for project guidance. Principal Z described working "hand in hand" with this trainer to support OGAP understanding and use at her school. The principal fundamentally believed that a team of people, rather than just herself, drove OGAP's life at Cedar—an approach we discuss in the next subsection, on distributed leadership.

2. OGAP leadership was distributed.

Cedar's principal described herself as "living and breathing" distributed leadership. "I have an amazing staff," she said, and "I trust their leadership in my absence. There is no doubt that if I'm not here, my building will run." She entrusted a good deal of responsibility for the day-to-day support of math instruction to a math teacher leader who was released from teaching students. This teacher leader had the time to tailor supports to individual teachers' needs and provide on-demand help.

Fully releasing a teacher typically involves district and school leaders making strategic decisions about how to prioritize scarce resources, or school leaders making their own allocation decisions. In this case, Cedar's principal carved out resources to release her math teacher leader and, in doing so, strongly facilitated OGAP use. The math teacher leader had previously taught using OGAP, and she was enthusiastic about the project. A teacher described her as "really effective in really trying to push the OGAP thinking" (Ms. M, fourth grade, Cedar).

To help sustain OGAP use at Cedar, the math teacher leader facilitated OGAP-focused PLC meetings, helped teachers to choose OGAP materials, modeled instruction, and set specific expectations for teachers' OGAP use. Several teachers noted that these expectations helped to sustain their use of the project. Rounding out the team of in-school OGAP leaders were grade-level leaders and other OGAP enthusiasts—"OGAP queens," as the principal called them. These individuals helped to provide a network of OGAP knowledge and experience for the faculty to draw upon and supported fellow teachers' understanding and use of OGAP.

3. Faculty engaged (repeatedly) in trainings.

OGAP professional development for Cedar's teachers and leaders involved a week of summer training as well as school-year workshops and related in-school supports from OGAP trainers. In the words of one teacher, training "is not just a one-time thing. It's constant here" (Ms. K, second grade,

Cedar). The ongoing nature of training helped teachers to deepen their practice over time and to seek answers to questions that arose during their use of OGAP in their classrooms.

It also helped that teachers did not have to travel when attending on-site professional development sessions; trainers brought their supports directly to the school. In-school professional development days, co-planned by the OGAP trainer and school leaders, allowed trainers to develop an understanding of the school context, see teachers in their classrooms, and even model instruction for teachers.

Cedar's principal and math teacher leader took pains to ensure that as many teachers were OGAP-trained as possible. Though attendance at OGAP summer training was not mandatory, teachers got the message that they were strongly encouraged to attend. According to the principal, "I needed to get everyone to go through the program. I think I did a pretty good job of getting most of us through there." In arranging trainings, the principal and trainers ensured that there were opportunities for backfill: that teachers who missed summer training could learn about the program during the school year. Both school leaders and teachers emphasized that having a mass of OGAP-trained teachers helped to suffuse project understanding and peer-to-peer project support throughout the school.

Leaders and teachers also noted that they enjoyed OGAP trainings. Faculty described trainings as "really engaging" (Ms. M, fourth grade, Cedar); "the presenters made it really fun. So time flew by" (Ms. A, kindergarten, Cedar). Trainings were also "really informative" (Ms. A). Professional development exposed participants to core content knowledge, research on student learning, and pedagogical strategies. The design and length of the summer intensive training sessions gave teachers space and time for epiphanies about their own approaches to learning math. In the words of Cedar's math teacher leader, "I feel like [the trainers] are very good at having the adults in the room as teachers have "ah-ha" moments about their own learning. I think the value of having it all week is awesome" (Ms. Q, math teacher leader).

This teacher leader noted that faculty at Cedar generally had "a pretty positive mindset with professional learning," and the principal agreed. In fact, the principal said that in hiring, she screened for faculty who would be willing to go above and beyond their teaching duties to take advantage of professional learning opportunities. She passed over candidates who did not appear interested in such opportunities and "built the culture here at [Cedar] where we take all the learning we can get" (Principal Z). Learning happened not only in trainings from OGAP but also in school-based meetings that brought teachers of the same grade together to practice and extend their professional learning.

4. Cedar protected "sacred" spaces of professional learning.

Roughly once a month, teachers at Cedar came together with their grade-level colleagues for OGAP-focused PLCs. They brought student work on OGAP problems and sorted it by student strategies using the OGAP frameworks that detailed different levels of problem-solving sophistication. They looked for patterns in students' strategies, strengths, and misconceptions, and they spoke about next instructional steps to address those patterns.

OGAP-focused PLCs grew teachers' understanding of and comfort with the project. Of significant value to teachers was that these meetings allowed them to *learn from their peers*, who brought different perspectives on their students' work—and even on their students' learning potential: "My colleagues will point out something about one of my students that I'll go back and I'll say, 'Oh my gosh, you're right. I didn't notice that.' So that's pretty cool too" (Ms. E, second grade, Cedar).

One fundamental goal of OGAP is to help teachers shift away from understanding their students' abilities as fixed; for Ms. C, PLCs provided a space to engage in this shift in mindset. For the principal—who was deeply invested in the notion that all children can learn, and who expected teachers to share this view—this time for professional learning was "sacred." Practically, PLCs were also an accountability mechanism; teachers knew they had to give students OGAP problems in advance of OGAP-focused meetings, which ensured at least baseline use of the project in their classrooms.

It was difficult to protect time for OGAP-focused PLCs. Teacher absences or the need to discuss other issues could easily impinge on the meetings. Yet the leaders at Cedar fought to prioritize these meetings, given how valuable they were: "You really have to have a grip on your PLC time. You really have to respect that. You have to have that time; no matter what's happening out here, this PLC has to happen. It's a matter of commitment to that time. . . . I would say to the principals, you've got to respect that time no matter what happens" (Principal Z).

To signal the importance of PLCs, the principal arranged teacher coverages to ensure that the meetings could happen as scheduled and sometimes sat in on them herself. In addition, the math teacher leader frequently facilitated OGAP-focused PLCs, lending them structure, expectations, and content expertise.

PLCs focused on math helped teachers to prioritize the subject area, and some individual teachers also mentioned that they fiercely protected their "math block" (instructional time for math in the classroom). In a district where elementary teachers tended to feel that literacy dominated, leaders and teachers at Cedar made conscious efforts to safeguard opportunities for math learning and instruction.

5. Cedar's teachers had time and space to collaboratively plan instruction.

At Cedar, teachers came together weekly with grade-team colleagues to collaboratively plan instruction. In general, this routine allowed colleagues to learn from one another and saved individuals time. Because teachers are chronically stretched thin, time-saving measures are critical. Specific to *OGAP*, Cedar teachers indicated that their use of the project was facilitated by collaborating about which OGAP math problems they should integrate into their instruction (or by having one person take the lead on choosing problems for the week). As a formative assessment system intended to be woven throughout existing instruction, OGAP can feel to some teachers like an added burden, but collaborative planning at Cedar reduced the feeling of being overwhelmed: "Some other people might think of [OGAP] as just something extra that they have to add, but if they used it the way that we use it, where we incorporate it into our actual lesson plan on a weekly basis, then it wouldn't feel like it's an added thing" (Ms. W, third grade, Cedar).

While having OGAP problems included in planning was helpful, teachers were not required to use those specific problems. They needed the flexibility to be able to adapt what they were given to meet their own classes' pacing and their students' needs. As one teacher described, if an OGAP problem selected by a grade team "doesn't work for your class or it's not something you wanted to do, then you can go find your own" (Ms. K, second grade, Cedar). English language learner (ELL) instructors also described changing which problems students solved and changing the format of problems, which included adding images to aid in student comprehension. The balance of having the ability to adapt the project to make it their own *and* being able to save time planning by working collaboratively seemed essential to Cedar teachers' success in using OGAP.

6. Cedar faculty understood how the project aligned with existing work and could be integrated into instruction.

At Cedar, OGAP aligned to existing routines in a few ways, including professional learning structures. Cedar teachers engaged in PLCs before OGAP came to the school, and the principal credited this familiarity with helping the project to take root: "I do believe that as a school we PLC, and because we PLC, OGAP fits that model."

Most teachers from Cedar adapted OGAP in their instructional responses by facilitating small groups. In this way they saw OGAP as fitting with their existing grouping routines. There was also coherence between OGAP's focus on student-driven conversations about math and the district's emphasis on student "number talks," or short discussions with students about how to solve math problems: "We're not really even thinking about it. 'Cause we have to do some kind of warm up, number talks, anyway" (Ms. U, first grade).

In terms of alignments between project work and existing curricula, there were initial challenges with OGAP that needed to be addressed. The PMLC tracked the take-up of OGAP in Philadelphia schools (see chapter 3) and noted that teachers struggled to understand how and where to fit OGAP problems into their math instruction. The Collaborative developed an online tool (OGAP Connections) that matched OGAP problems to specific points in the math curriculum widely used in Philadelphia schools. Cedar teachers took advantage of the tool: "I like how OGAP has collaborated where they synced together some of the prompts with what we're teaching at the time. So, we looked at the standards for the second quarter, and then I like how the OGAP has been more aligned to the standards that we're teaching" (Ms. A, kindergarten).

Curricular alignment is critical. Teachers in our research who thought OGAP did not "go with" their curriculum (or who framed it as some kind of competing curriculum) rarely engaged with the project. Even at Cedar, one teacher noted, "In the past . . . I don't know that we understood they could kind of go together" (Ms. U, first grade). Through deep, ongoing training and supports, in-school professional learning and planning opportunities, and the Connections tool, Cedar teachers eventually came to understand and take advantage of the alignment between OGAP and their math program. As Ms. S (second grade) said, "You can definitely find that connection between the problems. It makes it all coherent."

While coherence between a project and a curriculum is key, so too is curricular flexibility. Teachers at Cedar did not feel their curriculum had to dictate every moment of their math instruction. The school, according to the principal, should be "using [the curriculum] wisely. Picking and choosing what we want to use. . . . It's a resource." Principal Z came to this view in part because it was not working for her teachers to stick to lessons, activities, and pacing as prescribed; this approach did not allow her teachers to "go deep" with concepts and address students' current needs. The school's flexible approach to the curriculum offers another example of alignment: this time with the project's core tenets. Cedar teachers were familiar with the notion that they might need to pause regular instruction to respond differently than planned, in order to address student needs. This responsiveness is at the heart of OGAP's approach to math teaching and learning.

Implications Part II

Below we share six takeaways from the OGAP supports at Cedar described above. We believe that deep reform ownership comes from enacting these six elements in combination.[5] Our hypothesis, based on our understanding of OGAP implementation at Cedar and at other schools in our studies during project years 4 and 5 is that deep implementation can be threatened if key elements are not enacted in concert.[6] While we do not have the volume of data that would allow us to fully investigate this hypothesis, at no other school did we see evidence of such widespread use of OGAP, nor hear of such a systematic approach to supporting the project in multiple ways at once.

From our study of Cedar, we suggest that reform knowledge and support must be suffused throughout a school *and* coupled with time and space for teachers to learn, integrate, practice, and adapt the reform. Without the support of a principal trained in the reform (element 1), faculty may not receive signals about how important it is and may not get the support they need to prioritize it. If only the principal advocates for the reform—that is, if leadership is not distributed (element 2)—support can easily get pulled in other directions. If teachers are not given significant time to learn the reform (elements 3 and 4) and integrate it into their instruction (element 5), or if they do not understand how it aligns with their existing routines and curriculum in the first place (element 6), they are unlikely to sustain their efforts and engagement.

1. **Engaging principals in content-specific trainings can build deep understanding, enthusiasm, and commitment.** Principals need opportunities and time to build understanding of ambitious instructional reforms. Involving principals in professional development can accomplish several goals. It can strengthen content knowledge that principals need as leaders of instruction generally and as leaders of the specific reform. Given the heavy load of responsibilities principals face, particularly in districts with more demands than resources, time for deep content learning is rare and must be intentionally carved out. Giving principals time to learn the intricacies of the content and pedagogy underpinning the reform can also grow their enthusiasm and commitment, as well as their understanding of how to support the reform in their schools.

2. **Project leadership should be distributed.** The responsibility for leading a reform should not rest solely with a principal. Distributing leadership for a reform among teacher leaders and others able to play specific leadership roles can have several advantages. Ever-busy principals can rely on knowledgeable colleagues to foster enthusiasm and to support understanding and use of the reform. Support can be widespread and on-demand—particularly where there are resources to "fully release" a trained, highly-qualified teacher from teaching responsibilities to serve in a position such as a math teacher leader.

   Teacher leaders—especially those with classroom experience in the reform—can answer content-related questions for teachers, set expectations for project use, help teachers to understand pedagogical strategies, and even model how to translate reform recommendations into classroom practice. Other leaders can also include grade-level teachers, who can help to ensure that grade-specific reform supports are in close reach.

3. **All relevant faculty (educators and leaders) should engage in ongoing professional learning opportunities.** Professional development that has a shot at changing teaching practice cannot be a single event but, rather, a part of a process of continued learning. Ongoing professional development allows participants to deepen their knowledge and bring job-embedded problems of practice back to trainers and peers, to brainstorm solutions.

   On-site trainings offer several advantages, including that they allow reform staff to learn school contexts and teachers to remain in their buildings. It takes deliberate planning to arrange in-school and off-site training opportunities and conscious efforts to encourage attendance when trainings are not mandatory.

   Ensuring that everyone possible is exposed to the reform ideas—including through repeated "backfilling" for teachers who missed the initial training or for new faculty—can facilitate a widespread foundation of project understanding and helps to distribute reform leadership. Building a culture of ongoing professional learning is labor-intensive but necessary work—work that is made easier when trainings are engaging and profoundly instructive.

4. **"Sacred" spaces of professional learning in school should be protected.** In PLCs, teachers can engage in and reflect on the reform's ideas and their implications. These "sacred" spaces grow teachers' comfort with the instructional reform, offering them unique opportunities to closely examine student work and exchange ideas about instructional responses. Such exchanges can even lead to profound shifts in mindset—shifts toward understanding the concepts underlying the reform better, as well as ways to enhance student learning.

    Time for PLCs should be fiercely protected; as a school leader, "you really have to have a grip on your PLC time" to ensure that meetings aren't cancelled when the inevitable conflicts of the school day arise (Principal Z, Cedar). Teacher leaders (or other teachers trained to lead) can facilitate PLCs, and when the principal attends these meetings, it can send strong signals about the importance of these spaces for professional learning. Protecting these meetings can also send signals that a given content area is important; if literacy typically reigns supreme in professional development and instructional attention, math-focused PLCs can be a way of stressing the importance of a less-attended-to subject.

5. **Teachers may benefit from time to collaboratively plan instruction.** PLCs are typically not the place where teachers craft the fine details of their daily instruction. Giving teachers separate time to engage in collaborative planning can further facilitate deep ownership of an instructional reform. Teachers benefit from working with grade-level colleagues on the details of how and when to integrate reform-related materials and routines into their classes.

    Sharing the work of planning can deepen reform understanding and lessen the burden on individual teachers, who can rotate the responsibility for fleshing out and distributing lessons. Teachers emphasize that once they receive collaboratively planned lessons, they need to have the freedom to adapt them to address the strengths and needs of the students in their individual classrooms.

6. **Reformers and implementers should ensure coherence, and support alignments, between the project and teachers' existing work.** For feasibility, new reforms should be woven into existing demands; this may require adaptations to the project. Given all the instructional routines, concepts, materials, and even programs that teachers often need to address within a subject area, the reform should cohere with teachers' existing routines and curricula. Developers can support these efforts by creating tools that align elements of the reform to teachers' existing work, and district and school leaders can also support alignments.

The takeaways listed here offer suggestions of ways that school faculty, working in conjunction with district leaders and reform developers/staff, can build deep ownership of ambitious instructional reforms. In a related brief entitled *Six Lessons to Facilitate Deep Ownership of Ambitious Instructional Reforms*, we include tables of questions that reform developers/staff, district leaders, and school leaders can ask themselves as they strive to enact these supports *in conjunction* and cultivate deep reform ownership.[7] As the experience of Cedar Elementary shows, such efforts can lead to rewarding experiences for educators and deeper learning for students.

10

Supporting the Core

JONATHAN A. SUPOVITZ

The research on school reform is replete with underwhelming efforts to change the "instructional core."[1] The instructional core refers to the interactions among teachers, students, and materials, sometimes viewed as the "instructional triangle."[2] As a graduate student at Harvard in the mid-1990s, I was a research assistant for Richard Elmore and collected data for what became his seminal article on the challenges reformers face in changing the instructional core at scale.[3] In that piece Elmore examined a series of education reforms that showed great promise but eventually lost traction and asked, "How can good educational practice move beyond pockets of excellence to reach a much greater proportion of students and educators?" Part of his argument was that many reforms did not connect to "fundamental changes in the way knowledge is constructed ... the way students and teachers interact with each other around knowledge, or any of a variety of other stable conditions in the core. Hence, reforms seldom translate into changes in the fundamental conditions of teaching and learning for students and teachers."[4] Rereading Elmore's work, I come away thinking that the instructional triangle is the Bermuda Triangle of education reform.

One of the themes of the literature spawned by Elmore is the relative impermeability of classroom dynamics to outside influences. While organizational reforms seek to change the quality of teaching and learning, they don't seem to have much leverage on what happens inside classrooms. Rather than looking from the outside in, this five-year study of the Ongoing Assessment Project (OGAP) gave us the opportunity to look from the inside out. In this closing chapter I use the story of OGAP to ask what instructional reforms need from the surrounding system and how their instructional theory pushes against elements of the system in either their need for support, their desire for alignment, or protection against distractions.

OGAP has a particular theory about how students learn subject-matter content. Its tenets include that learning is an uneven and developmental journey toward fluency, rather than a switch that goes on from nonunderstanding to understanding; that students gain increasing fluency by being introduced to concepts and strategies that match their current levels of capability as their mental models evolve; and that having multiple opportunities to grapple with different types and contexts of problems deepens student understanding over time. Taken alone, these are not revolutionary ideas, but the system around them is nonetheless ill-equipped to nurture them.[5]

The implications of this conception of learning for teachers and teaching are profound. The teacher's role in such a system is to cyclically diagnose students' current schemas of understanding and use that knowledge to plan and enact subsequent instruction, moving students progressively toward deeper understanding. This iterative process requires a range of teacher knowledge, tools, processes, and supports: knowledge about the particular mathematics content area, the developmental learning process, and how to align instruction to different levels of understanding; tools such as OGAP's curated item bank and learning progressions; processes such as OGAP's technique of sorting student work by solution strategies and grade-level teacher meetings to collaboratively analyze and discuss student work; and ongoing support to help teachers develop their skill with the instructional approach. When we speak of OGAP as an ambitious instructional reform, this palette of knowledge, tools, processes, and supports is to what we refer. There are also important equity implications for this approach to teaching and learning. Grouping and reteaching strategies that clump together students with different levels of understanding (i.e., those who "didn't get it") are oblivious to the gradations of understanding within the group and therefore are less likely to increase the understanding of the range of students if they are each not brought forward from their current levels. It's too easy for marginalized kids to get lost in these groups.

First, the "good news," which is what OGAP trainers encourage teachers to first look for when examining student work. What did this project accomplish? The impacts of OGAP on teachers and students were consistently and significantly positive across different groups of schools, across grade levels, over time, and across renditions of the reform. The results presented in chapter 4 show that teachers trained in OGAP had persistently higher knowledge of formative assessment practices compared to teachers in schools that did not use OGAP and that they retained this knowledge over time. We also found that the students of teachers trained in OGAP's approach both scored higher and had more advanced solution strategies on a program-aligned assessment compared to peers taught by teachers who had not received OGAP training. Finally, we examined student performance on the Pennsylvania state assessment. Again, we found that the students of OGAP teachers scored significantly higher on the state test in most grade levels than did comparable students in schools not using OGAP. These results are particularly important for policymakers who are focused on improving student performance on their state examination. Across the five years of the project, we estimate that OGAP worked with about 1,000 teachers in grades K–8, and those teachers taught about 20,000 students. The program had scaled from its initial focus on grades 3–5 in 30 schools to working with all grades K–8 teachers in up to 40 schools a year, ultimately reaching 145 of the district's 163 elementary schools.

The program refinements the project team made over the five years undoubtedly contributed to these consistent impacts on teachers and students. The ongoing efforts to improve upon the elements of the reform to fit the particular context of the School District of Philadelphia (SDP) produced a series of enhancements to the design of the professional development experience and surrounding supports that augmented implementation and produced the strong evidence of teacher and student impacts. As Janine Remillard documented in the overview of OGAP in Philadelphia in chapter 3, the project tackled the challenge of continuous improvement by "tinkering" with changes. Using what she described as a design-based implementation research approach, the project formed the Philadelphia Mathematics Leadership Collaborative (PMLC) in 2016–2017—which was a partnership of the OGAP providers, the research team, and SDP leaders—to collaboratively plan adjustments and enhancements to OGAP delivery and support. These efforts produced a series of refinements that helped to improve the delivery of OGAP and supports. These included:

- •. Working with the district to have each school identify and position a math lead to be the liaison to OGAP, to support teachers' implementation, and to provide specific and ongoing training for these educators.
- Locating ongoing support in schools rather than at a central location. By bringing support closer to the classrooms and customizing training, OGAP was able to work with teachers in greater alignment with their learning needs. This approach is also consistent with OGAP's developmental philosophy of teaching children.
- Adding regular professional development sessions for school leaders and math leads to gain buy-in and better support for OGAP implementation. These quarterly sessions taught school leaders about OGAP's philosophy (a "formative mindset"), what to look for in classrooms when conducting visits/observations and how to talk to teachers and students about their work, and the importance of protecting regular grade-level teacher meeting time for teachers to bring, examine, and sort student work, to locate student solutions on the OGAP progressions, and to plan instructional next steps.
- Expanding to a whole-school math program once it became clear that supporting OGAP only in grades 3–5 was challenging to school leaders. This included developing OGAP frameworks and item banks

for grades K–2 and moving to a K–8 model to help schools more seamlessly support OGAP implementation.
- Building a bridge to the curriculum to make OGAP uptake easier. OGAP touted its ability to work with any curriculum, which gave it the advantage of not being tied to any curricular program, but the disadvantage was that it forced teachers to make the connections. Based on teacher feedback, the PMLC developed a series of curricular connections that allowed teachers to practice OGAP's formative assessment approach with the first activity of most chapters in the district's dominant mathematics curriculum.
- Working with the district's math director to align OGAP with the district's mathematics frameworks.
- Working with the district to allow teachers to use OGAP data to fulfill a district requirement that asked teachers to provide classroom-based evidence of their students' learning.

Despite these accomplishments, keeping things moving forward proved difficult. Perhaps the biggest challenge was maintaining a strong connection to district leadership. As Remillard pointed out in chapter 3, the project made a conscious choice to focus efforts on improving the experience in classrooms and schools, where instruction occurs and student learning is most influenced. To use a metaphor from education historian Larry Cuban, school systems are like hurricanes over the ocean—turbulent on the surface, but calm underneath.[6] Our experience was similar: from a program implementation perspective, there was more regularity in the schools than at the central office. This may have contributed to the difficulty we had in retaining district attention and support amid turnover at the central office. When our champions in the academics office left, we did not have the same visibility and broad base of support. This experience raised a dilemma for our work: by focusing so much attention on the locus of instructional improvement—classrooms and schools—we did not build enough capital to withstand turnover in the central office.

A retrospectively critical decision was to have OGAP funded as a subcontract to Carnegie Learning rather than directly with the district. The district's director of professional development wanted one provider to support math across all 160+ K–8 schools, and OGAP did not have the inclination or capacity. Based on the district's preferences, Carnegie summer training and ongoing school support were relatively generic math support. The original plan was for OGAP to train Carnegie Learning coaches to support OGAP teachers, but it quickly became apparent that this model was not going to be sufficient. This was the impetus for PMLC deciding to provide its own ongoing support to schools. Without realizing it, PMLC's support effort contradicted its goal to integrate with district supports, and unwittingly, OGAP had tied its success to that of the larger provider.

Thus, in 2018 when the SDP was reviewing the impacts of Carnegie Learning's work on students—looking for the black swan—they did not find evidence of improvements in math outcomes and concluded that the approach was not effective. As a subcontract to Carnegie Learning, OGAP was painted with the same brush. As we knew that the grant support was ending, we marshalled a campaign to raise awareness of the effectiveness of OGAP on teachers and student learning. We created an accessible brief that highlighted the number of teachers and students served by OGAP between 2014 and 2018, summarized the impacts of OGAP on student state test results, and included testimonials from teachers and principals in the district. We created a mailing list of district leaders (superintendent, chief academic officer, deputy chief of teaching and learning), school board members, members of the curriculum office, office of research and evaluation, and regional superintendents and sent electronic and hard copies to each. We met with district leaders to discuss the results and enlisted supportive teachers and principals to advocate for OGAP to their regional superintendents and other district colleagues. Alas, these efforts we not enough, and the district decided to work with teachers to create their own math framework, curriculum, and associated professional development which, after several years, was also scrapped, and the district is now rolling out yet another math curriculum.

Based upon the impact data and the testimonials of teachers and school leaders, there was a strong case to be made that here is a reform that is working—a program that should be nurtured and developed. Yet our focus on building instructional capacity in schools—where student learning lies—did not translate into influence in the district—where power perches. In this way, the black swan can be seen as a metaphor for the frailty of research evidence within the context of policymaking. On the one hand, policy makers are perpetually seeking evidence in the form of test score improvements because it validates confidence in the regimes and plans of leaders. But the evidence is not an end in itself; it is a means by which leaders justify (not test) their work. Evidence is just as easily glossed over or ignored if it doesn't align with the larger plans. This also extends to the relative rigor of different forms of evidence, which is lost in environments where the distinctions are not understood by decision makers. In the district policy world, descriptive trends can be more influential than carefully constructed causal research if they fit the narrative of decision makers and confirm motivated reasoning. This is because the evidence is not an end in itself; it is only valued insofar as it is a means to validate the improvement efforts of leaders. If there is no policy champion for the work that produced the evidence, then it will carry little sway regardless of its strength. For professional researchers who devote themselves to all the minutiae of evidentiary quality, this is a frustrating reality. In this case, the evidence was discounted because it was nested within the generic support the district contracted for and did not fit into the larger plans of the district.

This rebuff was somewhat ironic, because five years earlier OGAP did not start with the goal of spreading to all math classrooms across the district. Initially, the program focused on validating its hard-earned beliefs about the value of OGAP to produce strong (i.e., experimental) evidence that the program was effective. But after just one year of promising results, where the district looked at progress on the benchmark assessments in OGAP schools compared to other schools, the district opted to incorporate OGAP into its summer offerings for all schools. Our work with OGAP then shifted from a classic external research study to a program-research-practice partnership focusing on system connections and using data and observations to continuously strengthen the experience for teachers. This led to a more robust program with evolving ideas about how to support teachers after initial training—delivered at schools rather than centrally, customized to meet the needs of teachers in their own contexts, and recognizing that teacher mastery—like student fluency—takes time, practice, and ongoing support to accrue.

So, in concert with our shifting goals to scale up OGAP to more schools, we increasingly focused on the things that were needed at both the school and district levels to support strong implementation. Our focus on supporting instructional improvement made us highly attuned to OGAP's formative assessment philosophy, and we began to notice many ways that the developmental learning theory underlying OGAP was inconsistent with the systems and practices that were entrenched in the school system.

***

The prevailing view of school districts is that they have evolved and operate from a tradition that makes them prioritize efficiency and accountability more than instructional improvement. The historical evolution of the school district is the transition of locally run small systems to those of professional organizations that emphasize efficiency, routines, and standardized procedures.[7] Districts now tend to operate as bureaucratic systems, characterized by a top-down hierarchy of authority, clear divisions of labor, explicit rules and procedures, and both process- and outcome-based accountability.[8] In such systems, the designs for local activity are formulated at the top, with multiple structures and checks for faithful implementation, and too much deviation from the design is discouraged. Elements such as pacing guides and interim assessments are enacted as much as tools for monitoring as they are for support.

A primary characteristic of bureaucratic systems is a focus on performance. Education systems in particular revolve around a single measure of performance—annual state test results—as the dominant indicator of effectiveness. Taking cues from the top and rippling down through the system, much energy is devoted to improving and/or maintaining strong test score outcomes. This captures one of the major themes of this book: the "reality" within which instructional reforms enter is the powerful emphasis on performance that orients much of the activity in the system, and the pressure to achieve performance crowds out attention to the learning processes that produce performance. This performance orientation has also become imbued in the systems that are set up to "support" teaching. Yet this glosses over the fundamental fact that the processes that teachers use to develop the thinking of students that will ultimately produce performance is fundamentally different than the performance itself. It then follows that *systems designed to provide feedback to inform learning are necessarily different than systems that provide feedback on performance*. Moreover, both the systems and the leaders' words and actions to support the systems also convey messages about how learning occurs.

When we began to look more deeply at the degree to which the systems to support instruction reflected a learning orientation or a performance orientation, the distinction began to come into focus. The difference between learning and performance and its consequences are examined in several chapters of this book. In chapter 6, Ebby and D'Olier investigated teacher orientations toward formative assessment and related instructional decision-making. They looked at the extent to which teachers took a learning or performance orientation in their descriptions of the purpose of formative assessment and their examination of student work. They defined a performance orientation as teachers' emphasis on where student performance should be, where the solution of student work was the primary indicator of student understanding. By contrast they described a learning orientation as an emphasis on illuminating student thinking and that examining student work was a way for teachers to understand the approaches that students used to solve problems as a means to gain more insight into how to move students forward. They found that, even after participating in OGAP summer training, about 40 percent of the thirty-two teachers they studied had a performance orientation in the way they discussed their formative assessment practices. Further, when they asked teachers to make sense of their students' work, they found that over half of the teachers used a performance orientation to sort their student's work based on correctness rather than the sophistication of their solution approach. These findings suggest that a performance orientation is deeply ingrained in the professional understanding of a substantial proportion of teachers.

It's not particularly surprising that teachers would hold on to a performance orientation, even after their OGAP professional development, given what psychologist Robert Evans calls the "impulse towards conservativism" that creates headwinds for programs that seek to change the ways teachers teach, which includes the ways that people integrate new ideas into their existing belief systems as they try to make sense of different approaches.[9] This conservativism is sometimes misinterpreted as resistance to change but is really a coping mechanism to help teachers survive the constant cycling through of reform ideas. Another element underlying expectations for change is the steady work required to change teaching practice amid the current demands of actually teaching. As we saw in chapter 5, the first year of an instructional reform is often taken up just by grappling with the new ideas in the classroom and putting into place different kinds of school supports. This raises the question of whether a single year of training and support is sufficient to bring about durable changes in teaching practice.

When we paid attention, we also began to see that a performance orientation permeated the district's approach to professional development for teachers as well. The district director of professional development's theory of teacher learning was represented by his use of the "medical model" to describe teacher professional learning. From the perspective of the medical model, teacher training was a "treatment" and follow-up support was a "booster shot." In this paradigm, once teachers received training, they were "treated." But the medical model is a fundamentally flawed way to conceptualize teacher learning. Participating in professional development is not like taking a pill, and follow-up support is not like a booster shot. This metaphor leads to a performance orientation of "treating" people with an experience, which carries with it the assumption that once you have been treated, you have incorporated the intervention into your understanding, much like receiving an inoculation. But we know that learning is not a biological process, and we cannot assume that teaching produces learning in the way that taking medicine produces biological effects. District leaders that frame professional development using the medical metaphor risk a host of misconceptions.

To be fair, the district was in an "equity bind" with finite math professional development resources and the need to serve more than 160 elementary schools. Consequently, they designed the Summer Math Institutes to provide all schools with a week of summer math professional development and a year of support, rotating cohorts of about forty schools annually over the four years for which they had funding. Schools volunteered to participate each year, with the expectation that every school would participate over the course of the four years. The finite resources for math professional development fit nicely into the medical model and associated performance orientation.

PMLC had a fundamentally different notion of what was required to change teaching practice. They viewed the first year of professional development as just the initiation of the change process, which took multiple years in which to develop fluency. And as we saw in chapter 5, most schools were just beginning to engage with the reform in year one, and the adjustments of school components, like teacher meetings structured to support OGAP, were the slowest elements to change. PMLC advocated that the district set up a system for OGAP to work with teachers over several years to infuse the formative assessment mindset into the instructional approaches of teachers and to orient school leaders to this way of thinking. Our analysis of school and teacher take-up of OGAP (chapters 5 and 6) validated this assumption, indicating that participants were just beginning to make the shifts toward a learning orientation after the first year, and while we detected significant effects after the first year, there was still ample room for growth.

The second chapter that looked directly at the lack of alignment between the learning orientation of OGAP and the performance orientation of the system was chapter 7, which examined the logic underlying the district's benchmark assessment system. In this chapter we framed the performance-learning distinction as two underlying logics about how learning occurs and how data inform this process. We found that the benchmark system had more attributes of the performance logic than the learning logic, primarily because the data focused on the outcomes of learning rather than the processes that would inform instructional intervention. We saw the advocated uses of grouping students and reteaching based on the benchmark results as weak strategies for targeted instructional response because the information for grouping students would necessarily comingle students with different levels of understanding within groups and not provide for any information to inform what to emphasize when reteaching. In addition, as teachers noted, the data were not timely because, while the results were returned quickly after the assessment, they might represent topics taught several months ago. When we analyzed how teachers, school leaders, and district administrators viewed the purpose and utility of the district's benchmark system, we found that leaders viewed the system as primarily "formative assessment" information, yet teachers viewed it as very limited for instructional purposes and, rather, saw it as primarily a way to monitor teachers and hold them accountable for content coverage. Thus, we concluded that the benchmark assessment system was an example of a district support system with good intentions but that ultimately conveyed a performance orientation rather than a learning orientation.

These examples highlight the distinctions between learning and performance and show how their differences are conflated in the minds of educators and in the systems set up to support instructional improvement. I close this chapter by exploring ways leaders might rethink district systems and supports to emphasize the learning processes necessary to produce performance.

***

There have been longstanding calls for districts to better support instruction in classrooms. One way this has manifested is for districts to take a more customer service–oriented approach, which inverts the traditional hierarchy of their relationship.[10] But even then, it presumes that we understand what *support* means. The distinction between performance and learning can help leaders distinguish between an emphasis on how learning occurs and the outcomes of learning, that is, performance. The work of this book suggests that the capacity to produce performance is found in a learning orientation that focuses on building and supporting teachers' skills to decode their students' thinking and translate it into targeted instructional responses; that teacher understanding—just like student understanding—lies along a developmental continuum that needs to be introduced, supported, reinforced, and grown over time; that the data systems that districts adopt to support teachers should be time-sensitive and provide developmental data and not just outcomes. This requires district leaders to think differently about the experiences, tools, and resources they provide to help teachers better instruct students and school leaders to support teachers in their efforts.

There are several areas that district leaders can rethink to both better support instruction and signal the value of learning vis-à-vis performance. Foremost, this requires reframing and aligning the strategies employed by the organization to support the organizational mission of enhancing learning. Within this broader reset, areas of focus include the system for teacher learning, data systems, and accountability.

ALIGNING STRATEGY TO MISSION

If the mission of school districts is to enhance the students' learning, then it is incumbent upon leaders to align their support strategies and language with this mission. Looking from the classroom up, one of the lessons from this book is that the misalignment between learning processes and performance outcomes reduces coherence in the system and sends mixed messages to educators throughout the system. Shifting the way central office leaders frame their vision to prioritize learning is the first step in reorienting the mental models that underlie their vision.

A learning orientation requires leaders to be explicit about how they believe learning occurs and then to align system strategies to best support teachers and schools to enhance learning. They might ask, How can we best support teachers and school leaders to focus on learning processes rather than performance outcomes? How do we construct the elements of the system to support learning? What elements of the system send inconsistent messages that tacitly signal an undue emphasis on performance? How do we speak about the objectives for district success, and in what ways do we embed the different orientations into the messages we convey, the systems we develop, and the expectations we have? How do our language and other actions signal our belief about how to enhance learning in classrooms? Grappling with these questions may require a strategic realignment of the operational systems and processes to fit with the organization's mission and objectives. A shift to focus on learning processes might lead leaders to think differently about professional learning systems for teachers. It might lead leaders to think differently about the data systems they construct. It might lead to thinking differently about how time is allocated in schools and what teacher collaboration looks like. It might even lead to different ways of thinking about elements of the accountability system.

A learning orientation also requires leaders to create ways to signal their emphasis on learning. One of the reasons we hypothesized that teacher change was so challenging is that the longstanding emphasis on outcomes has taught teachers to adopt this as an instructional approach, with all its attendant limitations. While structures like professional development and data systems are central to this task, there is a more subtle underlying shift in the way leaders frame their messages to educators that both acknowledges the distinctions between learning processes and performance outcomes and also identifies and addresses inconsistencies in the system.

Perspectives and incentives are the two important concepts for leaders to consider. Everyone in an organization has their own perspective from their positionality and is responding to incentives embedded within the organizational culture. One way to interpret the differential attention to learning and performance in education systems is that the teachers and leaders are operating under different incentive structures. Leaders are incentivized by performance, and teachers are conflicted by the pass-through focus on performance and the learning processes they realize are at the core of their work. This leads people in different positions to see the same problems very differently and consequently to propose different solutions. Learning from teachers and trying to see the value of supports from their perspective can help leaders learn more about what it takes to enhance learning and ultimately produce higher levels of performance.

RETHINKING THE SYSTEM OF TEACHER LEARNING

This study also revealed a misalignment between the design of professional development delivery systems and contemporary understandings of how people learn. If learning was a relatively simple transmission process, then a summer session and a series of light follow-ups would be sufficient to change teacher practice, but there is abundant evidence pointing to the challenges of identifying impactful teacher professional development approaches to dissuade us of this notion.

There are at least three refinements to professional development systems that emerge from this study. First, professional development for teachers should be differentiated to align to where teachers are in their own development. Teachers, like all learners, come to professional development in different places and need different experiences and supports. Some teachers are currently very distant from a desired practice, while others are using some elements and not others, and others are already doing most of what is hoped for.[11] This differentiated approach reflects the way that the project provided ongoing support to teachers that was often different by schools and even grade levels of teachers. In this case, we found that schools needed different things: some schools needed more modeling of OGAP's form of teacher meetings; others needed stronger understanding of the OGAP frameworks and progressions; others needed modeling of lessons based on the findings from teacher meetings. Sometimes trainers did different activities for different grade levels within a school. By differentiating teacher professional development aligned to teacher needs, leaders can increase the likelihood that all teachers will enhance their teaching skills.

Second, leaders need to acknowledge that changing instruction takes time and repeated practice. Having teachers participate in professional development does not ensure that they will take up what is taught, and follow-up training does not necessarily increase the likelihood of change.

What we learned from our experience is that teacher learning, like student learning, requires time and repeated practice. If we apply the same expectations for teacher learning as we do for student learning, then we have to expect that teacher adoption of new practices will require ongoing efforts to master and incorporate effective approaches into teachers' repertoires.

Third, for supports to be contextualized, there will likely need to be adjustments to both the reform and the context. The context of every district and school is different. Regardless of whether a district builds its own professional development or "buys" it from an external provider, there will likely need to be adjustments to both the reform and the context to make it more effective. In this experience, OGAP made several design adjustments to strengthen the experience. For example, they brought follow-up training to the school sites rather than delivering it at a central location, which allowed for both more accessibility for teachers and more customization of the experience to meet the needs of the particular set of teachers; and they built connections to the adopted curriculum, which allowed teachers to practice and become more fluent with the formative assessment approach. There were adjustments needed in the school context too. For example, we found that the structure of teacher meetings in many schools did not readily adapt to OGAPs approach and that schools' math leads and principals had to adjust school schedules to adapt to them. Further, we found that while the program was focused on math instruction, helping principals understand the mindset behind formative assessment helped them to understand what to look for in math classes and to better support teacher implementation. This lesson of "mutual adaptation," or a willingness to flexibly adjust both the program design and the context, is likely to produce the deepest implementation and strongest results.[12]

FORMATIVE DATA SYSTEMS

If district leaders truly seek to provide formative feedback to teachers, they must rethink the data systems intended to support teachers. The takeaways from our analysis of the district benchmark system led to the conclusion that, from the teacher perspective, the system was more for accountability than it was to provide useful feedback for teachers to guide instruction. While it is beyond the scope of this chapter to design a data system to give teachers formative feedback on student learning, there are some key tenets to start thinking about. First, the system needs to provide feedback on student thinking rather than solely performance. As we found in our examination of the district's benchmark system, performance data provide teachers with little actionable information to inform instruction. It is in the student's thinking process that teachers can leverage that knowledge to bring student understanding forward. Second, the feedback needs to be more timely. The shelf life of instructionally useful information is relatively short, as teachers must match its application to students' current developmental thinking.

Technology offers some exciting prospects to address these shortcomings. The benchmark systems have developed to the point where students can take a test online and teachers can get the results immediately. Several test construction techniques could be used to move the assessment results from performance data to learning data. For example, multiple-choice items can be constructed to embed different developmental solution approaches and misconceptions into the response options, which can provide more information about student thinking than just getting an answer correct or incorrect. Additionally, large language-processing techniques can allow for the analysis of open-ended responses. Some of these ideas are likely to be beyond the scope of districts, and more appropriate for technology entrepreneurs, but hold promise to provide learning-oriented feedback.

While technological solutions can be beguiling, it is important to caution that these techniques should not replace building the capacity of teachers to analyze student work. The practice of critically analyzing student thinking processes that are represented by their work products and translating these insights into targeted instructional responses is a core practice of teaching that cannot be replaced. The craft of cyclical formative assessment to enhance learning demands a more skilled teaching force than rote practice.

Finally, but no less important, are the signals that districts send to teachers about learning via the way they construct their data systems. In our work we found that the benchmark system conveyed a performance way of thinking to teachers about how learning occurs that is in many ways antithetical to their job to foster learning in their students.

ACCOUNTABILITY

Lastly, there are important implications of a shift toward a learning orientation for accountability. The tradition of accountability is to focus on performance data, but the lessons from this book suggest that placing too high a priority on performance leads to reduced attention to learning and the mistaken notion that performance can be produced by focusing primarily on performance outcomes rather than learning processes. So how can we recalibrate accountability approaches to value learning and not just its product? We know much about the reifying dynamic of the relationship between a performance orientation and accountability,[13] but what does accountability look like from a learning orientation?

The press of accountability comes from many places. It comes from within ourselves, from our colleagues, and from external pressures.[14] The dynamics of these different locations can be reinforcing or counterbalancing. This suggests at least two avenues for infusing learning into local accountability: measures and messages.

First, we can pay more attention to the measures themselves. Designing assessments where the results can be decomposed into both correctness and solution strategies, as we did in the Learning Trajectory Assessment, as discussed in chapter 4 and the previous section on formative data systems, is one model of how to do this. On external assessments, the increasing emphasis on growth measures rather than single data points reflects a nudge toward a learning orientation in that it focuses on *change* in student understanding rather than at a single point in time. But even when assessing growth, the measures themselves are still opaque. The receptivity in many states toward local flexibility to include a broader array of measures beyond student outcomes is potentially another step toward a better balance between learning data and performance data.

Second, and perhaps even more impactful on a day-to-day basis, are the messages conveyed by leaders across the system and how they choose to talk about their priorities and construct various supports to enact their preferences. If leaders focus predominantly on performance in their communications and systems, then they signal their belief that learning occurs largely through behavioral means. By contrast, when leaders focus their attention on more contemporary understandings of how learning developmentally progresses, then educators internalize these messages, which, in turn, influences their own priorities and attention. The extent to which leaders emphasize the developmental learning processes of both adults and students comes across in myriad ways. They signal their predilections in such areas as the way they train district administrators and school leaders to support teaching and learning, how they build supports for learners at all levels, what they focus attention on in meetings and school and classroom observations, and even what accomplishments they choose to celebrate. In big ways and small, the messages of authority figures are a powerful form of accountability.

***

On the very first page of this book, I set up the contrast between two data meetings. One was district leaders looking at state test performance and wondering how all their work and efforts across the year to support schools and students through a variety of means were translating into student performance. The second data meeting was teachers in a professional learning community session examining student work samples and using the patterns and insights into student thinking processes to shape subsequent instructional next steps. I wondered how these two meetings were similar and different, and if the teacher meeting could have any impact on the large-scale trends that the district leaders were poring over. It turns out that these two forms of data—annual systemwide test results that are designed to summarize the entire year of learning and single-day classroom-contextualized data on student thinking—perfectly capture the contrast between performance and learning that represents one of the central dilemmas we have examined in this book. While on the surface they are both vignettes about adults examining student data, their purposes couldn't be more different. The different orientations reflected in both the form and purpose of the two sources of data and what the adults are looking for in them, capture the distinction between the performance orientation of leaders and district support systems and the learning orientation that can help teachers improve the students' learning. Attending to and synthesizing the inherent contradictions between learning and performance orientations in education systems holds important insights to successfully scale up instructional reforms.

Notes

Chapter 1

1. While white swans were well known in Europe up to the seventeenth century, black swans were thought to be nonexistent. The "discovery" of black swans by Europeans in Australia in 1697 led to the popularization of the metaphor that black swans represented rare, almost mythical occurrences.
2. Eric A. Hanushek, "The Impact of Differential Expenditures on School Performance," *Educational Researcher* 18, no. 4 (1989): 45–62.
3. Richard J. Murnane, "Interpreting the Evidence on Does Money Matter," *Harvard Journal on Legislation* 28 (1991): 457–64; David K. Cohen, Stephen W. Raudenbush, and Deborah Lowenberg Ball, "Resources, Instruction, and Research," *Educational Evaluation and Policy Analysis* 25, no. 2 (2003): 119–42; C. Kirabo Jackson, Rucker C. Johnson, and Claudia Persico, "The Effects of School Spending on Educational and Economic Outcomes: Evidence from School Finance Reforms," *National Bureau of Economic Research [NBER] Working Papers*, no. w20847 (2015).
4. Alfred Lubrano, "Among the 10 Largest Cities, Philly Has Highest Deep-Poverty Rate," *Philadelphia Inquirer*, September 30, 2015.
5. "A School Funding Formula for Philadelphia: Lessons from Urban Districts Across the United States," Pew Charitable Trust, 2015, https://www.pewtrusts.org/-/media/assets/2015/01/philadelphiaschoolfundingreportjanuary2015.pdf.
6. Kristen Graham, "Phila. School's Latest Budget Forecasts $80 Million Deficit," *Philadelphia Inquirer*, February 9, 2015.
7. Richard Elmore, "Getting to Scale with Good Educational Practice," *Harvard Educational Review* 66, no. 1 (1996): 1–27; Frederick M. Hess, *Spinning Wheels: The Politics of Urban School Reform* (Washington, DC: Brookings Institution Press, 1998).
8. The authors of chapters in this book use the terms *trajectory* and *progression* synonymously, and we do not distinguish between them.
9. D. Royce Sadler, "Formative Assessment and the Design of Instructional Systems," *Instructional Science* 18 (1989): 120.
10. Arkalgud Ramaprasad, "On the Definition of Feedback," *Behavioral Science* 28, no. 1 (1983): 4–13; Sadler, "Formative assessment," 120.

11. Ramaprasad, "On the Definition," 4.
12. Paul Black and Dylan Wiliam (1998). "Assessment and Classroom Learning," *Assessment in Education: Principles, Policy & Practice* 5, no. 1: 7–74.
13. Avraham N. Kluger and Angelo DeNisi, "The Effects of Feedback Interventions on Performance: A Historical Review, a Meta-analysis, and a Preliminary Feedback Intervention Theory," *Psychological Bulletin* 119, no. 2 (1996): 255.
14. Robert L. Bangert-Drowns et al., "The Instructional Effect of Feedback in Test-Like Events," *Review of Educational Research* 61, no. 2 (1991): 213–38.
15. *Taking Science to School: Learning and Teaching Science in Grades K-8* (Washington, DC: National Academies Press, National Research Council, 2007): 14.
16. Jere Confrey et al., "Equipartitioning/Splitting as a Foundation of Rational Number Reasoning Using Learning Trajectories," in *Proceedings of the 33rd Conference of the International Group for the Psychology of Mathematics Education*, ed. J. Novotna et al. (Thessaloniki, Greece: Psychology of Mathematics Education, 2009); Bruce Sherin and Karen Fuson, "Multiplication Strategies and the Appropriation of Computational Resources," *Journal for Research in Mathematics Education* 36, no. 4 (2005): 347–95; Catherine Ulrich, "Stages in Coordinating Units Additively and Multiplicatively (Part 1)," *For the Learning of Mathematics* 35, no 3 (2015): 2–7; Catherine Ulrich, "Stages in Coordinating Units Additively and Multiplicatively (Part 2)," *For the Learning of Mathematics* 36, no. 1 (2016): 34–39.
17. Vicky L. Kouba and Kathy Franklin, "Research into Practice: Multiplication and Division: Sense Making and Meaning" *Teaching Children Mathematics* 1, no. 9 (1995): 574–77.
18. B. Greer, "Multiplication and Division as Models of Situations," in *Handbook of Research on Mathematics Teaching and Learning*, ed. Douglas A. Grouws (Reston, VA: National Council of Teachers of Mathematics, 1992): 276–95.
19. P. Holt Wilson, Gemma F. Mojica, and Jere Confrey, "Learning Trajectories in Teacher Education: Supporting Teachers' Understandings of Students' Mathematical Thinking," *Journal of Mathematical Behavior* 32, no. 2 (2013): 103–21; Douglas H. Clements and Julie Sarama, *Building Blocks*, vols. 1–2 (Columbus, OH: McGraw-Hill Education, 2013).
20. Douglas H. Clements et al., "Mathematics Learned by Young Children in an Intervention Based on Learning Trajectories: A Large-Scale Cluster Randomized Trial," *Journal for Research in Mathematics Education* 42, no. 2 (2011):127–66; Douglas H. Clements et al., "Longitudinal Evaluation of a Scale-up Model for Teaching Mathematics with Trajectories and Technologies: Persistence of Effects in the Third Year," *American Educational Research Journal* 50, no. 4 (2013): 812–50.
21. Jonathan A. Supovitz, "Implementation as Iterative Refraction," in *The Implementation Gap: Understanding Reform in High Schools*, ed. Jonathan A. Supovitz and Elliot H. Weinbaum (New York: Teachers College Press, 2008).
22. Barry J. Fishman et al., "Design-Based Implementation Research: An Emerging Model for Transforming the Relationship of Research and Practice," *Teachers College Record* 115, no. 14 (2013): 136–56.
23. John D. Bransford, A. L. Brown, and R. R. Cocking, *How People Learn*, vol. 11 (Washington, DC: National Academy Press, 2000).
24. Na'ilah Suad Nasir et al., "Rethinking Learning: What the Interdisciplinary Science Tells Us," *Educational Researcher* 50, no. 8 (2021): 557–65.

25. Jal Mehta and Sarah Fine, *In Search of Deeper Learning: The Quest to Remake the American High School* (Cambridge, MA: Harvard University Press, 2019).
26. Linda Darling-Hammond, Maria E. Hyler, and Madelyn Gardner, *Effective Teacher Professional Development* (Palo Alto, CA: Learning Policy Institute, 2017).

Chapter 2

1. Paul Black et al., "Working Inside the Black Box: Assessment for Learning in the Classroom," *Phi Delta Kappan* 86, no. 1 (2004): 8–21.
2. Jeremy Kilpatrick, Jane Swan, and Bradford Findell, eds., *Adding It Up: How Children Learn Mathematics* (Washington, DC: National Academy Press, 2001).
3. The Vermont Math Partnership was funded by grants from the National Science Foundation (EHR-0227057) and US Department of Education (S366A20002).
4. *Assessment in Support of Student Learning: Bridging the Gap Between Large-scale and Classroom Assessment* (Washington, DC: National Academy Press, 2003); John Bransford, Ann Brown, and Rodney Cocking, eds., *How People Learn: Brain, Mind, Experience, and School* (Washington, DC: National Academy Press, 2001); James Pelligrino, Naomi Chudowsky, and Robert Glaser, eds., *Knowing What Students Know: The Science and Design of Educational Assessment* (Washington, DC: National Academy Press, 2000).
5. National Council of Teachers of Mathematics (NCTM), *Principles and Standards for School Mathematics* (Reston, VA: National Council of Teachers of Mathematics, 2000).
6. Caroline Ebby, Elizabeth Hulbert, and Rachel Broadhead, *A Focus on Addition and Subtraction: Bringing Research to the Classroom* (New York: Routledge, 2021).
7. Elizabeth Hulbert et al., *A Focus on Multiplication and Division: Bringing Research to the Classroom* (New York: Routledge, 2017).
8. Marjorie Petit et al., *A Focus on Fractions: Bringing Research to the Classroom*, 2nd ed. (New York: Routledge, 2015).
9. Marjorie Petit et al., *A Focus on Ratios and Proportions: Bringing Mathematics Education Research to the Classroom* (New York: Routledge, 2020).
10. Martin A. Simon, "Reconstructing Mathematics Pedagogy from a Constructivist Perspective," *Journal for Research in Mathematics Education* 26, no. 2 (1995): 114–45.
11. National Assessment Governing Board, *NAEP 2009 Science Framework* (ED-04-CO-0148), Washington, DC, September 2008, https://www.nagb.gov/content/dam/nagb/en/documents/publications/frameworks/science/2009-science-framework.pdf
12. Amy B. Ellis, Eric Weber, and Elise Lockwood, "The Case for Learning Trajectories Research," paper presented at the Joint Meeting of the International Group for the Psychology of Mathematics Education (PME) and the North American Chapter of the Psychology of Mathematics Education (PME-NA), Vancouver, Canada, July 15–20, 2014.
13. Joanne Lobato and C. David Walters, "A Taxonomy of Approaches to Learning Trajectories and Progressions," in *Compendium for Research in Mathematics Education*, ed. Jinfa Cai (Reston, VA: National Council of Teachers of Mathematics, 2017): 74–101.
14. Hulbert et al., *A Focus on Multiplication*.
15. Petit et al., *A Focus on Ratios*.

16. Kathleen A. Cramer, T. Post, and S. Currier, "Learning and Teaching Ratio and Proportion: Research Implications," in *Research Ideas for the Classroom: Middle Grades Mathematics*, ed. Douglas T. Owens (New York: Macmillan, 1993): 159–78; Edward Silver, OGAP National Advisory Meeting, Montpelier, VT, 2006.
17. Petit et al., *A Focus on Ratios*.
18. Dylan Wiliam, "What Is Assessment for Learning?," *Studies in Educational Evaluation* 37, no. 1 (2011): 3–14.

Chapter 3

1. David Tyack and Larry Cuban, *Tinkering Toward Utopia* (Cambridge, MA: Harvard University Press, 1995), 60.
2. William R. Penuel et al., "Organizing Research and Development at the Intersection of Learning, Implementation, and Design," *Educational Researcher* 40, no. 7 (2011): 331–37; Paul Cobb et al., *Systems for Instructional Improvement: Creating Coherence from the Classroom to the District Office* (Cambridge, MA: Harvard Education Press, 2018); Mary Kay Stein and Cynthia E. Coburn, "Architectures for Learning: A Comparative Analysis of Two Urban School Districts," *American Journal of Education* 114, no 4. (2008): 583–626.
3. Penuel et al., "Organizing Research and Development."
4. Penuel et al., 331.
5. Penuel et al., 332.
6. Cobb et al., *Systems for Instructional Improvement*.
7. Cynthia E. Coburn and Jennifer Lin Russell, "District Policy and Teachers' Social Networks," *Educational Evaluation and Policy Analysis* 30, no. 3 (2008): 203–35; Meredith I. Honig, "District Central Office Leadership as Teaching: How Central Office Administrators Support Principals' Development as Instructional Leaders," *Educational Administration Quarterly* 48, no. 4 (2012): 733–74.
8. Cobb et al., *Systems for Instructional Improvement*; Donald Peurach et. al., "From Mass Schooling to Education Systems: Changing Patterns in the Organization and Management of Instruction," *Review of Research in Education* 43, no. 1 (2019): 32–67.
9. Cobb et al., *Systems for Instructional Improvement*.
10. Meredith I. Honig and Lydia R. Rainey, *How School Districts Can Support Deeper Learning: The Need for Performance Alignment*, Deeper Learning Research Series (Boston: Jobs for the Future, 2015); Kenneth Leithwood, Characteristics of School Districts That Are Exceptionally Effective in Closing the Achievement Gap," *Leadership and Policy in Schools* 9, no. 3 (2010): 245–91.
11. Stein and Coburn, "Architectures for Learning."
12. David K. Cohen, Stephen W. Raudenbush, and Deborah Loewenberg Ball, "Resources, Instruction, and Research," *Educational Evaluation and Policy Analysis* 25, no. 2 (2003): 119–42; Mary M. Kennedy, "How Does Professional Development Improve Teaching?," *Review of Educational Research* 86, no. 4 (2016): 945–80.
13. Stein and Coburn, "Architectures for Learning," 584.
14. Caroline B. Ebby, Elizabeth T. Hulbert, and Rachel M. Broadhead, *A Focus on Addition and Subtraction: Bringing Mathematics Education Research to the Classroom* (New York: Routledge, 2021).

15. Although some schools dropped out over the three years of PMLC, the majority remained in the project, with a total of twenty-nine schools in the final year.
16. Cobb et al., *Systems for Instructional Improvement*.
17. Stein and Coburn, "Architectures for Learning."
18. Cobb et al., *Systems for Instructional Improvement*, 28.
19. Stein and Coburn, "Architectures for Learning."
20. Cobb et al., *Systems for Instructional Improvement*.
21. Stein and Coburn, "Architectures for Learning."
22. Stein and Coburn.
23. Penuel et al., "Organizing Research and Development."
24. Cobb et al., *Systems for Instructional Improvement*.
25. Stein and Coburn, "Architectures for Learning."
26. Responsive Math Teaching Project (RMT), "A Model for Developing Sustainable Math Instructional Leadership," CPRE Working Papers, April 2021, https://repository.upenn.edu/cpre_workingpapers/24.
27. Cobb et al., *Systems for Instructional Improvement*; Stein and Coburn, "Architectures for Learning."
28. David Cohen and Jal Mehta, "Why Reform Sometimes Succeeds: Understanding the Conditions That Produce Reforms That Last," *American Educational Research Journal* 54, no. 4 (2017): 644–90.
29. Cobb et al., *Systems for Instructional Improvement*.

Chapter 4
1. In 2019, only a sample of OGAP teachers were given the OGAP survey, which included the TASK.
2. In a few cases, we used the prior year's postadministration as the baseline for the next year.
3. For more details, see chapter 3. Teachers in these schools still had general mathematics support from Carnegie Learning and received biweekly OGAP Teacher Tips via email.
4. The response rates were considerably lower for this analysis, ranging from 62 percent for the treatment group and 26 percent for the comparison group.
5. For more details on the development of the LTA, see Jonathan A. Supovitz et al., "Experimental Impacts of Learning Trajectory–Oriented Formative Assessment on Student Problem-Solving Accuracy and Strategy Sophistication," *Journal for Research in Mathematics Education* 52, no. 4 (2021): 444–75.
6. "Mathematics Resources," Pennsylvania Department of Education," https://www.education.pa.gov/K-12/Assessment%20and%20Accountability/PSSA/Pages/Mathematics.aspx.

Chapter 5
1. Math lead teachers in K–8 schools tended to choose the Carnegie option, since it covered more grades that they were responsible for, while leaders from K–4 or K–5 schools chose either the OGAP or Carnegie options, often based on the grades in which they were teaching.
2. School-based teacher leaders (SBTLs) are teachers who support their peers across subjects, as opposed to math leads, who concentrate on mathematics.
3. One small middle school did not have a designated math lead.

Chapter 6

1. Mary M. Kennedy, "How Does Professional Development Improve Teaching?" *Review of Educational Research* 86, no. 4 (2016): 945–80.
2. David Clarke and Hilary Hollingsworth, "Elaborating a Model of Teacher Professional Growth," *Teaching and Teacher Education* 18, no. 8 (2002): 947–67.
3. Carol S. Dweck, *Mindset: The New Psychology of Success* (New York: Random House, 2006); Carol S. Dweck and Ellen L. Leggett, "A Social-Cognitive Approach to Motivation and Personality," *Psychological Review* 95, no. 2 (1988): 256.
4. Karl E. Weick, *Sensemaking in Organizations* (Thousand Oaks, CA: Sage, 1995).
5. James P. Spillane and David B. Miele, "Evidence in Practice: A Framing of the Terrain," *Teachers College Record* 109, no. 13 (2007): 46–73.
6. Karl E. Weick, Kathleen M. Sutcliffe, and David Obstfeld, "Organizing and the Process of Sensemaking," *Organization Science* 16, no. 4 (2005): 409–21.
7. Spillane and Miele, "Evidence in Practice."
8. Chris Argyris and Donald A. Schön, *Theory in Practice: Increasing Professional Effectiveness* (San Francisco, CA: Jossey-Bass, 1974).
9. Sidney Strauss, "Teachers' Pedagogical Content Knowledge About Children's Minds and Learning: Implications for Teacher Education," *Educational Psychologist* 28, no. 3 (1993): 279–90.
10. Dweck, *Mindset*.
11. Dweck and Leggett, "A Social-Cognitive Approach"; Elaine S. Elliott and Carol S. Dweck, "Goals: An Approach to Motivation and Achievement," *Journal of Personality and Social Psychology* 54, no. 1 (1988): 5.
12. Caroline B. Ebby, Janine Remillard, and Jordan H. D'Olier, "Pathways for Analyzing and Responding to Student Work for Formative Assessment: The Role of Teachers' Goals for Student Learning," CPRE Working Papers, 2019, https://repository.upenn.edu/handle/20.500.14332/8470.
13. This instructional model, sometimes referred to as guided-math, drew heavily from popular approaches to elementary literacy instruction.
14. Elizabeth T. Hulbert et al., *A Focus on Multiplication and Division: Bringing Mathematics Education Research to the Classroom* (New York: Taylor & Francis, 2023), 36.
15. Caroline B. Ebby, Elizabeth T. Hulbert., and Rachel Broadhead, *A Focus on Addition and Subtraction: Bringing Mathematics Education Research to the Classroom* (New York: Taylor & Francis, 2021).
16. Spillane and Miele, "Evidence in Practice."
17. Larry Cuban, *How Teachers Taught: Constancy and Change in American Classrooms, 1890–1980*, 2nd ed. (New York: Teachers College Press, 1993); James P. Spillane, Brian J. Reiser, and Todd Reimer, "Policy Implementation and Cognition: Reframing and Refocusing Implementation Research," *Review of Educational Research* 72, no. 3 (2002): 387–431; Jonathan A. Supovitz, *The Case for District-Based Reform: Leading, Building, and Sustaining School Improvement* (Cambridge, MA: Harvard Education Press, 2006).
18. David K. Cohen, "A Revolution in One Classroom: The Case of Mrs. Oublier," *Educational Evaluation and Policy Analysis* 12, no. 3 (1990): 312.
19. Spillane and Miele, "Evidence in Practice," 52.
20. Chris Argyris and Donald A. Schon, *Theory in Practice: Increasing Professional Effectiveness* (San Francisco, CA: Jossey Bass, 1974); Valerie K. Otero, "Moving Beyond

the 'Get It or Don't' Conception of Formative Assessment," *Journal of Teacher Education* 57, no. 3 (2006): 247–55; Strauss, "Teachers' Pedagogical Content Knowledge."
21. Clarke and Hollingsworth, "Elaborating a Model."

Chapter 7
1. Amanda Datnow and Lea Hubbard, "Teachers' Use of Assessment Data to Inform Instruction: Lessons from the Past and Prospects for the Future," *Teachers College Record* 117, no. 4 (2015): 1–26.
2. Spyros Konstantopoulos et al., "Effects of Interim Assessments on Student Achievement: Evidence from a Large-Scale Experiment," *Journal of Research on Educational Effectiveness* 9, no. 1 (2016): 188–208.
3. Lauren B. Resnick and Megan Williams Hall, "Learning Organizations for Sustainable Education Reform," *Daedalus* 127, no. 4 (1998): 89–118.
4. Jal Mehta and Sarah Fine, *In Search of Deeper Learning: The Quest to Remake the American High School* (Cambridge, MA: Harvard University Press, 2019).
5. Carol S. Dweck and David S. Yeager, "Mindsets: A View from Two Eras," *Perspectives on Psychological Science* 14, no. 3 (2019): 481–96.
6. John D. Bransford, Ann L. Brown, and Rodney R. Cocking, eds., *How People Learn*, vol. 11 (Washington, DC: National Academy Press, 2000).
7. Dweck and Yeager, "Mindsets."
8. "Benchmark 1 Information—November 2017," The School District of Philadelphia, https://www.philasd.org/curriculum/wp-content/uploads/sites/825/2017/10/Benchmark_1_Information_Memo_10-30-17.doc.
9. "School District of Philadelphia: Academic Office Benchmark Data Protocol," The School District of Philadelphia, https://www.philasd.org/curriculum/wp-content/uploads/sites/825/2017/10/Benchmark_Data_Protocol_1.doc.

Chapter 8
1. Paul Berman and Milbrey Wallin McLaughlin, *Federal Programs Supporting Educational Change*, vol. 1, *A Model of Educational Change* (Santa Monica, CA: RAND Corporation, 1974); Russell F. Waugh and Keith F. Punch, "Teacher Receptivity to System-Wide Change," *British Educational Research Journal* 11, no. 2 (1985): 113–21.
2. Berman and McLaughlin, *Federal Programs*, 17.
3. We use the tree name pseudonyms introduced in chapter 5.
4. School leaders encompassed the following individuals: principals, assistant principals, math lead teachers (MLT), and school-based teacher leaders (SBTLs); in some instances, we interviewed teachers individually because of scheduling constraints. At other times, they may have been the only teacher of math for their grade level.
5. Pew Charitable Trust, "Philadelphia's Poor: Experiences from Below the Poverty Line," September 26, 2018, https://www.pewtrusts.org/en/research-and-analysis/reports/2018/09/26/philadelphias-poor-experiences-from-below-the-poverty-line.
6. Abigail Gray et al., "Discipline in Context: Suspension, Climate, and PBIS in the School District of Philadelphia," Research Report no. RR 2017–4, Consortium for Policy Research in Education, University of Pennsylvania, 2017.

Chapter 9

1. Paul Berman and Milbrey W. McLaughlin, *Federal Programs Supporting Educational Change: Volume VIII: Implementing and Sustaining Innovations*, R-1589/8-HEW, RAND, 1978; Charles M. Payne, *So Much Reform, so Little Change: The Persistence of Failure in Urban Schools* (Cambridge, MA: Harvard Education Press, 2008); David Tyack and Larry Cuban, *Tinkering Toward Utopia: A Century of Public School Reform* (Cambridge, MA: Harvard University Press, 1995).
2. We use the same tree pseudonyms that were introduced in chapter 5.
3. Nicole M. Deterding and Mary C. Waters, "Flexible Coding of In-depth Interviews: A 21st Century Approach," *Sociological Methods and Research* 50, no. 2 (2021): 708–39; Herbert J. Rubin and Irene S. Rubin, *Qualitative Interviewing: The Art of Hearing Data*, 3rd ed. (Thousand Oaks, CA: SAGE, 2012); Johnny Saldaña, *The Coding Manual for Qualitative Researchers*, 3rd ed. (Thousand Oaks, CA: SAGE, 2016).
4. See Adrianne Flack et al., "OGAP Implementation in Five Philadelphia K–8 Schools: How Teachers and Leaders Engaged with Customized Implementation Supports," paper prepared for the Annual Meeting of the American Educational Research Association, April 2019.
5. Jill C. Pierce and Jonathan A. Supovitz, *Six Lessons to Facilitate Deep Ownership of Ambitious Instructional Reforms* (Philadelphia: Research for Action, 2020).
6. Flack et al., "OGAP Implementation"; Adrianne Flack et al., "A Report on Persistence: Teachers' Engagements with OGAP Beyond the First Year of Implementation," unpublished manuscript, 2019.
7. Pierce and Supovitz, *Six Lessons*.

Chapter 10

1. Robert Evans, *The Human Side of School Change: Reform, Resistance, and the Real-Life Problems of Innovation* (New York: John Wiley & Sons, 2001); James Hiebert, "The Constantly Underestimated Challenge of Improving Mathematics Instruction," in *Vital Directions for Mathematics Education Research*, ed. Kieth R. Leathman (New York: Springer, 2013), 45–56; David Tyack and William Tobin, "The 'Grammar' of Schooling: Why Has It Been so Hard to Change?" *American Educational Research Journal* 31, no. 3 (1994): 453–79.
2. David K. Cohen and Deborah Loewenberg Ball, "Instruction, Capacity, and Improvement," CPRE Research Report Series no. RR-43, Consortium for Policy Research in Education (1999).
3. Richard Elmore, "Getting to Scale with Good Educational Practice," *Harvard Educational Review* 66, no. 1 (1996): 1.
4. Elmore, "Getting to Scale," 3.
5. John H. Bransford, Ann L. Brown, and Rodney R. Cocking, *How People Learn*, vol. 11 (Washington, DC: National Academy Press, 2000).
6. Larry Cuban, "How Did Teachers Teach, 1890–1980," *Theory into Practice* 22, no. 3 (1983): 159–65.
7. Joel H. Spring, *The American School, 1642–1985: Varieties of Historical Interpretation of the Foundations and Development of American Education* (New York: Longman, 1986).
8. Max Weber, *Economy and Society: An Outline of Interpretive Sociology* (Berkley: University of California Press, 1978).

9. Evans, *The Human Side of School Change*.
10. Stacey Childress, Richard Elmore, and Allen Grossman, "How to Manage Urban School Districts," *Harvard Business Review* 84, no. 11 (2006): 55.
11. Jonathan A. Supovitz, *The Case for District-Based Reform: Leading, Building, and Sustaining School Improvement* (Cambridge, MA: Harvard Education Press, 2006).
12. Paul Berman et al., *An Exploratory Study of School District Adaptation* (Santa Monica, CA: Rand, 1979).
13. Daniel Koretz, *The Testing Charade: Pretending to Make Schools Better* (Chicago: University of Chicago Press, 2017).
14. Charles Abelmann et al., *When Accountability Knocks, Will Anyone Answer?* (Philadelphia: Consortium for Policy Research in Education, 1999).

Acknowledgments

This book would not have been possible without the contributions of many amazing and dedicated people. First, we want to acknowledge the support of our first National Science Foundation program officer, Karen Denise King, who championed our work until her untimely death on Christmas Eve, 2019. This work is part of her enduring legacy.

Countless teachers and school leaders in the School District of Philadelphia (SDP) and Upper Darby School District engaged in the work and gave us their candid feedback to improve the initiative. From the SDP, Cheryl Logan, Chris Schaeffer, Tonya Wolford, and Joshua Taton provided the necessary support and attention to give OGAP a place to grow in the district. Many OGAP trainers, including Beth Hulbert, Mary Abele Austin, Fran Huntoon, Penny Stearns, Karen Reinhardt, Marianne Srock, and other members of the national training team, provided high-quality professional learning for teachers, visited schools, and nurtured their development over the course of the project.

Beyond the chapter authors, a host of researchers at the Consortium for Policy Research in Education (CPRE) at the University of Pennsylvania and Research for Action in Philadelphia supported this work, including Toscha Blalock, Sia Brown, Tesla Dubois, Nicole Fletcher, Abby Gray, Lydia Kulina, Hayden Lyons, Robert Nathenson, John Phillips, Cecile Sam, Phil Sirinides, and Kelly Sloane. Without the skills, insights, and dedication of these team members, this work would not have reached its potential. Bridget

Goldhahn and Yolanda Green also provided amazing communications and project support. Finally, a legion of master's students and others provided detailed scoring of student work. They are all 2,5 (correct and highly sophisticated).

This work was supported by three grants from the National Science Foundation: Using Research-Based Formative Assessment to Improve Mathematics Teaching and Learning, grant no. 1316527; Systemic Formative Assessment to Promote Mathematics Learning in Urban Elementary Schools, grant no. 1621333; Developing Formative Assessment Tools and Resources for Additive Reasoning, grant no. 1620888. The opinions, findings, and recommendations expressed are those of the authors and do not necessarily reflect the views of the National Science Foundation.

About the Editor and Contributors

Jonathan A. Supovitz is a professor of education policy and leadership at the University of Pennsylvania's Graduate School of Education and the director of the Consortium for Policy Research in Education, a community of leading education policy scholars from across the United States. Dr. Supovitz is an accomplished mixed-method researcher and evaluator and has over ten thousand academic citations of educational studies and evaluations of national, state, district, and school reform efforts. He has been a lead and coinvestigator of numerous Institute of Education Sciences, National Science Foundation, and other philanthropy-sponsored research projects and has presented his work nationally and internationally. His books include *Challenging Standards* (with James Spillane, Rowman & Littlefield, 2015), *The Implementation Gap* (with Elliot Weinbaum, Teacher College Press, 2008), and *The Case for District-Based Reform* (Harvard Education Press, 2005). He is also the lead author of an examination of the Common Core debate on Twitter, which is publicly available on the award-winning website www.hashtagcommoncore.com. Supovitz holds a doctorate in education policy and research methods from Harvard University; an MA in public policy from Duke University; and a BA in history from the University of California, Berkeley. He was a high school teacher in Boston, Massachusetts and Queretaro, Mexico.

Jordan D'Olier is an experienced teacher with a demonstrated history of working in the education management industry. As an advanced doctoral student at the Graduate School of Education at the University of Pennsylvania, Jordan led professional development and research investigations on the study of OGAP in Philadelphia. He holds an MBA in organizational leadership from the Wharton School.

Caroline B. Ebby is a senior researcher at the Consortium for Policy Research in Education (CPRE) and an adjunct professor at the Graduate School of Education at the University of Pennsylvania, where she designs, facilitates, and studies professional learning experiences for preservice and in-service teachers. Her work focuses on using formative assessment to inform and improve mathematics teaching and build teachers' capacity for responsive and inclusive mathematics instruction through research-practice partnerships with K–8 schools. A member of the OGAP national training team, she led the expansion of OGAP tools and routines to grades K–2 in additive reasoning and has coauthored three books for practitioners on additive, fractional, and multiplicative reasoning.

Adrianne Flack, EdD, is an assessment and accreditation professional specializing in sub-baccalaureate programs in career and technical and education. Currently, she serves as the director of assessment at the Pennsylvania Institute of Technology and was formerly the director of planning, assessment, accountability and institutional research at Thaddeus Stevens College of Technology. As a former research specialist at the Consortium for Policy Research (CPRE), Dr. Flack led the qualitative component of the OGAP implementation study. Dr. Flack has taught developmental reading and writing courses as well as research method coursework and academic writing at the graduate level. She is an adjunct assistant professor in the Division of Literacy Studies at the University of Pennsylvania Graduate School of Education.

Brittan Hallar has fifteen years of combined government and nonprofit expertise, with a strong commitment to supporting the development of research, evaluation, and information technology processes to improve outcomes for children and families. Brittan currently serves as the chief of performance management and technology in Philadelphia's Office of Children and Families, leading the design, management, and implementation of a diverse portfolio of data-driven strategies to improve effective services for children and families in Philadelphia. Brittan holds a PhD in science education from the University of Georgia and throughout her career has focused on STEM education, education equity, and actionable research and evaluation.

Brittany L. Hess is a mathematics educator and researcher at the University of Pennsylvania Graduate School of Education. She specializes in the development of instructional mathematics leadership to facilitate a more student-centered, responsive style of teaching. Drawing on her own experiences as a teacher in Philadelphia public schools, she has worked with teachers and leaders throughout the district to support the use of formative assessment to drive instruction, collaboratively plan and debrief responsive mathematics lessons, and assist in the transition to a new mathematics curriculum.

Elizabeth Hulbert is a developer and president of the Ongoing Assessment Project (OGAP). She coordinates and oversees all the professional development for OGAP and is on the national facilitator team. Beth's work over the past twenty-five years has been focused on working with teachers to improve mathematics teaching and learning through a focus on effective instructional strategies, including content-focused formative assessment. Previously, she was the mathematics coordinator for a school district in Vermont for sixteen years and an elementary classroom teacher and special educator.

Christian Kolouch was a research associate at the Consortium for Policy Research in Education (CPRE) at the University of Pennsylvania, where he contributed to the study of OGAP in Philadelphia. He was a main contributor to the #commoncore Project, which examined how social media influences the politics of education.

Robert Laird is passionately interested in the intersections among teacher knowledge, teacher instructional decisions, and student learning at both the individual classroom and system levels. Bob was one of the founders and a senior partner for the Ongoing Assessment Project (OGAP). Bob was intimately involved in the development of tools and processes used in OGAP trainings and coauthored several books on fractions, multiplicative reasoning, and proportional reasoning. Bob also served on the leadership team for the Vermont Mathematics Initiative (VMI), a master's degree program for K–12 mathematics teachers. There, he oversaw VMI's teaching/learning and action research strands and served as a course instructor.

Katrina Morrison, EdD, is a graduate of the University of Pennsylvania's Teaching, Learning, and Teacher Education doctoral program. She has practiced research and evaluation for sixteen years. She is currently a policy scientist at the University of Delaware's Center for Research in Education and Social Policy (CRESP) and health equity lead in the Delaware Clinical and Translational Research ACCEL Program. Her work focuses on research, evaluation, and teaching in the areas of education and health. Prior to becoming an active researcher, evaluator, and faculty member, she was a high school humanities teacher and a K–12 teacher supervisor in the School District of Philadelphia.

Marjorie Petit's primary work for the past twenty years has been supporting the development and implementation of the Ongoing Assessment Project (OGAP), focused on additive reasoning, fractions, multiplicative reasoning, and proportionality. She has coauthored a number of books translating mathematics education research for practitioners, including *A Focus on Fractions* (2022), *A Focus on Ratios and Proportions* (2020), and *A Focus on Multiplication and Division* (2022). She served as Vermont's deputy commissioner of education from 1996 to 2000 and acting commissioner of education during 2000. Marge has served on a number of national advisory boards, projects, and panels during her career.

Jill C. Pierce is a research education analyst at Research Triangle Institute, International (RTI). She works at the Center for Education Evaluation and Research within RTI's Education Practice Area. Pierce specializes in pre-K through twelfth-grade education issues, leading qualitative research and evaluation activities on mixed-methods studies. Pierce taught English language arts in Brooklyn, and she is passionate about giving voice to how school community members experience education initiatives.

Janine T. Remillard is a professor of education at the University of Pennsylvania's Graduate School of Education, where she serves as the chair of the Learning, Teaching, and Literacies Division, and faculty member in the Urban Teaching Apprenticeship Program. Her teaching and research focus is on mathematics teacher learning and classroom practices, teacher education, and the role of tools in supporting teacher learning. She has a strong commitment to teaching and learning in urban contexts and making mathematics humanizing for teachers and students. She cofounded the Community Based Mathematics Project, a hub for developing and sharing locally relevant and social justice–oriented mathematics lessons that teachers can modify to fit the needs of their classrooms. Her most recent book, *Elementary Mathematics Curriculum Materials: Designs for Student Learning and Teacher Enactment*, was published in 2020.

Maurice Spillane is a data analyst who specializes in quantitative methods, statistical analysis, and data visualization. From 2016 to 2022, he served as a research specialist at the Consortium for Policy Research and Education (CPRE). He is currently a manager of data analytics and insights at a Fortune 5 health-care company. Maurice earned his master's degree in social science from the National University of Ireland–Maynooth and a bachelor's degree in social work from Dundalk Institute of Technology.

Index

accountability, 17–18, 50, 58, 161, 242, 252–253
assessments. *See also* benchmark assessments; formative assessment; Learning Trajectory Assessment (LTA); learning trajectory-oriented formative assessment (LTOFA)
    benchmarking and, 17, 156–159
    long-cycle, 157–158
    medium-cycle, 157–158
    preassessment, 13
    short-cycle, 157–158

behaviorism, 15
benchmark assessments
    content coverage and, 171–174, 178
    in district assessment systems, 156–159
    grouping and, 166–171, 178
    investigation of use of, 164–166
    as learning vs. performance measures, 159–166
    as modeling form of state test, 175–176
    in Philadelphia, 162–164
    reteaching and, 166–171, 178
    system feedback with, 174–175
benchmarking, 17
"black swans," 1
bureaucratic systems, 242–243

CAO. *See* chief academic officer (CAO)
capacity, teacher, 188
capacity building, 61–62
Carnegie Learning, 51, 56, 67–70, 108–109, 239–240

champions, 68–70
chief academic officer (CAO), 68–69
classroom dynamics, 236
Common Core State Standards, 86
Consortium for Policy Research in Education (CPRE), 6, 13, 26–27, 45–46, 49, 54–55, 57, 60, 66, 68, 185
constructivism, 15
content areas, 24–25
CPRE. *See* Consortium for Policy Research in Education (CPRE)
curricular alignment, 228–229
curriculum pacing, 16

DBIR. *See* design-based implementation research (DBIR)
design-based implementation research (DBIR), 47–48, 70–71
discussions, student, about math, 217–218

educational system, impeding instructional improvement efforts, 15–18
education production function, 2–3
Elmore, Richard, 235
enVision, 12–13, 64–65
e-tools, 13–14, 26–27, 44, 63–66
Evans, Robert, 244

feedback, 8, 158, 174–175, 177, 179
feedback interventions, 9
formative assessment, 6, 8–10
    as accountability measure, 58
    espoused models for, 135–137, 141–148

formative assessment (cont.)
  as guiding principle, 23–24
  hybrid model and, 140–141
  instruction and, 38–39
  integration of, 27–30
  in-use models for, 137–148
  learning and, 17
  learning orientation and, 138–139
  mindset, 50
  misinterpretation of, by teachers, 58
  performance orientation and, 139–140
  problem contexts and, 31
  in teacher uptake, 119–122
formative data systems, 250–252

goals
  learning, 130
  performance, 130
grouping, 166–171, 178
groups, in math teaching, 216–217

instructional core
  defined, 235
  supporting, 235–253
instructional improvement, 4, 15–19, 46–48, 57–61
interim assessment, 17
IRT. *See* item response theory (IRT)
item response theory (IRT), 86

leaders, school, 59–61
leadership distribution, 224, 231
learning
  formative assessment and, 27–30
  logic, 160, 177–178
  medical model of, 244
  multilevel, 11–15
  performance vs., 159–161, 170
  progressions, 38–39
  sacred spaces of professional, 226–227, 232
learning orientation, 138–139, 144–146, 148–151, 243, 247–248
Learning Trajectory Assessment (LTA), 74–76, 85–90, 98–99, 102
learning trajectory-oriented formative assessment (LTOFA), 6, 10, 28–30, 77, 129–151
learning trajectory/progression (LT/P), 30
lenses, framing, 47–49
LTA. *See* Learning Trajectory Assessment (LTA)

LTOFA. *See* learning trajectory-oriented formative assessment (LTOFA)
LT/P. *See* learning trajectory/progression (LT/P)

MathCounts Institute (MCI), 51, 70, 105, 108
math discussions, 217–218
mathematical thinking, 212–213
mathematics, renewed attention on, 50–51
math teacher leader, 51
math teaching tools, 215–217
MCI. *See* MathCounts Institute (MCI)
mission, aligning strategy with, 247–249
multiplicative framework, 112–117

National Council of Teachers of Mathematics, 21–22
National Research Council, 21–23
National Science Foundation (NSF), 46, 50, 69
NCLB. *See* No Child Left Behind (NCLB)
No Child Left Behind (NCLB), 21, 50
NSF. *See* National Science Foundation (NSF)

OGAP. *See* Ongoing Assessment Project (OGAP)
OGAP Curriculum Connection, 63–66
Ongoing Assessment Project (OGAP), 1, 3–4
  alignment of, with existing work, 228–229
  as ambitious, 7–8
  conceptual framework for, 23–24
  content areas in, 24–25
  continuous improvement model, 25–26
  Curriculum Connection, 63–64
  decision-making on adoption of, 188–189, 194–195
  development of, 21–22
  essential ideas of, 5–6
  evolution of, 26–27
  guiding principles of, 24
  impeding adoption of, 123–125
  implementation, challenges in, 192–193
  implementation, internal capacity to support, 201–203
  implementation, investigation of, 110–112
  implementation, leadership beliefs about, 203
  implementation, perceptions of, 193–194, 198–199
  implementation, principals' role in supporting, 199–201
  implementation, reality of, 190–193, 196–198
  implementation, stories of, 187–205

implementation, supports for, 107–108, 122–123
inception of, 22–25
learning orientation and, 144–146
Learning Trajectory Assessment and, 88–90
as making a difference, 73–94
MathCounts Institute and, 105
math enhancement from, 210–211
multilevel learning and, 11–15
multiplicative framework, 112–117
ongoing support for, 108–110
Pennsylvania System of School Assessment and, 90–93
persistence with, 207–233
in Philadelphia, 45–72
professional learning communities and, 39–41, 52–53, 117–119
Ratio and Proportion Framework, 31
scaling up, 41–43
students and, 85–88
student thinking and, 35–38
TASK and, 80–85
teachers and, 74–85
as valued by educators, 209–220

PD. *See* professional development (PD)
Pennsylvania System of School Assessment (PSSA), 74–75, 90–93, 100–101, 103
performance
  bureaucracy and, 242–243
  logic, 159–161, 170, 177–178
  metrics, 17
  orientation, 139–140, 146–148, 243
Philadelphia Mathematics Leadership Collaborative (PMLC), 12, 14, 27, 53–54, 58–59, 68, 76, 94, 109–110, 181–182, 238, 245. *See also* School District of Philadelphia (SDP)
PLCs. *See* professional learning communities (PLCs)
PMLC. *See* Philadelphia Mathematics Leadership Collaborative (PMLC)
preassessment, 13
precarity, 66–70
problem contexts, 30–35
problem-solving strategies, of students, 211–214
problem structures, 30–35
professional development (PD), 16, 25, 28, 53–54, 60–61, 121, 130, 184–186, 249–250. *See also* trainings

professionalism, teacher, 204–205
professional learning, interconnected model of, 129–130
professional learning communities (PLCs), 39–41, 52–53, 106, 117–120, 126, 133, 183, 197–198, 204, 228
proximal development, 177
PSSA. *See* Pennsylvania System of School Assessment (PSSA)

randomized controlled trial (RCT), 50, 53, 57, 182
RCT. *See* randomized controlled trial (RCT)
Responsive Math Teaching Project, 71
reteaching, 166–171, 178

SBTL. *See* school-based teacher leader (SBTL)
scaling up, 41–43
school-based teacher leader (SBTL), 109, 259n2
school district, 66–70
School District of Philadelphia (SDP), 3–5, 27, 45–72, 107, 161
SMI. *See* Summer Math Institute (SMI)
strategy, aligning mission and, 247–249
student(s)
  discussions about math, 217–218
  growth, evidence of, 213–214
  Ongoing Assessment Project and, 85–88
  problem-solving strategies of, 211–214
  schemas of, 236
  thinking, 35–38
  understanding, 214
Summer Math Institute (SMI), 51, 54–56, 58–59, 61, 67–68, 245

TASK. *See* Teacher Assessment of Student Knowledge (TASK)
Teacher Assessment of Student Knowledge (TASK), 74–85, 93, 95–97, 102
teacher capacity, 188
teacher collaboration, 203–204, 232–233
teachers. *See also* professional learning communities (PLCs)
  buy-in of, 124–125
  curricula and, 218–219
  learning trajectory-oriented formative assessment and, 129–151
  Ongoing Assessment Project and, 74–86
  as overburdened, 124
  professionalism of, 204–205

teachers (cont.)
　rethinking system of learning for, 249–250
　sacred spaces of learning for, 226–227, 232
　student schemas and, 236
　tools, traction and, 62–66
　traction, 62–66

trainings, 222–226. *See also* professional development (PD)

urban districts, large, 41–43

Vermont Mathematics Partnership (VMP), 22–23